XOLELA MANGCU

THE
ARROGANCE
OF POWER

South Africa's Leadership Meltdown

TAFELBERG

Tafelberg
An imprint of NB Publishers
40 Heerengracht, Cape Town, 8000
www.tafelberg.com
© 2014 author

Set in Plantin
Cover design Michiel Botha
Book design by Nazli Jacobs
Edited by Riaan de Villiers
Proofread by Jacqueline Sheasby
Index by George Claassen

Printed and bound by Paarl Media Paarl
Jan van Riebeeck Drive, Paarl, South Africa
First edition, first printing 2014

ISBN-13: 978-0-624-07077-1
Epub-ISBN: 978-0-624-07078-8
Mobi-ISBN: 978-0-624-07079-5

To the memory of my late grandmother
Rose Noteya Nodress 'Antinti' Tyamzashe (1886–1981)
and my late aunt
Nomvula Mangcu Tyamzashe (1923–1986)
for opening my eyes to the world.

Table of Contents

V – THE ZUMA SURGE

VI – TRIUMPHALISM AND ITS DISCONTENTS

VII – REALIGN OR PERISH

Introduction

'Choose your president carefully, because at the end of the day no one can save him from himself.'– Richard Neustadt, *Presidential Power and Modern Presidents: The Politics of Leadership from Roosevelt to Reagan (1991)*

South Africa does not have a tradition of presidential histories. As a result, we have no body of knowledge about the sources and limitations of presidential authority. We know hardly anything about the temperaments of the men who have occupied the highest public office in the land or of what informs their decision-making. We also don't have a great biographical tradition, although we fare better in this respect than with presidential histories. The reasons for this inattention to presidential scholarship may be deeply rooted in our history. But it may also have to do with the false belief that we elect political parties, not individuals, to govern us. If political parties are our only interest, why bother about individuals? In fact, talking about the individual qualities of our leaders is positively discouraged in our political culture. Yet the political culture of the past 20 years has been significantly shaped by the actions of individual leaders, often with dire consequences. Therein lies the irony: we tell ourselves that individuals do not matter even as our collective attention is focused on their depredations.

The absence of presidential scholarship deprives future presidents of any guides to how they should conduct themselves, or how we should evaluate their performance. Even though the inclusive elections of 1994 gave us the right to govern – and misgovern – ourselves, we remain dependent on politicians' evaluations of their own performance, and on annual media report cards. Invariably, politicians trot out statistics about electricity connections, roads, houses, clinics and schools, all of which goes under the rubric of 'service delivery'.

From Thabo Mbeki to Jacob Zuma, the refrain has been that of a 'better life for all'. Zuma has added a twist to this by proclaiming that 'we are better off than we were before'. Compared to what? Apartheid? Of course, that was the whole point of the liberation struggle. And who, in their right mind, could be against a better life for anybody? But that is hardly the stuff that moves one to action.

With such banalities as a substitute for national purpose, it is difficult to argue against success, especially when you mark your own script as the ruling party. But I also remember reading from Julius Nyerere, one of our continent's greatest leaders, that government services are not the be-all and end-all of development, but only its means: 'People cannot be developed; they can only develop themselves,' he wrote in *Freedom and Development* (1974). 'For, while it is possible for an outsider to build a man's house, an outsider cannot give the man pride and self-confidence in himself as a human being. Those things a man has to create in himself by his own actions.'

It is this sense of self-reliant development that gives people a sense of dignity, or what the Canadian philosopher Charles Taylor calls 'self-defining freedom'. Steve Biko described this conception of freedom as follows: 'Freedom is the ability to define oneself according to one's possibilities, held back not by law but by God and natural surroundings.' He went on to implement this vision through the programmes of self-reliant development formulated for the black consciousness movement.

Contrary to this vision of Nyerere and Biko – and of Immanuel

Kant, who believed we are made human not by satisfying our desires but by attaining human dignity – black people remain a dependent class in South Africa. Those who do not find jobs in the formal economy are warehoused by their millions in the social grants system, deprived of the dignity that comes from self-reliant development. This is an unsustainable set of social and economic arrangements, not only for the inequality it produces but also for the social resentment it generates. This, in turn, produces the political instability glibly referred to as 'service delivery protests'. Protests and strikes go on for months on end without any leaders showing up, because they have become afraid of their people. At the heart of our leadership malaise is the absence of a common national purpose, and a collective failure of imagination.

There was a time when Thabo Mbeki's African Renaissance promised to provide an inspirational public philosophy for transforming our society. However, no sooner had its author announced those lofty ideals than he was distracted by controversies that had little to do with the purpose of the liberation struggle, namely to move the ordinary masses of black people towards self-reliant development and self-fulfilling freedom. I have often wondered what we could have achieved in pursuit of that purpose with the energy and resources that were instead expended on controversies about HIV/AIDS, the arms deal, Guptagate, Nkandla, and countless other costly distractions. Those are the opportunity costs of the endless controversies that have dogged our national leadership over the past twenty years.

The media do better in generating discussions of values, but this is indirectly through exposés of the corruption and malfeasance in the corridors of power. I have been fortunate to be part of a group of columnists who have engaged directly with the broader political and moral questions of our time. We've been able to do so because we have been removed from the daily grind of news reportage. And moral questions are unavoidable when hundreds of thousands of people die from HIV/AIDS while their government denies the cause of their death, and thus refuses to do anything about it. As columnists, we have had to step back from what the American historian and public intellectual Richard Hofstadter characterised as 'the meaning *in* a situation' to rather reflect on 'the meaning of the situation as a whole'.

The columns collected in this volume are drawn from those written over a 15-year period, from just before Thabo Mbeki's ascent to the presidency in 1999 until just before our fifth inclusive national and provincial elections in May 2014, effectively covering Mbeki's entire nine-year presidency up to his resignation in 2008, and Jacob Zuma's since then. In the absence of detailed presidential scholarship, they provide a week-by-week account of how this eventful history unfolded. I hope they will show that the quantitative decline in electoral support for the ruling African National Congress (ANC) from 1994 to 2014 did not happen overnight or without reason; it has been the result of qualitative decline in leadership over time. On a weekly basis, I watched ANC leaders slowly eat away at the high levels of trust they enjoyed among the majority of the population.

While the ANC has received a mandate to govern for another five years, the quantitative decline in its support over time – with its share of the vote dropping from almost 70 per cent under Thabo Mbeki in 2004 to 65 per cent and 62 per cent under Jacob Zuma in 2009 and 2014 respectively – should worry anyone who is concerned about its future. In the 2014 elections, the party had to pull out all the stops to hold on to Gauteng, eventually by a mere 53 per cent. This should worry the party, because Gauteng is not only the country's economic heartland but also its most populous province, and the most representative of the South

African population. The ANC's support also declined in all the other major metropolitan areas. This should also worry the ANC because, as the political scientist Francis Fukuyama has put it, 'while governments can enact policies that have the effect of depleting social capital, they have great difficulties understanding how to build it again.'

At the heart of this narrative, though, is the conduct of two presidents: Thabo Mbeki and Jacob Zuma. It is the closest an outsider can get to a presidential history. Hopefully, those who have been in the bowels of the presidential system in this period will one day emerge to tell us what really happened – without the usual public spin – and how the grievous mistakes made could be avoided in the future. Maybe the leaders themselves will come clean one day. I wouldn't bet on it, though; there is always the danger of legal action.

In many ways, this book built itself. The narrative structure tells it all – initial promise, followed by inexplicable failures and grave disappointment. It starts with my excitement about Mbeki's African Renaissance, quickly followed by detours into all the dark corners where Mbeki took us during his eight years in office. The same emotional ups-and-downs characterise my approach to Zuma's administration – initial excitement, followed by great disillusionment.

The columns also throw the spotlight on us, the citizens. I hope they show what happens when good men and women give up their power to speak out against wrongdoing. As the British philosopher Isaiah Berlin once put it: 'Happy are those who live under a discipline which they accept without question, who freely obey the orders of leaders, spiritual or temporal, whose word is fully acceptable as unbreakable law. That may make for contentment, but not for understanding what it means to be human.'

But it was Matthew Arnold – Berlin's predecessor at Oxford – who provided the prescient observation that 'there is a natural current . . . in human affairs, [that] . . . will not let us rivet our faith upon any one man and his doings. It makes us see not only his good side, but also how much in him was of necessity limited and transient; nay, it even feels a pleasure, a sense of an increased freedom, and of an ampler future, in so doing.' That is how South Africans responded to Mbeki, and that is how they will still respond to Zuma, or whichever leader takes their trust and goodwill for granted. That at least is what the results of the 2014 elections seem to signal.

Writing a newspaper column over such an extended period of time comes with its own hazards. First, it is a public reflection of oneself. You can tell someone's personality by the columns they write. Many of my critics have complained about the way in which I insert myself in the story. I am not a shrink, so I can't say why this is the case. It could be a bad case of narcissism, or that I like to claim my own voice. Two other factors may have contributed, though. When I started my doctoral studies – and there we go again, I hear you say – my supervisor complained that he could not hear my voice. He would not read my dissertation until I had learnt to write in the first person. The other reason could be related to what The Kennedy School of Government's Marshall Ganz has said about narrative:

Some of us may think our personal stories don't matter, that others won't care, or that we shouldn't talk about ourselves so much. On the contrary, if we do public work, we have a responsibility to give a public account of ourselves – where we came from, why we do what we do, and where we think we are going. . . . If we don't author our story, others will – and they may tell our story in ways we may not like. Not because they are malevolent, but because others try to make sense of who we are by drawing on their experience of people whom they consider to be like us.

So that is perhaps why my writings will be punctuated with references to my family, my home town of Ginsberg in the Eastern Cape, Steve Biko, black consciousness, and the life of the mind – so that the reader can know where I am coming from, so to speak, thus to better engage about where we both need to go.

In writing these columns, I have been guided by my own inner voice, for better and for worse. In the process, I have earned as many enemies as friends, neither of whom are ever permanent. There are at least two personal criticisms that I have never really addressed. The first is that I don't have the slightest clue about the politics of the ANC. This jibe has often been accompanied by an invitation to join the party, and stop criticising from the outside. I could have done that a long time ago. I have indeed thought about the opportunity costs of not being in the ANC. After all, I could have pleaded fealty to the party and turned into an instant tycoon, no questions asked. I could have done the same for the opposition Democratic Alliance (DA), for that matter. But I think something dies in you when you do that. But I don't know – I've never tried.

The second criticism is that I have been made a multimillionaire several times over by the billionaire ANC politician Tokyo Sexwale, which is why I was so excited about him as an alternative to both Mbeki and Zuma. It's hard to refute such allegations without showing how little money I have in the bank. The truth is that I've never seen, smelled or counted a million rand in my entire life. In the celebrated remark of a Gauteng politician (no names, no pack-drill): 'I've never ever seen the door of a million.'

I cannot possibly address all these criticisms, just as those who have been at the sharp end of my pen could not – which is why the

17

door for conversation between citizens and leaders should always stay open, a quality that has proven to be a major distinction between good leaders and bad ones. The only thing I can say in my defence is that my writings are motivated by a sense of shame about the direction we have taken over the past 20 years. Not only are we trapped in the path laid down for us by the system of apartheid; there does not seem to be any imaginative responses to it on the horizon. And, as Benedict Anderson has remarked, 'if you cannot be ashamed for your country, then you do not love it.'

A presidential chronology

In **1991,** at the ANC's 48th national conference held in Durban, Nelson Mandela was elected as president, succeeding Oliver Tambo, who was elected as national chairperson. Walter Sisulu was elected as deputy president.

Following the ANC's election victory in **April 1994,** the national assembly elected Mandela as South African president. He appointed the leader of the National Party (NP), former president F W de Klerk, as his first deputy president, and Thabo Mbeki as the second.

In **December 1994,** at the ANC's 49th national conference held in Bloemfontein, Mandela was re-elected as president, and Thabo Mbeki as deputy president.

In **1996,** following the NP's withdrawal from the government of national unity, Mbeki became the sole South African deputy president.

In **1997,** Mandela announced that he intended to retire as South African president in 1999 and would not be available for re-election as ANC president. In December, at the ANC's 50th national conference held at Mafikeng, Mbeki was elected as president, and Jacob Zuma as deputy president.

In June **1999**, following the ANC's victory in the general election since the transition to democracy, the national assembly elected Mbeki as South African president. He appointed Zuma as deputy president.

In December **2002**, at the ANC's 51st national conference held at Stellenbosch, Mbeki was re-elected as president, and Zuma was elected as deputy president.

In April **2004**, following the ANC's third election victory since the transition to democracy, Mbeki was re-elected as South African president for a second and final term.

On 30 May **2005**, the Durban businessman Schabir Shaik was found guilty on charges of fraud and corruption relating to financial transactions between himself and Zuma. On 14 June, Mbeki dismissed Zuma as South African deputy president, and Zuma resigned as a member of parliament.

In **2007**, Zuma mounted a campaign to contest the presidency of the ANC. In December 2007, at the ANC's 52nd national conference held at Polokwane in Limpopo, Zuma was elected as president, thereby unseating Mbeki. Kgalema Motlanthe was elected as deputy president.

On 4 **August 2008**, Zuma appeared in the Pietermaritzburg High Court on 16 charges of racketeering, money laundering, corruption and fraud. On 12 September 2008, Judge Chris Nicholson ruled the charges were unlawful on procedural grounds, and added there was reason to believe the decision to charge Zuma had been politically motivated.

On 20 **September 2008**, the ANC national executive committee announced it had decided to recall Mbeki. The next day, on 21 September 2008, Mbeki resigned as South African president. Motlanthe was elected as interim president until the 2009 elections.

On 12 **January 2009**, acting upon an appeal by Mbeki, the Supreme Court of Appeal overturned Judge Nicholson's ruling that Zuma had been unfairly charged and that Mbeki and other members of his cabinet had interfered with the prosecution process. This meant that the charges against Zuma were automatically reinstated. On 6 April 2009, however, the NPA announced a decision to drop all charges against Zuma.

In **May 2009**, following the ANC's victory in the fourth general election since the transition to democracy, parliament elected Zuma as South African president.

In **2012**, at the ANC's national conference held at Mangaung in the Free State, Zuma was re-elected as president, and Cyril Ramaphosa as deputy president.

In **2014**, following the ANC's victory in the fifth general election since the transition, Zuma was re-elected as South African president for his second and final term. He appointed Ramaphosa as deputy president.

I
THE PROMISE

Seeking common national values

Mail & Guardian, 5 June 1998

South Africa's transformation project has been framed almost exclusively in political and economic terms. The introduction of a constitutional democracy has been followed by an even greater focus on economic growth. While all of this is understandable and desirable, relatively little attention has been given to our public values. And yet the success of our democracy will probably be determined by the extent to which our political, administrative and policy institutions are informed by the values, aspirations and motivations of ordinary South Africans. This in itself requires that our leaders undertake the difficult task of distilling what might be termed common-denominator values among the many world views that characterise South African life. If Jawaharlal Nehru could frame a sense of public values for India, Julius Nyerere for Tanzania, or James Madison and Thomas Jefferson for the United States, then surely our national leaders should be able to do the same for South Africa.

In many ways, Deputy President Thabo Mbeki has started on that path by calling for a national consensus, which he describes as the 'African Renaissance'. The success of the African Renaissance as a national ethos will, in turn, depend on the extent to which it matches the common aspirations of South Africans across political, economic and cultural divides. Equally important will be the means that are adopted to achieve such a national consensus – that is, the end values must be consistent with the democratic means that most South Africans cherish. How can this balance be achieved in practical terms? I suggest four policy steps.

25

First, we must create a deliberative process of public purpose-building that is pluralistic and even clamorous, reflecting the diversity of our society. This must be something that appeals to the idealism of most people, and must be conducted on a scale that parallels what other countries have achieved. An example that comes to mind is the framing of the United States constitution, and the adoption of its Declaration of Independence. The National Endowment for the Humanities – a federal government agency – recently sponsored a National Conversation on American Pluralism and Identity aimed at engaging the American public on the paradox of pursuing a shared American identity in the midst of pluralist diversity.

Even those who ascribe America's success to its purposelessness, and even to the exploitation and exclusion of racial minorities, now argue for a common purpose because of changed conditions. As the American political theorist Benjamin Barber has put it in his book *A Passion for Democracy: American Essays* (2000): 'The new pressures of ecology, transnationalism, and resource scarcity in combination with the apparent bankruptcy of privatism, materialism, and economic individualism – [as well as] the pathologies and the ambivalent promises of our modernity – create conditions more inviting to the generation of public purposes and a public spirit than any America has ever known.'

Several books have also come out to celebrate India's enduring democracy 50 years after independence – a feat which they attribute to Nehru's concept of unity in diversity. India continues to withstand the fundamentalist threat, and will most likely withstand its current woes, because of its democratic tradition. We have also seen the rather belated, if grudging, recognition of the nation-building legacy of Nyerere in Tanzania. In December 1996, even the conservative *Wall Street Journal* observed that: 'Mr Nyerere may have been a poor economist, but he was a skilled nation-builder. He fused Tanzania's 120 tribes into a cohesive state, preventing tribal conflicts plaguing so much of Africa.'

South Africa can draw some lessons from these examples without committing the mistakes that those countries made in their economic policies. We can at least agree that successful democracies are those that draw from their pluralist diversity in creating broadly shared understandings. We have shown that we can do this by drafting and adopting what is arguably the best constitution in the world. But we need to go beyond the formalism and rights orientation of the constitutional process to build a positive cultural *leitmotif* that also pays attention to our collective responsibilities in the new society.

Second, a project of purpose-building must be conducted by public intellectuals who can be both supportive and critical of the national government. Public intellectuals are particularly suited to this role because they combine moral commitment to progressive ends with a commitment to objective analyses and procedures. Their role would be to build a moral consensus that is preceded by an open airing of different viewpoints. But who and where are the public intellectuals? Black intellectuals have particular perspectives that can inform a national conversation on the public purpose. They represent values and world experiences that have historically been locked out of the knowledge–ideas complex in South Africa. It is indeed worrisome that the subject of black intellectual empowerment has not received the same level of national attention and visibility as political and economic empowerment. I submit that unless the ideas of black people are part of this knowledge–ideas complex, our freedom will be incomplete. Ideas do matter, and those who control ideas ultimately shape the policies that govern our lives.

One idea that is part of our living experience as black people, and underlies the process of reconciliation, is that of *Ubuntu* (African humanism). *Ubuntu* is also eminently compatible with the idea of self-reliant and people-centred development. It is such congruence between public values and public policies that will ultimately provide the basis for effective governance. It has, of course, been argued that *Ubuntu* is a myth which papers over the atrocities that blacks have perpetrated on each other. But, just as the existence of slavery and racist segregation does not make democracy any less desirable in the West, *Ubuntu* remains a 'necessary myth'.

Third, to prevent ossification of the deliberative process, the debate must also be conducted through multiple institutions: the media, policy institutes, and community forums. Members of the public must be encouraged to air their views in newspapers and on radio and television call-in shows. I can anticipate fears that this would immediately cede the process to the control of a generally hostile media. Perhaps it is time to explore more creative ways for inclusive public deliberation. One possibility is private funding of new policy institutes – by the new black millionaires. This would not be just a matter of social responsibility, but a pragmatic investment in the generation of new ideas.

Fourth, it is imperative that we develop the next generation of South African intellectuals. To be a public intellectual should be just as prestigious among young people as being a doctor or a lawyer. Perhaps a project of public purpose-building could be the beginning of such intellectual participation by young people in the formulation of their country's new identity. Then they could say to future generations that they were there – at the country's founding!

An alternative to snob democracy
Mail & Guardian, 30 April 1999

The political transformation of the past ten years will no doubt go down in history as one of the most important events of the millennium – on par with the French, American, Indian, Chinese, and Russian revolutions. Some of our leading scholars have taken to talking about the 'maturing' and 'consolidation' of our democracy, and rightly so. But self-congratulation has to be accompanied by a willingness to talk frankly about our shortcomings as well.

There is a foundational flaw in our democracy that goes back to the early days of the transition, but has become a defining characteristic of our political culture. While the political transition itself was the result of mass mobilisation in the townships and villages of this country, the negotiations process was, at times, a secretive affair whose outcome hinged on the bargaining skills of the leaders of the various political parties, mainly the ANC and the National Party (NP).

Having delegated power upwards during the negotiations, we then invested in a number of political and institutional support systems consistent with the overall emphasis on elite decision-making. The centralisation of authority in national leadership; the dominant role of political parties as containers of debate, discontent and disagreement; the party list system; the concomitant emphasis on what Nelson Mandela and Thabo Mbeki would do for us; and the language of delivery, are but a few manifestations of an increasingly top-down political system.

All these developments run the risk of producing a split national identity. The one side would comprise a group of political and economic elites who would, by virtue of their proximate race/class distance from power, become the real, active citizens. The other would comprise a passive population that would be nothing more than what the Indian scholar Partha Chatterjee has called 'empirical objects of government policy, not citizens who participate in the sovereignty of the state.'

Promises of delivery would become nothing less than 'the opiate of the masses' – the only language that the government could use to talk with its constituencies. In less than a decade, we would have gone full circle from the mass clamour for democratic participation to the elite model of democracy normally associated with political snobs such as Edmund Burke and Joseph Schumpeter.

It will, of course, be argued that the negotiated transition was the only way we could have drawn back from the abyss of interminable racial violence. But that's only half the answer. A full answer would have to suggest how we can build on the progress of the past to deepen democratic participation in the future. As the Yale University political scientist Ian Shapiro argues: 'The problem with negotiated transitions is not that the institutions are imposed from above, but rather that they are not imposed in a sufficiently thoroughgoing fashion.'

And so, for me, the most important question surrounding our second set of inclusive national and provincial elections is not which party to vote for – since they all operate within the same elite model of democracy – but whether we can start talking about alternative models of democracy in this country. It seems to me that we need to go beyond the conception of democracy as the mere right to choose our leaders – which is a necessary but insufficient condition for democratic participation – to some kind of direct, participatory, and communicative democracy.

As Steve Biko put it in *I Write What I Like* (1978): 'In a government where democracy is allowed to work, one of the principles that are normally entrenched is a feedback system, a discussion between those who formulate policy and those who must perceive, accept or reject policy. In other words, there must be a system of education, political education, and this does not necessarily go with literacy.'

Or, as our own great writer Es'kia Mphahlele wrote more recently, before his death in 2008: 'We are wrong in thinking that because the government is democratically elected, therefore there is democracy. Democracy is about the relationship between the politicians and their constituencies, and the "African renaissance" must therefore go to the heart of the people in making them think democratically.'

Participation is the cardinal principle of democracy – not only because of its intrinsic value, but also because it increases the political efficacy of citizens by giving them direct training in the policies and tools of governance. Almost 200 years ago, John Stuart Mill suggested that this kind of democratic training is best obtainable at the local level, where citizens can make decisions about issues they can immediately relate to, and then generalise that knowledge to the broader, national political system.

The best example of this in this country is the black consciousness movement of the 1970s. Many of our current leaders in the public, private and non-profit sectors received their leadership training through the political education and development programmes of organisations such as Black Community Programmes – even if some of them would now disavow black consciousness politics. But, even if people do not agree with the substance of black consciousness, we can at least go back to the veritable tradition of conscientisation that was the hallmark and signal achievement of that movement.

As the development economist Albert Hirschman once observed, the social energies that are aroused in the course of a social movement do not disappear when that movement does, but are kept in storage and become available to fuel later and sometimes different social movements. Or, as the Brown University social scientist Ashu Varshney has put it: 'While futures are indeed created, they are not typically created on a clean slate. It is hard for nations to leave their pasts behind. The more pertinent issue is: how does a nation reconstruct its past? Which traditions should be revived, and which ones dropped? The ideological task is to retrieve that which is valuable, and to make this selective retrieval a political reality.'

If black consciousness contributed to our current crop of leaders, we should ask ourselves how we can contribute to the development of future leaders in this country. I doubt very much if such contributions will happen through the procedural view of democracy as showing up at the polls once every five years. A long-term view would suggest a balance between the vertical politics of elite representation bequeathed to us by the negotiations process with a more horizontal politics of direct democracy that comes from deep within our own history.

Can the president fulfil his tryst with destiny?
Sunday Independent, 20 June 1999

'Long years ago we made a tryst with destiny, and now the time comes when we shall redeem our pledge.' – Jawaharlal Nehru, address to the Indian parliament on the eve of India's independence, 14 August 1947

'The people have spoken.' That was president-elect Thabo Mbeki's humble, dignified and assertive refrain at the ANC's post-election victory rally at Gallagher Estate in Midrand. While not as exultant as Jawaharlal Nehru's 'tryst with destiny' speech, or

John F Kennedy's 'ask not what your country can do for you', Mbeki's words will be remembered nonetheless for their self-assured and declarative message. Mbeki will no doubt interpret what the people have said to mean an overwhelming mandate for the ANC. But I hope he will take a broader approach, as he hinted he would when he described his own inauguration as 'a festival and a celebration of democracy'.

While there really was no mystery about which party would win the elections, voters kept on saying they were coming out in large numbers to protect South Africa's young democracy. They stood in queues for hours on end, braving the cold, and jumping through all the administrative hoops to affirm their right to vote. In that respect, this election was a referendum about the condition of our democracy. As Mbeki kept saying, 'democracy is alive and well in South Africa'.

The policy question, though, is: now that Mbeki has obtained the overwhelming mandate of the people, how will he sustain their interest in democracy until the next elections and beyond? Will he use his party's dominant position to deepen the roots of democracy? Whether Mbeki can link his party's interest to the national interest of building a democratic society will depend in turn on whether he can do what Mahatma Gandhi called 'building bridges' with the people. His biggest challenge will be that of building unity and forging a national identity in a country riven by racial and economic inequality. But if Nehru could forge a pluralistic modern Indian identity in India, the world's largest and most diverse society, Mbeki can learn from India's imperfect experience and Nehru's personal experiences, which are remarkably similar to his, and brilliantly portrayed in Nehru's autobiography *The Discovery of India* (1946), written in prison before independence.

Like Nehru, whose father was one of the founding fathers of

the Indian National Congress, Mbeki also comes from 'struggle royalty'. While his intellectual and organisational abilities are widely recognised, this 'pedigree' is also an important leadership asset. Notwithstanding Nelson Mandela's protestations about the focus on him as an individual, the truth is that people yearn for some kind of inspirational leadership that gives them hope and faith in democracy, above and beyond brick and mortar issues. As Mbeki pointed out in his inaugural address, it is now up to him and all of us to advance the democratic ideals of his father's generation.

Both Nehru and Mbeki can be described as detribalised intellectuals who were educated outside their traditional communities, but given the historical responsibility of building democracy in their societies. Nehru was educated at two of England's most prestigious institutions: Harrow and Cambridge. Once, at a public rally with the great Mahatma Gandhi, he asked: 'What do I have in common with these people?' Mbeki was educated at the University of Sussex, and hobnobbed with members of British high society. His attendance last December of a ceremony to welcome him back to his home at Idutywa in the Eastern Cape after many years in exile was perhaps an attempt to start building bridges with his traditional roots. Hopefully, he will take Gandhi's and even Mandela's connection with traditional communities more seriously than Nehru was ever able to, without pretending to be what he is not.

Much has been said about Mbeki's 'formality' as an impediment to his ability to connect with the people. But it's also important that Mbeki should be himself, and he may be surprised to learn that people like him just the way he is. Gimmicks such as dressing informally will go only a certain distance. What is more important is whether he comes across as a leader who is respectful of the people.

Mbeki should muster his personal strengths and abilities to keep to the former, for that is where his legacy lies. What people will most appreciate is his respect for their ideas, and their ways of doing things. One practical suggestion is for him to go back to the townships and villages he visited during the election campaign to engage people directly in the policy process. If he could do it in the short space of an election campaign, he can surely do it during the term of his administration.

Finally, if Mbeki is going to translate the overwhelming vote for the ANC into a victory for our society, he should also build bridges with civil society. As the American political philosopher Michael Walzer has noted: 'No state can survive if it is alienated from civil society. . . . The production and reproduction of loyalty, civility, political competence and trust in authority are never the work of the state alone, and the effort to go it alone – one meaning of totalitarianism – is doomed to failure.'

Also instructive for Mbeki on this matter would be the following remarks by Mwalimu Julius Nyerere at a workshop I organised in October 1997 at the Rockefeller Foundation's conference centre in Bellagio, Italy:

We committed two basic mistakes in Tanzania. First, we abolished local government. We thought local officials did not have the vision that we had at the national level. They seemed not to realise how urgent the business of transformation was. I had been writing all these things about freedom and participation and yet taking away power from down there and centralising it in national government because I thought things would move quicker. That was one basic mistake. Second, we abolished the cooperative movement. During the process of the liberation struggle we had built up a strong cooperative movement as an economic power base for the people, and now we were abolishing it. However, it soon became clear that we could not sustain the path of a centralised bureaucracy. We had to make government responsive and accountable to the people. That's when I started calling for a multiparty democracy. I had thought I could reform the party from within, but the inertia of corruption was too heavy. The pressure had to come from outside. In addition to political parties, we had to build self-governing communities and people's organisations.

Mbeki's historical responsibility is therefore to make sure that we don't make the same mistakes. There's one final international parallel I would like to draw. Just as Thomas Jefferson followed George Washington in founding the United States, and Nehru followed in Gandhi's footsteps, Mbeki follows in the steps of the towering Nelson Mandela. Like those other 'crown princes', Mbeki has an historic opportunity to help us develop a positive national consciousness and identity. That is his tryst with destiny. Whether or not he will fulfil it will be for future generations to tell. It is that long-term perspective which differentiates nation-builders from party builders.

Will he who strikes the presidential pose add body to democracy's slight frame?
Sunday Independent, 27 June 1999

'Material poverty is bad enough; coupled with spiritual poverty, it kills.' – Steve Biko, *I Write What I Like* (1976)

'People, especially, poor and degraded people, are also hungry for meaning, identity, and self-worth.' – Cornel West, *Race Matters* (1992)

Last week, I suggested that Thabo Mbeki's inauguration speech had not been as exultant and inspirational as it should have been. He seemed tired, unrehearsed, and just out of it – even though the content of the speech was serious enough to make tears well up in one's eyes.

This week, in his 'state of the nation' address to parliament, we saw a different Mbeki: relaxed, poised, and clearly familiar with the subject at hand. I have seen American presidents give 'state of the union' speeches before, and this one must rank up there with the best. Mbeki's last such performance was his 'I am an African' speech to parliament in 1996. All of this leads me to one conclusion: Mbeki is much more at home in the formal setting of parliament than at mass gatherings. Maybe his aides should think about having him give his most important addresses in parliament. This was vintage Mbeki at his brilliant best: articulate, consistent, and analytical. In fact, I would go on to suggest that some of this is what he should have said at his inauguration.

For the first time, I heard him articulate a vision for South Africa, which he described as the 'caring society'. He spoke of the need to 'give birth to something new, good and beautiful to replace the old order's law of the jungle'. Yes, Mbeki has been on the stump before, talking about the need for moral regeneration as the basis of the African Renaissance. But until now he has never – at least as head of state – spoken systematically about the African Renaissance as the basis of what the French philosopher Jean-Jacques Rousseau called the 'civil religion': a new set of values for our common national identity. I have always maintained that South Africa's ability to project the African Renaissance across the continent will ultimately depend on us asking ourselves what it means to be South African and African.

I am therefore heartened by the fact that Mbeki will be bringing issues of nation-building and linguistic pluralism to the centre of his governance. I was also heartened to hear the president say that 'no one should feel that sense of alienation which drives people into peripheral existence'. As the American political theorist Michael Walzer has written: 'When minorities are free to celebrate their histories, remember their dead, and shape in part the education of their children, they are more likely to be harmless than when they are unfree.'

As South Africans, we have done a great job with developing procedural democracy – elections, constitutions, courts, and so on. What we need now is to fill these structures with content. What Mbeki can help us do is to build a more substantive democracy, with clearly identifiable public values. Moving from vision to policy, Mbeki outlined in his speech a laundry list of policy initiatives that make broad generalists such as myself yawn and, like some members of parliament, drop off to sleep. Here too Mbeki demonstrated a level of comfort with policy that most heads of state do not have. The only other president I can think of with such a grasp of public policy is America's Bill Clinton.

Mbeki also did what he does best. He is perhaps one of the finest practitioners of the art of co-option – ask the Azanian People's Organisation (AZAPO) and the Pan Africanist Congress (PAC) how he co-opted their language of pan-Africanism and turned them into ineffective opposition parties in the black community. He deprived the opposition parties of anything to fault him on. After all, who could be against added efforts to combat crime, or enhanced services for the disabled? Tony Leon, leader of the official opposition, had to battle to find something negative to say about the speech. By the way, our opposition leaders should know that it is okay to applaud during a state-of-the-nation address. Afterwards, they can go to the media and give their responses. This is about the nation and not just party politics, and Mbeki is the country's president, not just the ANC's.

What Mbeki has done brilliantly is to take his broad vision of *faranani,* or partnership, and extend it beyond the policy arena. For far too long we have been talking about service delivery outside a broader philosophical vision of ourselves as a society, such as the caring or people-centred society he spoke about. I have argued before that service delivery is a potentially dangerous concept if separated from issues of self-reliance and long-term capacity-building. The philosophical concept of *faranani* should be used to call on communities to assume greater responsibility for their own development. What we need is a mind-shift at the level of the community – from a democracy based on claim-making to one based on carrying out our responsibilities as citizens. This can be done through the co-operative movements which Mbeki spoke about.

Those who wish him well, and I include myself among them, find Mbeki frustrating. On the one hand, he has the potential to be one of the greatest African leaders, and a true visionary for South Africa. On the other, he seems guarded, held back by who knows what. Paradoxically, Mbeki should realise that his success lies in letting others take ownership of his agenda. Otherwise, we will continue to get flashes of brilliance only – like we did this time around.

The potential for Thabo's 'renaissance'
Mail & Guardian, 2–8 July 1999

'Where are the black intellectuals?', Thabo Mbeki has often asked. I would urge him to consider an even larger and prior question: where is the intellectual environment required for the emergence of those intellectuals?

It is a known fact that black people have historically been excluded from what I have previously called the 'knowledge–ideas complex'. It consists of interlocking, mutually supportive and impenetrable relationships among white intellectuals, in fields ranging from literary criticism to urban planning. Because of their strategic position at the cusp of intellectual and cultural production, white intellectuals have been able to disproportionately project their values on to our public morality and public policies. Our constitution, bill of rights, and the rules and rituals of political decision-making have a liberal western outlook. Happily, the values of justice and fairness enshrined in the constitution coincide with the values of most South Africans.

But why should black people continue to be coincidental in shaping the national political culture? Are there ways of increasing black participation in its making? Moving from a procedural democracy comprising western-type institutions to a more substantive democracy might create new spaces for black intellectuals. Creating a proper intellectual environment is therefore inextricably tied to a larger question: where is the social vision that challenges intellectuals to bring out the best in them? How might we then begin to facilitate greater black intellectual participation in the endeavour of nation-building?

Let's start with the question of a social vision, and end with some ideas on what we can do about the intellectual environment. The absence of a social vision has undermined black intellectual participation in public life in many ways. For example, during our recent elections, I noticed a racial division of labour in the public discourse. White political parties and intellectuals dominated the discussion of broader democratic values and principles. In the words of my fellow columnist Steven Friedman, the right issues were being raised by the wrong people. However dubious their motivations were for opposing an ANC two-thirds majority, their language was framed in terms of democratic principles. Black parties and intellectuals, on the other hand, seemed stuck in the discourse of delivery, as if they had become more knowledgeable about building houses than building nations.

This is not to say that there isn't a tiny minority of black scholars working on issues of democracy, but rather to ask whether we have anything resembling the substantive society-wide discussions that took place among the French *philosophes* in the 18th century; in the 13 states of pre-independence United States; in India in the 1950s; and in South Africa itself during the struggle against apartheid.

All of that energy has dissipated under the weight of post-apartheid technocracy and materialism. Winning government contracts has become more important than reading and writing – the essence of the intellectual function.

Getting to the intellectual environment, I am struck by the absence of institutions in which people of ideas can get together to engage each other and the public on the democratic experience. We talk to each other only through newspapers, radio, television and, for the lucky few, the Internet. The ideas that float in the public domain are never followed up and interrogated in any indepth manner with members of the public. If South Africa is ever going to be the winning nation that Mbeki talks about, we have to know how to become a learning society first – in the manner that organisational gurus talk about learning organisations.

One practical suggestion would be to introduce topics such as nation-building and pluralism in the agendas of existing community forums. Members of parliament could also use their constituency meetings to talk about issues that pertain to our identity as a nation. Something drastic should also be done about the state of university salaries; as long as universities remain underfunded, the perception will continue that the intellectual function is not a priority in our national development. Young people will continue to shun academic careers for as long as they see them as not prestigious or lucrative enough.

Perhaps Mbeki and the minister of education, Kader Asmal, should have a tête-à-tête about how the state of the universities prevents the emergence of a black intellectual class – most of whose members do not have inheritances like their white counterparts. But being black is not a sufficient condition in and of itself for playing a progressive role in the articulation of a new national identity. Black intellectuals should learn some lessons from the negative example of black economic empowerment; we should avoid a situation where a group of self-anointed elites become the high priests of black intellectual life. Nor should we allow envy and petty jealousies – that great affliction of formerly oppressed people everywhere – to interfere with intellectual collaboration.

One of the weirdest things I have heard is that there is a growing divide in our intellectual community between those who have attended American and European universities and those who remained behind, or attended African universities. Seemingly, the latter are the true intellectual arbiters of the African experience, while the former are pawns in a grand white scheme to deny Africa its true intellectuals. Rubbish; let's just get on with it.

We should also be careful that black self-determination does not turn into a blind black jingoism. The challenge is to make sure that a healthy black nationalism is not turned into a degenerate anti-whiteism. People like Steve Biko and Robert Sobukwe were able to avoid that fate through their relationships with whites. We should challenge the dictionary-based, and therefore static, definitions of who Africans are that have come from some black scholars. We need definitions that evolve and express our changing circumstances, aspirations, and position in the world.

It is that improvisational approach to identity that made it possible for Biko and his black consciousness comrades to redefine blackness to include coloureds and Indians. That is why Malcolm X came back from Mecca a changed man – less essentialistic about the white man as the 'devil'. Just as we speak of Arabian-Africans like Colonel Muammar Gadaffi, we should be able to talk of Jewish-Africans, Italian-Africans, or whatever. Improvisation, adaptation, hospitality, generosity and inclusion are at the heart of the African personality, encapsulated in the notion of *Ubuntu*. Black intellectuals have the potential to bring those values to bear on the process of generating a new social vision for South Africa. But that's all it is at this point: a potential.

Mbeki, visionary at large, is the manager at home
Sunday Independent, 6 February 2000

In his seminal article 'Managers and Leaders: Are They Different?', the Harvard University leadership guru Abe Zaleznik argues that managers and leaders are indeed different kinds of personalities. Managers value stability, predictability, efficiency, and rational control over organisational processes. They are infatuated with strategy. Leaders, on the other hand, are in a constant process of what Joseph Schumpeter called 'creative destruction'. In fact, leadership arises out of the ability to mobilise people around what may initially seem to be hopeless causes.

While managers rely on mounds of strategy manuals to guide their action, leaders inspire change through sheer talent, imagination, intuition, and effective relationships with followers. Drawing on William James's classic work *The Varieties of Religious Experience: A Study in Human Nature* (1902), Zaleznik describes managers as once-born people for their reluctance to venture beyond inherited patterns, and leaders as twice-born people for their restless search for change. To paraphrase the late Robert Kennedy, managers see things as they are, and ask why; leaders see things as they never were, and ask why not.

President Thabo Mbeki possesses both leadership and managerial qualities, but displays them at different levels. He has been a visionary leader on the global stage. South Africa and the African continent at large could not have asked for a better spokesperson in world forums – whether we are talking about the United Nations, the European Union, the G-8, the Commonwealth or the World Economic Forum. He has almost single-handedly placed the idea of the African Renaissance at the centre of global policy discussions.

As South Africans, we should be thankful for the manner in which he has shepherded our country back into the community of nations, establishing important bilateral relations with powerful nations such as the United States, Britain, and China. His experience as head of the ANC's international mission in exile helped hone the grace, comfort, skills and talent he shows at these forums. However, the opposite is true of the president's performance on the domestic front, where he has acted more like a manager concerned with strategic problem-solving. Here, he has followed a frenetic pace of institution-building, administrative reform, and legislative enactments.

While the president has shown bold leadership in respect of racial transformation, he has been more guarded on the economic front. Given that there is greater consensus on the need for racial redress than there is around economic policy, the managerial strategist in him knows which fight not to pick. The managerial mystique extends beyond economic policy to domestic policy in general. There is a widely held perception that the president is a stickler for detail. Cabinet ministers are like managers directly accountable to the chief executive. As it happens in many organisations, daily transactional leadership has been substituted for long-term visionary and inspirational leadership around issues of values. This is what James MacGregor Burns would call 'transformational leadership'. The privileging of strategic details gains a momentum of its own, and detracts from the development of an overarching *leitmotif* for the country. Loyalty, survival, and 'not rocking the boat'– the hallmarks of managerialism – take precedence over risk-taking, experimentation and innovation – the hallmarks of leadership.

And so, here we are with a president whose leadership potential, at least on the domestic front, remains half-fulfilled: a global leader of the African Renaissance shrouded in managerial mystique at home, a leader of racial transformation held back by the strategic managerialism of economic and domestic policy.

Plot debacle suggests opposition is the new treason
Sunday Independent, 29 April 2001

I was at a private dinner with former United States president Bill Clinton in Johannesburg the other day when my cellphone rang. What a rude intrusion, I thought, as I fumbled for the phone. It was one of my friends. 'Hey man, turn on the TV! The minister of safety and security, Steve Tshwete, is alleging that Cyril Ramaphosa, Tokyo Sexwale and Mathews Phosa have been spreading rumours that Thabo Mbeki was involved in the murder of Chris Hani!'

Here we go again, I thought. Our politics have become an embarrassment, a joke and a farce. Our political leaders have given official sanction to the insidious and deadly politics of rumour-mongering. One of the dinner guests asked: 'What if the movement hotheads just decide to go and shoot the alleged plotters?' After all, we come from a history of blind loyalty during the anti-apartheid struggle in which the slightest disagreement could lead to instant death. All that was needed to eliminate a political enemy was for someone to shout '*impimpi!*' (informer). And how long would it take before we all got caught up in ever-widening intrigues about who's plotting against whom? Are we really becoming just another banana republic in which power is wielded through political intrigue? What price political power?

I believe the answers to these questions will be revealed in how the public responds to Tshwete's allegations. Let me begin with the scarier response. The day after the minister's remarks, I got into my car and drove to my home town of Ginsberg in Eastern Cape. As soon as I arrived, I stopped off at one of my favourite watering holes, and found tongues wagging. One guy said: '*Kungaqhuma kubasiwe* (there is no smoke without fire); the minister would not have said it if it wasn't true. Those three guys are ambitious.' Another one chimed in: 'Thabo must now get the support of the Xhosa people.' And then a conspiratorial masterpiece that could have come out of a John le Carré novel: 'You see, Cyril, Tokyo and Mathews were involved in the arms deal, and Thabo wanted to expose them. That is why they want to remove him.' All this would be comical if it wasn't so dangerous.

By contrast, Nelson Mandela has shown us the way to respond to this politics of innuendo. Ever the honourable statesman, he spoke for many people when he came out in defence of the integrity of the three alleged 'plotters'. I suppose he was demonstrating, as only he knows how, that democratic leadership is first and foremost about building trust, and not about sowing suspicion and division.

The political economist Albert Hirschman once drew a distinction between social capital such as trust and financial capital such as money. Whereas money decreases with frequent use, trust accumulates through frequent use. The question then is whether Mbeki and his party have done enough to build the social trust necessary for citizens to compete openly for political office without fear of being labelled plotters. Mbeki and the ANC must face the challenge that democratically elected leaders face all around the world: they must either shape up or ship out. And we must get to a point where that is a ready sanction for our leaders. Challenges to leadership should be viewed as democratic contestation instead of 'plots'.

Countdown to the politics of adaptation has begun
Sunday Independent, 6 May 2001

The other night, I watched the ANC MP Mnyamezeli Booi on television congratulating the minister of safety and security, Steve Tshwete, on a job well done. I have known 'Nyamie' since our days in the student movement in the mid-1980s. His loyalty to the ANC was unshakeable, and by the looks of things it still is. My incredulity at his song of praise for the minister was therefore tempered by my prior understanding of this long-standing loyalty.

For Nyamie, organisational survival supersedes considerations about the external environment to which the organisation must appeal for support. Implicit in the primacy of the organisation over society is a deeply held belief in the indispensability of the ANC. As if attesting to this, Tshwete treated parliament as nothing more than a temporary inconvenience, declaring: 'I have to fly to Pretoria now.'

He could do this because he has the backing of the party bosses in parliament. But, contrary to the leadership's expectations, the insistence on unity has often led to party fragmentation as voters compete over interests. As the sociologist Alvin Gouldner cautioned, 'organisational survival is possible only in icy stasis in which security, continuity, and stability are the key terms'. Needless to say, the ANC members of the portfolio committee on safety and security chose to err on the side of 'icy stasis' and let him off the hook.

I welcome the attempts by the head of the ANC presidency, Smuts Ngonyama, to own up to the damage that the minister's statements have done to the country. But the instinct for organisational face-saving kept showing through his retractions, which sometimes sounded like 'non-retraction retractions'. I mean, it's rather ludicrous for the ANC leadership to commit a major blunder such as implicating three senior public figures in a plot to oust the president, and then to turn around and blame the media. It is equally irresponsible to suggest that Tshwete's comments were a matter of opinion. As for the argument that Tshwete did not have the benefit of hindsight that his critics have, may I simply suggest that we elect leaders precisely because they presumably exercise the political judgment needed to avert political disasters?

I have deliberately juxtaposed Nyamie's and Smuts's responses to suggest a choice for the president, the person where the buck ultimately stops. The choice is between the politics of organisational survival which has inevitably culminated in the current politics of intrigue on the one hand, and a politics of adaptation in which the party leadership goes beyond its narrow organisational concerns to address those of the broader society on the other. I submit that the mounting crises in the ruling party and government are intricately bound up with the politics of organisational survival.

And yet, potential crises will only be averted when there is a more open, less defensive organisational culture within the ANC. The question is whether the president will embrace and lead this politics of adaptation, or this will require a new leader. Mbeki has three more years to either dig us further into this rut or to permanently lead us out of it. The countdown begins.

Hybrid child Mbeki would do well to use selective retrieval
Sunday Independent, 13 January 2002

Ninety years of a struggle that culminated in a victory over one of the most heinous political systems of the 20th century do indeed call for a celebration. But history is important also because it can serve as a guide to present and future action. Indeed, a cursory look into the history of the ANC has helped me develop my own theory of President Thabo Mbeki's leadership. The essence of my theory is that Mbeki is a hybrid child of the three different strands of African nationalism that have evolved since the late 19th century.

The first strand goes back to the early conservatism of ANC founders such as John Dube and Pixley ka Seme. Those leaders studied in the United States and became part of a growing global African nationalism led by people such as W E B Du Bois and Booker T Washington. Those early ANC leaders had a complete disdain for any notion of a radical mass politics. Dube even warned that 'unless there is radical change soon, herein lies a fertile breeding ground for hot-headed agitators amongst us Natives, who might prove to be a bigger menace to this country than is generally realized today. Let us all labour to forestall them.' How does this early history link to Mbeki's leadership today, and what historical lessons can the president take from it?

There is indeed in Mbeki's leadership style the patrician, cerebral politics of those early leaders. Contrary to the dismay we often express about tensions between the president and his socialist alliance partners, the historical record shows this is not a new tension in the ANC. After all, Mbeki's idol Pixley ka Seme ousted the ANC president Josiah Gumede because Gumede suggested links with the Soviet Union. But Seme also presided over the most precipitous decline of the ANC. As Gail Gerhardt has put it: 'Under his autocratic leadership, the ANC had declined in the 1930s into an annual conclave of his own sycophantic personal followers.' The first historical lesson is that the current president must avoid Seme's fate, much as he admires him.

Paradoxically, the second strand of African nationalism to inform Mbeki's leadership comes from the radical nationalism of the ANC Youth League of Anton Muziwakhe Lembede, A P Mda, Robert Sobukwe, Nelson Mandela and Walter Sisulu. This generation ushered in the mass politics of the 1940s and 1950s. The more radical among them formed the PAC. Mbeki's critique of white racism could only have come from the legacy of this generation. Seme would have recoiled at such audacity. But even for this second generation of nationalists, ideas such as pan-Africanism were still the domain of the political elites. It is of no small social significance that Sobukwe was called 'Prof'. The historical lesson for Mbeki from this period is that even the most radical nationalism is not exempt from the demands of political decentralisation.

If the president is to overcome the limitations of the two nationalisms, he must look to the third strand of the community-based cultural nationalism of the black consciousness movement. This movement produced a new cultural vision of society through everyday popular culture, even though the movement itself was started by student elites. That's the way to go, Mr President! As an academic friend of mine puts it: 'While futures are indeed created, they are not typically created on a clean slate. It is hard for nations to leave their pasts behind. The ideological task is to retrieve that which is valuable, and to make this selective retrieval a political reality.'

II
THE STUMBLE

Many intellectuals choose loyalty over Mbeki's bad books
Sunday Times, 13 February 2000

Reading has been my passion since I was a five-year-old boy reading stories to older kids in my Eastern Cape home town of Ginsberg, to the days I spent at the Strand Bookshop in New York, where you can buy a 100-year-old classic for five dollars. I am therefore heartened to know that we have a president who reads. But my delight in the president's challenge to black intellectuals to read, issued in an interview with the *Sunday Times*, goes beyond the narrow subject of intellectuals having to read the proper journals in their field. My interest in what he said (or, perhaps more accurately, in what he did not say) is the relationship between the life of the mind and nation-building in general.

In his celebrated book *Imagined Communities: Reflections on the Origin and Spread of Nationalism* (1991), Benedict Anderson writes about the centrality of reading in the evolution of modern nationhood. As early as the 16th century, newspaper reading was a mass ceremony that connected people to one another. The paradox of the ceremony was that while it was performed in what Anderson calls 'the private lair of the skull', each reader was aware of the millions of others engaged in the same activity, thus 'creating that remarkable confidence of community in anonymity which is the hallmark of modern nations'. Books, too, played a major role in the raging struggles between dynastic and popular rule in an emerging Europe. Martin Luther became the first bestselling author when he translated his biblical theses into German in 1517, creating a mass readership and a popular literature that led to the dethronement of Latin and the decline of the Vatican's power and influence.

Reading also played an important role among the French *philosophes* who inspired France's revolutionary leaders; the salons of Paris were lively incubators of the ideas that gave France its enduring identity. Similarly, early English writers like John Locke engaged the public in discussions of the relationship between liberty and power in the coffee houses of England. As James MacGregor Burns has noted: 'It was in such coffee-houses and clubs that theorist and practitioner, government minister and academic critic, preacher and pamphleteer argued and perhaps shaped the practical applications of the ideas of the great intellectual leaders of an earlier century.'

Intellectuals have been at the centre of all social revolutions simply because every revolution or renaissance requires changes in cultural assumptions about the world. It is therefore not surprising that the president should sound so frustrated about black intellectuals not reading. In his scheme of things, they should be driving the cultural renewal. It is also heartening to hear the president urging intellectuals not to be intimidated by him. For intellectual life cannot be just about loyalty. The life of the intellectual is constantly torn between the quarrels of the ancients and the moderns. The ancients value loyalty, the moderns value critical analysis. Both are equally necessary to a democracy. One of the enduring lessons I learnt from my English I professor at Wits University was that there was no singular way of interpreting a poem or a prose. The practice of 'brainstorming' a sonnet allowed me to develop confidence in my own ideas.

But the 'brainstorming' is done within an overall story line – and the president should also acknowledge that the story line of the African Renaissance is hardly characterised by the give and take of the French salons and the English coffee houses. It needs to reach our townships and our villages as a grassroots *imvuselelo* (renaissance). One often senses a creeping anti-intellectualism in broader South African society. Business deals dominate our public life. Any discussion of ideas for their own sake is frowned upon as being too theoretical and intangible.

And here one wonders whether the president should not bear some of the responsibility for the anti-intellectualism he laments. His entire governing philosophy is based on the practical delivery of services. It is not clear to me, for example, to what extent intellectual ideas enter government policy-making – and here I'm not talking about consultants' reports written to ingratiate themselves with department heads, so as to get the next contract. I am talking about policy-makers reading books about philosophy, politics, economics, and so on. Please don't say you don't have the time. The president seems to manage.

The challenge is to make government itself a learning organisation. Even more importantly, the challenge is to make ours a reading nation, and accept the consequence that citizens of such a nation will always challenge power-wielders. That is why the first things despots do is to ban books. They fear the questions that come from knowledge. Seemingly, our president is not scared by this, which should be welcomed as a positive sign for our democracy.

There are intellectuals out there – some ensconced in government – who spend a great deal of time reading. Yet they dare not speak out because of the social and economic costs of doing so. There are widely held perceptions – real or imagined – that no one dare cross the president. Fearing that they may be branded as counter-revolutionaries, lose their cushy jobs in government, be forced to take their kids out of private school, or give up the Mercedes-Benz, many intellectuals will just not bother to engage the president intellectually.

It only makes things worse when the president sarcastically refers to his intellectual critics as those who think they are 'the clever among us'. In his famous book *Exit, Voice and Loyalty* (1970), Albert Hirschman suggested that individual citizens could decide either to ignore the debates of their societies, or openly voice their opinions. In many cases, they simply choose loyalty. And that, I suggest, is the real problem, Mr President.

While the AIDS sceptics investigate, let us act with caution
Sunday Independent, 9 April 2000

The present debacle over whether HIV causes AIDS relives old debates about the relationship between knowledge and action in policy analysis. Despite the appearance of a critical engagement with the global orthodoxy that HIV causes AIDS, President Thabo Mbeki, the minister of heath, Manto Tshabalala-Msimang, and the AIDS dissidents are reviving a rather conservative strain in the philosophy of knowledge. They are reviving what may be called rational positivism – a philosophy of knowledge that says we can act only on the basis of observable facts.

Rational positivism reached its heyday in the 1950s when social scientists insisted on rational models as a prerequisite for policy intervention. However, this obsessive search for incontrovertible evidence resulted in inaction. A break with this insistence on full knowledge was initiated by the father of modern policy analysis, Herbert Simon, himself a rationalist of sorts. Simon argued that decision-makers always operated under conditions of 'bounded rationality'. Instead of maximising data collection in the hope of full knowledge, we are better off 'satisficing', which meant taking the course of action that seemed good enough, given the limits of our knowledge. He concluded that 'the first step, and perhaps not the least important, is the test of common sense'.

Unfortunately, common sense is the least common thing in the current discourse on AIDS in South Africa. Like the rational positivists of yore, the AIDS dissidents and our political leaders seem to be suggesting that until such time that we have empirically isolated the virus and its linkage to AIDS, there is very little we can do.

Common sense would tell us that most of the time human beings act on the basis of suppositions and inferences. We don't have empirical knowledge of many of the things we believe in – from the existence of God to knowing whether a business venture will pay off. After years of studying development projects, the American political economist Albert Hirschman found that it was ignorance which drove people to undertake new ventures. To the rational, scientific notion that we should wait until all the information has come in, let me suggest a counterproposal: while the AIDS sceptics investigate, let us err on the side of the assumption that there is a deadly relationship between HIV and AIDS which is killing many people in this country, every single day.

Let me put it this way: if the AIDS dissidents, the president, and the minister of health are correct, the world would be forever indebted to them for their incredible foresight in exposing what would have been the greatest scam in the history of medicine. But if they are wrong, they would have been terribly wrong. The real question is whether we are going to stand by while they undertake such weighty decisions on our behalf. Amartya Sen once said that one of the reasons famines don't happen in democracies is because people are always on the alert. Equally, what is at stake in South Africa is the ability of our democracy to prevent a potential disaster.

By the way, I can't help observing that while we are often the first to accept global economic orthodoxies, we are last in accepting a global social orthodoxy on which our very existence depends. Could the reason for this contradiction be that global economic orthodoxies (which are no more empirically verifiable) promise money – while social orthodoxies involve spending it?

Time to talk openly about why we are feeling let down
Sunday Independent, 23 July 2000

A friend from Australia was here last week, attending the Urban Futures conference at Wits University. Naturally, she was curious to know how I was doing. And then she asked: 'How are things in South Africa?' Momentarily, I was torn between the impulse to defend the gains we had made since 1994 and the need to talk about the malaise gripping our political culture. And so I sought refuge in the obfuscatory power of words. 'A bit of an anti-climax,' I said, rather half-heartedly.

Later that day, I heard people ask the same question over and over again – 'what's wrong with the president?' – obviously referring to the HIV/AIDS debacle. In bars, shebeens and private homes, people are asking the same question: 'How did we get here? Did we have to go down this path? Did our head of state have to get mired in these medical minutiae about HIV and AIDS?' And: 'What about Parks Mankahlana, the presidential advisor who has died from complications caused by the disease?'

More important than direct answers to these questions – because only the president really knows – are the implications of what happens to a broader political culture when people can only speak in hushed tones in the privacy of their bedrooms. Here, the Eastern European experience is instructive for South Africans. The anarchy that wreaked havoc in Russia and Eastern Europe was largely attributable to the historical absence of civic institutions that could ensure the building of common institutions and common values as the basis of their new democracies. The lack of an open public sphere engendered a culture of mutual suspicion, paranoia and distrust; people spoke in codes even in their own homes.

What the Eastern European experience also demonstrates is that governments don't only fall or fail because of external assaults from their opponents; they also implode because of a lack of internal supports in the ordinary citizenry. This withdrawal of support is not necessarily a vocalised eruption, but plays itself out through a surreptitious process of drift. You can see this drift when people merely look at and applaud a president without listening any more. Unless something drastic happens, the HIV/AIDS debacle could be the Achilles' heel that produces such a drift in our society, and turns us into another Eastern Europe.

Two years ago, I excitedly praised President Thabo Mbeki for placing us on a path of nation-building reminiscent of people such as Jefferson, Nehru and Nyerere. I was one of those young people who were enthused and energised by this new intellectual head of state. Perhaps naively, I saw his trumpet call for an African Renaissance as a 'project of public purpose-building that could be the beginning of intellectual participation by young people in the formulation of their country's new identity'. From my youth I had always cherished the idea of government by the best and brightest. Lately, however, I have also felt a twinge of disappointment.

Perhaps I should have made room for the possibility of disappointment. After all, I also wrote that 'the African Renaissance as a national ethos will, in turn, depend on the extent to which it matches the common aspirations of South Africans across political, economic and cultural divides. Equally important are the means that are adopted to achieve the national consensus.' This is the message that former President Nelson Mandela gave to the current president and the ANC last week: 'It is necessary for us to start talking about commitment to the people. We must turn that into practice, and go into the areas where we stay and live. . . . If the president or deputy president goes to these houses, you will be surprised at the response you will get.'

Indeed, that is the only way in which the president and government can recapture our hearts and our imagination, and save himself and our generation from being remembered by the world and our children as the Great Disappointment.

Individual views of intellectuals provide a mirror for change
Sunday Independent, 20 August 2000

Last week, President Thabo Mbeki gave a seminal speech on the role of black intellectuals in South Africa – although we were distracted from its content by his broadside against the leader of the DA, Tony Leon. I don't know why the president keeps throwing the spotlight on Leon, and I'm sure Tony loves the publicity. Seems like he dangles the bait, and the president swallows it hook, line and sinker. Anyway, back to the subject of black intellectuals.

Drawing on a range of historical figures from Amílcar Cabral to Ngugi wa Thiong'o, the president described the black intellectual class as a confused group standing midway between the white ruling class and the black majority population. He asked: 'What then of our own petite bourgeoisie, which emerged out of foreign domination and which aspires to a way of life which is similar if not identical with that of the foreign minority? . . . Where is the black intelligentsia now, given that the victory over white minority domination, scored through their joint action with the native masses, has created the conditions for them to pursue their class interests, without let or hindrance?' He then calls on black intellectuals to stop being the 'foot-lickers' of their former enemies, and join the African revolution.

Mbeki's expectation of black intellectuals could generously be put within the classic Gramscian understanding of the intellectual function. In Gramsci's formulation, 'every social group creates together with itself, organically, one or more strata of its own intellectuals which give it homogeneity and an awareness of its own function not only in the economic but also in the social and political fields.'

At about the same time that the president was musing in public about the whereabouts of black intellectuals, I was being asked the same question at a community meeting in Ginsberg in the Eastern Cape. I had been going on about the virtues of local economic development when a younger man asked me: 'Xolela, what are you doing to bring back the intellectual debates we used to have in this community?'

He was referring to the days when we read every book we could lay our hands on, and entered in spirited debates about different approaches to struggle. If the president is closer to Gramsci in seeking to create a new class of intellectuals that will define a new transformative project, the young man is closer to C Wright Mills or Edward Said – or Karl Marx, who saw the role of intellectuals as 'a ruthless critique of everything and anything under the sun'. Mills argued that the role of intellectuals is 'to detect and state problems as potential issues for probable publics'. Said made a similar point by arguing that the *raison d'etre* of intellectuals is 'to represent all those people and issues that are routinely forgotten or swept under the rug' – whether by corporations or governments.

'The intellectual,' Said observed, 'always stands between loneliness and alignment . . . this is not always a matter of being a critic of government, but rather of thinking of the intellectual vocation as maintaining a state of constant alertness, of a perpetual willingness not to let half-truths or received ideas steer one along.' Said concluded that 'the intellectual will not adjust to domesticity or to humdrum routine'.

South Africa desperately needs a synthesis between the president's and the young man's vision of intellectual life. While black intellectuals ought to be part of the transformative project in a broader sense, they should retain their individuality, and ought not to be reduced to mere functionaries or competent bureaucrats. The expression of their individuality ought not be seen as mere foot-licking, but an attempt to provide a mirror to those in power.

HIV/AIDS debacle has damaged our collective identity
Sunday Independent, 24 September 2000

I could not sleep the other night because of a heavy feeling of worry lodged deep within my chest. I tossed and turned for hours, thinking about our public problems. And so, at three in the morning, I got up, made myself a cup of coffee, and wrote these angst-laden words:

What is happening to our country is sad. Very, very sad. We fought and arrived at freedom with such great promise. Remember those images of the great Madiba walking out of Pollsmoor, fist raised in triumph; the long queues of black voters broadcast all over the world; and the exhilaration of development-speak in the early 1990s?

At about that time, some of us left to study so we could become part of the greatest nation-building project of the late 20th century. Hardly a decade after the so-called 'miracle', we have landed with an equally miraculous thud – a political thud that has lodged itself in my chest and wakes me up at three in the morning. I must admit that I have never felt such a loss of political efficacy. As Carole Pateman pointed out in her classic work *Participation and Democratic Theory* (1970), democracy is above all about the political efficacy of citizens. Even under apartheid, I had some efficacy, some agency. I was part of something, and I could have an impact. Now all I can do is write these angst-laden words. I'm depressed. It is as if we are dying a slow collective death, dying of an internal bleeding that we all suspect but dare not diagnose.

Besides this, I am bothered by what economists would call the opportunity costs of our transition. We will probably never be able to tell what we have lost by embarking on our current path – until, of course, the death counts from HIV/AIDS start piling up. AIDS has all the makings of our own Vietnam, and worse. I can't think of any set of policies that have done more damage to our international and collective self-esteem than those on HIV/AIDS, with our economic policies a close second. Now we have proposals to bring the immoral conscription policies of the past back into our national life.

I have often suggested that the greatest challenge we face as a nation is not only the quantitative aspects of governance – how much you can deliver over a certain period of time. I make bold to say that even more important is the quality of our decision-making processes; our political culture. Of central importance in any political culture is the willingness of leaders to make midstream corrections and changes in direction. But this requires thinking about government both as a learning system capable of correcting its mistakes, and a system of public learning capable of increasing the political efficacy of its citizens. The one lesson of history in this process of public learning is that the quality of public policy decisions ultimately depends on our ability to learn together. Our public policy problems are a classic illustration of the one great lesson of history: because of their refusal to learn, governments are too often their own worst enemies, and citizens get the governments they deserve. We ignore this lesson at our peril.

So much for my sleep-talking. But I feel better now after getting all this off my chest. Try it; it's good for you, and good for our democracy.

AIDS drugs case gives Mbeki a chance to learn from Clinton
Sunday Independent, 11 March 2001

'If I am driving a car in desperate haste, come to a rickety bridge, and must make up my mind whether it will bear my weight, some principles of engineering would no doubt be useful. But even so I can scarcely afford to stop to survey and calculate. To be useful to me in a crisis such knowledge must have given rise to a semi-instinctive skill.' – Isaiah Berlin, *The Sense of Reality: Studies in Ideas and Their History* (1998)

I am tempted to suggest that the case brought by 39 pharmaceutical companies against the government's importation of generic anti-AIDS drugs provides an opportunity for President Thabo Mbeki to redefine his leadership strategy, away from a concern with practical policy details to a more general engagement with transcendent moral values of life and death. In that sense, his leadership would be more a matter of providing general

66

direction, parameters and values than the development and application of specific policies. The experience of former United States president Bill Clinton is instructive in this regard. Clinton's first years in office were marked by one political *faux pas* after another. That was partly because Clinton, a formidable intellectual in his own right, confused policy expertise with political leadership. His ambitious health care and welfare reform proposals did not fail because they were technically inferior. They failed because they were presented, rightly or wrongly, by their opponents as antithetical to the American value system.

Clinton's response was to assemble a formidable team of political and communications advisers, including the conservative whizz-kid Dick Morris. In no time, he re-emerged as a centrist who had appropriated some of his opponents' values discourse. His critics on the left mistook his responsiveness to public opinion for a lack of principle. But he did exactly what great American presidents such as Franklin Roosevelt had done. As the American writer and historian Garry Wills has put it with respect to Roosevelt: 'If Roosevelt had power, it came from his responsiveness to public opinion.' He realised that 'great leadership is not a zero-sum game'. Great leaders accumulate power by giving it away.

One way for Mbeki to accumulate power by giving it away would be to invite people to play their own part in the discussion of social values. Indeed, steadily and encouragingly, our public intellectuals are engaging in discussions of values. The advantage of a values discussion is that it has a broader invitational appeal, and therefore a salutary effect on our democracy. It is the invitational nature of his radio show that makes Tim Modise such an important feature of our democracy. He has accumulated his power in the best sense of that term by giving it away, by making us feel we have a voice. The president could use the bully pulpit of his office to the same effect.

I am also driven to the suggestion for a redefinition of presidential leadership towards an engagement with social values by the violent events of recent weeks. Hardly a week passes without headlines about some kind of mob violence. Typically, in this technocratic democracy of ours, policy analysts have even proffered privatisation as the solution. The logic seems to be that our problems will be lessened if we just get the trains to run on time, lock up the criminals and throw away the keys, or just burn them alive.

And yet, political leadership about values is needed precisely because we do not want to revert to a Hobbesian state of nature where children can rampage through Johannesburg destroying the hard-earned goods of their mothers and fathers. I suggest we need much more than policy. We may well be in need of a national discussion on social values between the president and the country's community and youth leaders.

The thought police ignore our history of moral reasoning
Sunday Independent, 13 May 2001

'I, Xolela Mangcu, being of sound mind, do solemnly swear that I have not now or at any time in the past colluded with rightwing forces or white liberals to undermine the democratically elected government of President Thabo Mbeki. I also swear that, as far as I can recall, I do not have any puppet-master pulling the strings behind every thought or word that originates from my pen. However, it is always possible that I suffer from a serious case of false consciousness, and that I have been unwittingly duped into this conspiracy.

'In order to assuage the fears of the Thought Police, I henceforth give up any autonomous moral reasoning that could be confused with the rightwing or white liberal plot against the president. I fully recognise that being black demands that I denounce any claim to independent expression and democratic citizenship. This is an irony by which I pledge to live, so that I may remain authentically black!'

This is the kind of ingratiating claptrap one would expect from intellectuals facing persecution in Eastern Europe. But now I fear that black intellectuals will feel compelled to offer such ingratiating assurances following the revelation of another plot against the president, allegedly by the country's black commentators. According to an advertisement placed in the *Sunday Times* last week by a group of business people sympathetic to Mbeki, there is a coalition of rightwing forces made up white so-called liberal politicians that is conspiring to undermine the president. 'Separately from them', the ad reads, 'there are a few black commentators who unwittingly contribute to this campaign.' Now, the HIV/AIDS 'dissident' David Rasnick has suggested that the veteran journalist and political activist Mathatha Tsedu is suffering from a similar case of false consciousness by being oblivious to a CIA/FBI/National Security Agency plot against the President. Welcome to the Pandora's box of conspiracy theories as political theory! Scary, if you ask me.

The advertisement, however, raises an important point about the moral autonomy of black people. It relies on a logic of black authenticity that urges black people to put solidarity with their leaders or heroes above everything else. In this case, the history of racial oppression is used as a form of racial blackmail, or what the writer Mothobi Mutloatse has described as 'the liberation handcuffs that have given us Mugabe, Nujoma, and now Chiluba'.

However, like Steve Biko before him, the distinguished African-

American scholar Cornel West defines blackness as a political and ethical construct: 'appeals to black authenticity ignore this fact; such appeals hide and conceal the political and ethical dimensions of blackness.' Indeed, throughout the struggle against apartheid, political solidarity was always tied to moral reasoning. That is why the vast majority of black people were appalled by barbaric acts such as 'necklacing'.

What is troubling about the new political culture is that political solidarity is being separated from, and assumed to trump, moral reasoning. As black intellectuals, we are asked to be party to that separation, but only on the side of political solidarity. According to this logic, black intellectuals should have shut up when the minister of safety and security, Steve Tshwete, implicated senior public figures in a plot to oust the president. Gone is the sense of fairness that has always informed our political struggle.

Are we not as black people entitled to our own autonomous sense of right and wrong about such matters without being manipulated by white people? And why should those who speak in the name of black authenticity predicate the moral integrity of black people on the actions of whites? Strange, very strange.

History, morality, values do not count for much in SA
Business Day, 29 May 2001

I choked with emotion while reading Sipho Mthathi's letter to *Business Day* on Monday ('Join us, do not spit in our faces'). Mthathi, the literacy co-ordinator for the Treatment Action Campaign (TAC), was responding to an article in which, among other things, Christine Qunta had accused the HIV/AIDS activist Zackie

Achmat of being a publicity-seeker. I was deeply pained by Qunta's article because I have always known Zackie to be a man of integrity. Mthathi's letter poignantly captures the pain of ordinary South Africans living with HIV/AIDS, a pain exacerbated by their political, social and economic distance from the levers of power.

The import of the letter extends far beyond the person of Christine Qunta. It is a collector's item that historians must keep if only to remind us of these cynical times. Mthathi writes that the 'deprivation of many already poor black women as a result of AIDS should be better understood by black women like Qunta who have skills to read and analyse situations. It is therefore tragic that many black middle class women and men, such as her, have been so silent on AIDS and the deaths of over 600 mostly black people daily.'

She continues: 'Qunta's article reinforces my sense of betrayal by many of our successful women leaders and those in Parliament who, despite the power vested in them by voting them into government, blindly join the boys' club which laments human rights activists as unpatriotic when they should be leading us to a better life for all.' She concludes with this plea: 'We wish our brothers and sisters in the elite, like Qunta and health minister Manto Tshabalala-Msimang, would work with us to save lives and give hope, instead of spitting in our faces.' We may be tempted to shoot the messenger, but the truth will remain long after he is gone, a lesson that our long and brutal history should have taught us by now.

Maybe, however, highbrow concepts such as history, morality and values do not amount for much in our money-crazed society. Judging by the frequency of corruption scandals among senior government officials, you would think we are living in Thomas Harding's 'tragedy of the commons', where each individual has to extract as many deals as possible before the public trough runs dry. I must say I read with utter dismay President Thabo Mbeki's assertion in his weekly letter to the ANC that these scandals are a fictitious creation of racist 'fishers of men' who seek to portray the black government as corrupt. The president sustains this assertion by employing a smart legalistic flourish. Because the government was responsible only for the awarding of main contracts in the arms deal, he argues, it cannot be held responsible for the shenanigans surrounding subcontracts. In one deft move, he has proven himself to be more creative than his 'fishers of men', bracketing from consideration the real crux of the corruption allegations.

But if we refuse to be distracted by this creative device, we confront the morass of corruption among the high and mighty, whether this is in cases where wrongdoing has been admitted by Tony Yengeni and Mosiuoa Lekota, or where the investigations are still under way in the cases of Deputy President Jacob Zuma and the recent revelations of a Nigerian oil deal secured in our name. I submit, Mr President, that the real fiction would be to look the other way simply because these are our black brothers and sisters. With race as a cover, our public life has become much more than fiction; it has become a tragicomedy.

And while I am on the subject of creativity, Mr President, I may as well point to the fiction that you have created around Zimbabwe. I suspect Zimbabweans suffering Mugabe's wrath will not be amused by your statement that 'the economic crisis currently affecting Zimbabwe did not originate from the desperate actions of a reckless political leadership . . . it arose from a genuine concern to meet the needs of the black poor'. Neither will they be terribly impressed with the statement by the minister of foreign affairs, Nkosazana Dlamini-Zuma, that 'we will never condemn Zimbabwe'. What will it take for the government to wake up to the reality of the monstrosity that is Robert Mugabe? To merely repeat the mantra that Zimbabweans will solve their problems is at best a non sequitur.

From where I sit in this theatre of the absurd, the real world of make-believe is to be found in the government's stance on HIV/AIDS, Zimbabwe, corruption, and the economic policies that have let loose joblessness, poverty, inequality, and hopelessness throughout our land. As in Zimbabwe, when the consequences of these policies hit our streets, we shall no longer talk of fiction, because – in the American poet and musician Gil Scott-Heron's prophetic words, 'the revolution will not be televised'.

Mbeki ends up fighting battles that should be left to others
Sunday Independent, 24 June 2001

'I suppose you guys have to write about this stuff,' one of my friends intoned, half-inquisitively. He was referring to the incident in which President Thabo Mbeki pushed – or slapped? – the president of the ANC Women's League, Winnie Madikizela-Mandela. 'Our leaders don't make it any easier, do they,' I replied. Earlier in the week, a fellow panelist on a radio talk-show asked me a similar question: 'Do we really have to talk about this stuff?'

I must indeed confess that for those of us not interested in 'gotcha' journalism, writing about this 'stuff' is really tiresome. One is never sure how long to bask in the afterglow of the president's policy successes before a political blunder erupts as if out of nowhere. I am now convinced that this rather vicious cycle of policy successes and self-inflicted wounds requires a structural solution. 'Stress' is the word that keeps cropping up in analyses

73

of Mbeki's mistakes. But what is leadership if it is not the management of the social stress that results from competing social values and aspirations? However, the mistake that leaders often make is to internalise the social stress, and make it their own; they react with undue haste and anger to the slightest provocation by their opponents.

The opposition loves this personal assumption of conflict because it is a potential minefield for developing caricatures of the leader. It is equally tempting for the leader to personally take the battle to the opposition camp. Remember, we come from a long history of strong leaders – from Afrikaner leaders such as Jan Smuts, J B M Hertzog, Hendrik Verwoerd and P W Botha to our own Nelson Mandela. Unfortunately, Mbeki's image as a philosopher-king does nothing to break with this historical leadership mould, and he ends up having to fight all kinds of battles, with all the mishaps that this entails.

A repetition of these mishaps can eventually narrow the scope of a leader's vision. The leader may develop self-doubt, and so may his followers. Even the strongest and brightest among us are not immune to indecision. As Harvard University's Ronald Heifetz has put it: 'Leadership cannot be exercised alone. The lone warrior model of leadership is heroic suicide. Each of us has blind spots that require the vision of others.'

In a rebuke of Plato's philosopher-king model of leadership, the American journalist and historian Garry Wills argues that the paradox of great intellectual leaders such as Socrates is that their leadership came from an absence of knowledge: 'the great teacher is the strategically ignorant person'. In line with this, the late Mwalimu Julius Nyerere defined leadership as the ability to say, 'I don't know'.

Heifetz advises leaders to adopt the following strategy: 'Engaged in the dance, it is nearly impossible to get a sense of the patterns made by everyone on the floor. To discern the larger patterns on the dance floor, we have to stop moving and get on the balcony.'

Similarly, I would urge the president to remould himself as a facilitating leader who periodically walks out onto the balcony and comes back to remind the citizenry of the broader values for which we stand, while allowing us to do the actual work. In the process, he should revamp his office with the best and the brightest kids on the block. They may not be members of his party, but they are out there. I see them every day.

We must take the initiative when our leaders fail us on AIDS
Sunday Independent, 9 December 2001

In his book *A Passion for Democracy: American Essays* (2000), the political theorist Benjamin Barber provides a model of leadership that could play a very useful role in the way in which we confront the HIV/AIDS pandemic in this country. The defining characteristic of this leadership model is the cultivation of consensus. Barber identifies two kinds of consensus-seeking leaders. The first are authoritarian leaders who inculcate consensus by inducing fear among the citizenry. In this approach, consensus and coercion are indistinguishable. The others are authoritative leaders who 'inculcate consensus only by discovering it, and maintain it only by respecting it'. Those leaders are incapable of defying the consensus reached by the people. And if they must defy it, they must do so from within the empirical realities of the people they serve.

Sure, we are not living under authoritarian rule. If anything, the TAC's court action against the government is a salutary indicator of the strength of our constitutional system of government. Somehow, it has increasingly become the judiciary's burden to unburden us of the follies of our politicians. And I do wish the TAC all the success in the world in this life-and-death court action. One of the most tragic ironies of our times is that one of the great political movements of the 20th century is being taken to court by its citizens over a life-and-death issue such as HIV/AIDS. I daresay that the HIV/AIDS challenge goes to the heart of our democracy's ability to listen to the consensus of pain reached expressly and tacitly by its people. Thus, while we may not live under authoritarian rule, we certainly do not live under the authoritative rule that respects the consensus that our people have reached on HIV/AIDS, a consensus buffeted by the empirical reality of their unending deaths.

While I applaud former president Nelson Mandela and Archbishop Desmond Tutu imploring President Thabo Mbeki to take leadership on this issue, I have personally given up on that possibility.

I feel very sad about that conclusion because, as Tutu said last week, the president has so much going for him on other fronts. We should perhaps see the president's failure on this most important front as a challenge to our own understandings of leadership. To paraphrase Barber, we have become 'a society of dependent hypochondriacs who think themselves capable of being healthy only when they are under the doctor's care'.

Now that the doctor-in-chief is not convinced of the cause of the mounting deaths, we seem rudderless. But HIV/AIDS will, sooner or later, rudely awaken us to our responsibilities to our children. We might as well take up the cudgels sooner rather than

76

later. We should all follow the example set by people like Mandela, Tutu, Nthato Motlana and the TAC, and respect the consensus on HIV/AIDS reached by our people through their own empirical reality of death. We need more leadership voices from within the ANC's National Executive Committee (NEC). Or has the NEC become such an elective oligarchy that not a single member, other than Mandela, has the courage and integrity to speak out openly on such a defining issue for our children and our nation? Surely, the deaths of our children are more important than political loyalty or fiscal austerity? Or have we all become so callous as to allow bureaucratic power and political self-interest to blunt the moral sensibilities of *Ubuntu* that have always informed our very identity as a caring and feeling people?

Blind acceptance of authority can only weaken democracy
Sunday Independent, 27 January 2002

A spectre is haunting our country. It's the spectre of authoritarianism. This formulation is a paraphrase of Edward Shils's famous opening line in his essay 'The Theory of the Mass Society'. Shils was addressing the spectre or ghost of mob rule in modern democratic societies. Early sociologists spent a lot of time worrying about the tendency for society to become a uniform, undifferentiated mass under the spell of one man. This concern was shown to be justified as countries such as Germany, Russia, and Italy developed various forms of mob rule. Apartheid itself was based on a strong civil society of religious, educational and media institutions. Civil society can thus easily translate into a fear-inspiring culture of civic authoritarianism. So where am I going with this historical preface?

Well, last Wednesday I was asked to participate in a discussion of President Thabo Mbeki's call for volunteerism on Tim Modise's television show. I made the mistake of suggesting that volunteer programmes had a greater chance of success when they were constructed as national programmes, rather than party-political ones. We have seen on our own continent the tragic consequences of party-led volunteerism. Jomo Kenyatta's Harambee, Hastings Kamuzu Banda's Young Pioneers, Swaziland's Lusekwane, and Leabua Jonathan's Youth League are just a few examples of how such party-political programmes can be used to terrorise citizens into joining the party. These are historical lessons that those of us who work in the public sphere have a responsibility to warn against.

Unfortunately, there's a growing tendency to describe such warnings as unpatriotic or being 'against the President'. You can tell that the spectre of authoritarianism is creeping into your country when people feel they have to build a personality cult around the head of state, subsuming all manner of independent thinking, identity and individuality into that of the uniform mass.

The trouble with the ghost of authoritarianism is that it is insatiable, making no distinction between the guilty and the innocent, friends and enemies, and devouring its own children in the end. Nuances, modifications, questions, suggestions, however benign, are instinctively viewed as threats to authority. Citizens themselves begin to internalise what the political philosopher Hannah Arendt has described as 'a self-coercive force of logicality' that demands nothing but absolute obedience to authority. Being 99 per cent loyal will not suffice; it must be 100 per cent. I cannot imagine such an obsequious life. For as long as I can remember, I have always asked questions of my parents, my teachers, my employers, my political and community leaders, everyone.

In analysing the spectre of authoritarianism, we often limit our gaze to the behaviour of people in positions of authority. While they must indeed do all they can to discourage this development, the even bigger task is for all of us to re-examine our own understandings of authority, and what it means for future citizenship. It would indeed be tragic if we started hush-hushing our children whenever they posed questions to those in authority. Such a political culture would amount to no less than stunting their development as moral beings.

As the British philosopher Isaiah Berlin noted in the *Crooked Timber of Humanity: Chapters in the History of Ideas* (1992): 'Happy are those who live under a discipline which they accept without question, who freely obey the orders of leaders, spiritual or temporal, whose word is fully acceptable as unbreakable law. That may make for contentment, but not for understanding what it means to be human.'

Spare our children this nightmare of preventable death
Sunday Independent, 3 February 2002

'The promise was so beautiful. Even those who were too young to understand it all knew that at last something new was being born. It was there. We were not deceived about that. How could such a thing turn so completely into this other thing? Could there have been no other way?' – Ayi Kwei Armah, *The Beautyful Ones Are Not Yet Born* (1968)

Tomorrow is my birthday, but my gift has already come – in the form of a dream. It takes me back to my childhood, kneeling on the dusty floor of our community hall in Ginsberg with other children, waiting for the performance to begin. The tall and lanky poet Steve Bantu Biko appears, dressed in a bright blue dashiki. The odd thing is that he keeps to one side of the stage, and looks up to the sky as if talking to God. His face is smooth and unblemished, and he looks remarkably like his mother, Ma-Mcethe. I am so excited that this man who has had such a hold on my life has finally arrived back from exile – the last of the returnees. But to my great disappointment, I realise that he is dead, even as he continues to recite his poetry.

Yes, I do think we have for too long exiled Biko from our national life. He is reappearing on our public stage through the cultural activities of what Zakes Mda calls 'Biko's Children'. These are youth artists plying their consciousness-raising poetry at various underground venues, waiting to come to centre stage when we are ready to listen. But power still prevents us from listening. And, as the political scientist Karl Deutsch once warned, you know people are blinded by power when they can afford not to learn or to listen.

It is also very significant that Biko's mother appears in my dream. Ma-Mcethe had an expansive understanding of motherhood. All the children of this country were her children, and her son often said he too was a child of every other mother. This extended sense of parenthood defined what it meant to be black. We need that collective sensibility now as our babies perish from the preventable scourge of HIV/AIDS. When I was born, my parents could say with a certain degree of confidence that I would live to be an adult. Today, our government stands culpable of failing to provide that certainty to the innocent babies who will be born, and just as quickly die, as I celebrate my birthday tomorrow.

In desperation, I can only say, come back Biko – if not in

person, then in spirit. Come back so that our children can also dream the dreams we used to dream, the dreams we still hold in our heads, the dreams that wake us up at night. But wake them not to this nightmare of preventable death, where their birthdays serve as mere rituals for the confirmation of their deaths.

Oh, the people we have become, so soon after our freedom. As the Ghanaian writer Ayi Kwei Armah put it: 'How horribly rapid everything has been, from the days when men were not ashamed to talk of souls and of suffering and of hope, to these low days of smiles that will never again be sly enough to hide the knowledge of betrayal and deceit. There is something of an irresistible horror in such quick decay.'

Mbeki talked the talk – now he must walk the walk
Sunday Independent, 10 February 2002

Brilliant, absolutely brilliant! That was my reaction to President Thabo Mbeki's State of the Nation Address. Tears of pride filled my eyes as the president gave a comprehensive address that was couched in the language of values. In reviewing the speech, I went back to a column I wrote following the president's address last year. I argued then that a language of values was needed to address the state of the nation. By going back to the basics of *Vuk'uzenzele* (wake up and do it for yourself), the president affirmed and articulated the long-standing value orientation that 'no one should do for us what we can do for ourselves'. It is indeed of no small symbolic significance that both Rebecca Kotane and Nontsikelelo Biko were in the audience, to bear witness to a contemporary articulation of the dreams of their late husbands.

With due respect to the South Africans living in America who came up with the concept of *Vuk'uzenzele*, I would have been happier if the president had situated it in the historiography of self-help in our own communities since the 19th century.

I was also happy to hear the president re-issue the call to volunteerism he made at the 90th ANC anniversary, but this time as president of the nation, calling on all of us to contribute what we can in our respective communities by helping children to register for social grants, contributing to our schools, and participating in a process of moral regeneration. These are the spiritual foundations upon which all national identities are built. And, as the social science research of the past decade shows, the quality of political and economic development of nations depends on their civic values. For these reasons, it was actually saddening to see almost all the opposition parties groping, in a pathetic knee-jerk fashion, for something negative to say about the speech, despite its transcendent appeal. By so doing, they confuse cynicism with criticism. In the hurly-burly of a clamorous political year, a state of the nation address, especially when it is delivered as well as it was on Friday, gives us a moment of collective reflection, not sectarian genuflection.

There were also some tentative shifts in the president's position on policy issues. After giving a free commercial for Stellenbosch University, he spoke candidly about the government's shortcoming in respect of HIV/AIDS. What he ought to do now is to walk the talk through greater spending on an epidemic that could be a tinderbox of not only his but all of our undoing. He signalled a shift towards a great focus on job creation through an expanded community works programme, and spoke forthrightly about what ought to happen in Zimbabwe. I get a sense that Mbeki is a very cautious man. But maybe with a public that is mobilised and engaged around transcendent values, he will feel freer to take the leaps of faith that are always the hallmarks of great leaders.

All in all, Mbeki was in his best element on Friday. As the gallery burst out with the song '*Nanko U Thabo Uyasibiza*', I felt that he had spoken to me, to all of us, to this nation, and its antecedent values. But then again, I have felt like that before. Now is the time for the president to think creatively about how to extend this uplifting moment beyond the pomp and pageantry of parliament.

Clinging to the rollercoaster ride that is HIV/Aids policy
Sunday Independent, 24 February 2002

We are governed by politicians who don't know how to bask in the glow of their own success. Hardly a couple of weeks have passed since President Thabo Mbeki received rave reviews for his state of the nation address. Some of us even excitedly pronounced significant shifts in the government's policies on HIV/AIDS, which is why the increase in spending for HIV/AIDS in this year's budget has been interpreted as a logical extension of the President's pronouncements in parliament.

Enter health minister Manto Tshabalala-Msimang, acting like the court jester of the new republic. All earthly kingdoms are entitled to their court jesters. But rarely, if ever, do court jesters have license over human life. Their function is to amuse rulers and ridicule critics – except that nobody is sure of what the current rulers think, and the critics are unlikely to be fobbed off that easily. Oh, the sorry spectacle of a court jester without a public court. But then again, when all else fails, the party will provide the court for its own jesters. The public be damned, literally and figuratively!

At the very least, the jesters can count on the audience of the man whose rugby kit I used to carry as a little boy: Smuts Ngonyama. Ngonyama lambasted Gauteng premier Mbhazima Shilowa for 'jumping the mark' in announcing an expanded programme for his province. Frankly, 'Bra' Smuts, we need more than jumps to catch up with the HIV/AIDS mark. We need leaps and bounds!

But Shilowa also forgot the oldest rule in party politics, namely the 'iron law of oligarchy.' At all times, the party before the public! Not even former President Nelson Mandela could escape the grip of the iron law. How sad to see the indignity of the world's greatest living freedom fighter being wrapped over the knuckles for speaking out on a matter of conscience. Sadder still to see him overcompensate by saying that the government's HIV/AIDS programme is the best in the world.

But if a larger-than-life figure like Mandela cannot escape the iron law of the party, why should Shilowa think he can? It cannot be that Shilowa is more courageous than Madiba, nor can he be less vulnerable to the iron law of the party. This leads me to a less than generous conclusion about Shilowa's actions. Like those of us who gave rave reviews about the president's speech, Shilowa pounced on the slightest indicator of a policy shift in the ANC, perhaps more out of hope than *realpolitik*. But the government's latest announcement that it will challenge a court ruling that it should roll out Nevirapene is a slap in the face of such hopefulness. We may have reached a dead-end in this debacle. If anything, these latest developments expose those of us who were quick to provide rave reviews of the president's pronouncements on HIV/AIDS for the utter fools we have been. What a rollercoaster ride this has been, trying to keep up with the government on HIV/AIDS. It must be an even bumpier ride for those living with HIV/AIDS.

The only way we can redeem ourselves for raising false hopes among those living with AIDS is to stay at the crest of the wave of hope and support whatever alliances of hope on HIV/AIDS emerge inside the ANC. As the Brazilian scholar and activist Paulo Freire once said: 'Any attempt to do without hope in the struggle to improve the world is a frivolous illusion.' Now is the time to do the right thing – *ke nako*!

Loyal cadre slips up as country dies of haemorrhage
Sunday Independent, 31 March 2002

Mr Loyal Cadre is a senior member of the ANC's NEC. He receives notice of a special meeting to debate the government's position on HIV/AIDS. Arguing the government's position that there is no demonstrable link between HIV and AIDS is the revolutionary Peter Mokaba of 'Kill the Boer, Kill the Farmer' fame.

Representing the mainstream view that HIV causes AIDS is the distinguished Oxford-educated immunologist Professor Malegapuru William Makgoba. Mokaba brings down the roof with a foot-stomping, chest-beating, fire-eating oration entitled 'Castro, Hlongwane, Caravans, Cats, Geese, Foot-and-Mouth, and Statistics: HIV and the Struggle to Humanise the African'. As someone used to the quiet din of the laboratory, Professor Makgoba is visibly shaken by the taunts and jibes from the other side. He nervously stammers through his presentation, 'How HIV Fulfils Koch's Hypothesis as a Causative Agent of AIDS'. The vote is a mere formality, and Mokaba trounces Makgoba by 100–0. The meeting adjourns, and everyone is invited for cocktails, caviar, whisky and wine. A queue forms to congratulate Mokaba: *'umshayile mfowethu, icabanga ukuthi i-clever le-outie'* (you fixed him right, he thinks he's clever).

Mr Loyd Cadre drives home to find his daughter, Renaissance, elated that she's been admitted to study for her PhD in medicine at Oxford. Now she needs advice about the challenges of Oxford. Comrade Mokaba, his oratory notwithstanding, is not exactly the person Mr Cadre has in mind. So he reluctantly calls Makgoba, who, following the afternoon's events, has decided to return to Oxford. Makgoba graciously agrees to take Renaissance under his wing. Mr Cadre thanks the professor profusely, and then says: 'Please, please, please, Prof, this conversation never happened.'

A couple of months later, the government appoints Comrade Mokaba as the new minister of health in recognition of his understanding of '*ama*-issues' and '*ama*-dynamics'. After all, as Thomas Kuhn once said, scientific breakthroughs are often brought about by outsiders like Comrade Mokaba. Comrade Mokaba might just be entered in the Guinness Book of Records for initiating both a militant youth revolution and a medical breakthrough. A first for the African Renaissance!

In the meantime, Renaissance does exceptionally well at Oxford. As a child of the revolution, she wants to enter the public service. Mr Cadre knows that with her mainstream views on HIV/AIDS she has no chance in hell: 'Stay where you are, my child. Others have already left, deprived of the capacity to dream by me and my generation.' And then he goes into a long history of how Africa exiled bright minds like the Kenyan academic Ali Mazrui to the West: 'History has a cruel way of repeating itself,' he concludes. But still his historical consciousness is not persuasive enough to distract him from the possibility that he too might still become minister of health. It is the mere allure of the job that makes him live up to his name, the one and only Loyal Cadre.

Despite his exterior bravado, his guilt is privately eating away at him. And then one evening the national broadcaster announces that Mr Cadre has died of internal bleeding, and that the country itself has long died of a brain haemorrhage, which 'Doctor' Mokaba was never able to diagnose. Mr Cadre's relatives send out urgent messages to Professor Makgoba and Renaissance to come back for yet another shot at an African Renaissance, the third one since Nkrumah and Mbeki. 'It is time to catch up with the world again,' the national broadcaster announces to an inattentive audience.

What happens when the racial and tribal cover is blown?
Business Day, 3 July 2003

President Thabo Mbeki's frequent references to race to explain the actions of his opponents, and his eulogy for Kaiser Matanzima, former president of the 'homeland' of Transkei, have given me cause to pause and ask: has there been an ideological reversal on the concepts of race and tribe within the ANC? After all, we have always known the ANC to be a 'progressive', 'modernist' organisation that transcends primordial categories of race and tribe. What occasioned this turnaround?

I remember vividly the debates that I, as a student leader in the black consciousness movement, used to have with ANC student leaders about their avowed principle of non-racialism. They argued fervently that we were engaged in a class struggle, and that race had nothing to do with it. That class analysis owed its origins to the long-standing dominance of the South African Communist Party (SACP) in the politics of the ANC. The ANC depended for its resources on the SACP's direct access to the Soviet Union. If you wanted to make it into the leadership of the ANC, you had to join the party. Even as people like Oliver Tambo went into exile to set up u-Mkhonto weSizwe, the real power lay with communists such as Moses Kotane. The breakaway of the PAC in protest against the communist influence further eroded whatever nationalist power base Tambo might have hoped for. However, the arrival of exiles from the black consciousness movement in the 1970s strengthened Tambo's hand. Tambo then formed Okhela, an alternative group led by radical whites such as Breyten Breytenbach, to counter the influence of the SACP. One of Breytenbach's objectives when he was arrested was to arrange for Steve Biko to come out to Belgium for a meeting with Tambo.

Tambo's hand was further strengthened by the decline of the Soviet Union. Suddenly, a number of ANC leading lights, including heir apparent Thabo Mbeki, resigned from the SACP. One would have expected the ascendant nationalists to join forces with the black consciousness movement internally in the 1980s. But the communists had already cornered the domestic political scene, especially through the trade union movement. Hence the paradox in the 1990s of a nationalist leadership in exile, and a socialist leadership in the trade unions at home. The nationalist exiles captured power and began to reformulate the ideological terrain; hence the president's constant emphasis on race.

The problem of course is that these appeals to racial solidarity have come back in the context of conservative economic policies that are producing rampant joblessness among blacks. Racial solidarity may well come in handy for the short-term purposes of the 2004 elections.

Let me turn to an explanation of the ANC's awkward embrace of the institution of traditional leadership. In a brilliant doctoral thesis on traditional leadership, Lungisile Ntsebeza, an academic at the University of the Western Cape, builds on Mahmood Mamdani's thesis that post-colonial Africa, including South

Africa, deracialised without detribalising. Post-colonial states institutionalised chieftaincy, and left many rural dwellers under the rule of unelected leaders. Mamdani argues that this created an iniquitous situation of urban citizens and rural subjects. People like Govan Mbeki and local activists in the 1980s had long argued that chiefs had outlived their usefulness. How did it happen that these formerly discredited institutions would have their role enshrined in the constitution, have their own house of traditional leaders, and receive salaries and support from the state?

Ntsebeza argues that the ANC never really had a strong base in the rural areas, and thus needed 'traditional' infrastructure to bolster its support in the post-apartheid period. But, as with the turn to race, the embrace of tribe also takes place in the context of a conservative economic orthodoxy. This orthodoxy has meant that the government has very little money to create rural institutions and promote rural development. Ntsebeza concludes that 'the recognition of the institution of traditional leadership was by and large influenced by political and reconciliation considerations, rather than influenced by popular support. The recognition of the institution was part of the highly political arena of choosing and consolidating alliances between elites, to the exclusion of ordinary rural people, and ignoring realities on the ground.'

But then again, who knows when the chickens of rural poverty will come home to roost, and everyone will be taking to the rooftops to declaim: 'The emperor of capitalism has no tribal clothes in which to hide any longer?' The ANC may have revised its stance on race and tribe to mediate the impact of its conservative economic policies. Sooner or later, though, the capitalist emperor will really have no racial or tribal clothes in which to hide.

Cryptic Mbeki runs risk of losing touch with common people

Sunday Independent, 12 February 2004

I have never met President Thabo Mbeki. I am told, though, that he possesses a formidable intellect, allowing him to hold his own among world leaders. He is suave, articulate and generally genteel, save for the moment when he pushed Winnie Madikizela-Mandela in her face, or when he seemed flustered by a question about HIV/AIDS on television last Sunday night. When the SABC journalist Redi Direko asked him whether he became irritated by questions about HIV/AIDS, the president responded: 'No, it does not irritate me. What irritates me is why people do not want to think.'

This particular response betrays an all-too-common flaw among a certain category of intellectuals. In his book *Certain Trumpets: The Nature of Leadership* (2013), the American journalist and author Garry Wills identifies two types of intellectuals. The first are those who engage in a rigorous and lonely quest for the absolute truth, and end up frustrated with those who 'do not want to think'. Wills cites the case of the great 20th century philosopher Ludwig Wittgenstein as an example: 'Unlike Socrates, who engaged citizens in philosophical self-examination at public meeting places, Wittgenstein could not bring himself, very often, to meet with a small circle of students. He feared that not even those select Cambridge philosophers would understand him.'

However, an intellectual president does not have the luxury to behave like Wittgenstein, whether about HIV/AIDS or any other matter. He also has to attend to the business of the nation. How then to be an intellectual and a president at the same time? For that you must pursue what Wills describes as the second type of intellectual excellence, namely to work towards 'a less exacting but more accessible truth'. The father of administrative science, Herbert Simon, called this 'satisficing' – making decisions on the basis of imperfect information. In many ways one could say that the government's strategy on HIV/AIDS follows the latter kind of intellectual inquiry – until, of course, the president or minister of health lapses into solipsistic arguments that leave us all agape, perhaps because we 'do not want to think'.

The model of the intellectual president as a latter-day Wittgenstein would hamper his ability to communicate in other dimensions as well. As Wills puts it, 'calls are always going down the vasty deep; but what spirits will respond?' Our president seems to feel frustrated because no one understands him. Instead of calling forth the energies of the people, he becomes self-absorbed. His speeches take on a particular predictable and uninspiring pattern.

First, there is the usual acknowledgement of the struggle family in the parliamentary gallery; then the characteristic quote from a poet or writer, preferably white, either W E B Yates, John Dunne, Ingrid Jonker, Willie Esterhuyse, Rian Malan, or a white couple now living in America who are suddenly crazy about the spirit of *Vuk'uzenzele*. I must say though that the least attractive of the president's rhetorical devices is the by now familiar refrain: 'There are some among us . . . ' In Xhosa, it's called '*uku-kwekwa*', and it's not a very nice way of talking.

The reality is that when the president says 'there are some among us who are not as mature as Rian Malan', we know he is referring to opposition leader Tony Leon. Why doesn't he say so? And then there's the reference to 'we are on course . . . ', and the constant refrain of 'as President Mandela said ten years ago . . .' Frankly, I don't know if comparing the present government's current achievements to a dysfunctional apartheid government is the proper benchmark for measuring social progress. We could only do better.

I suspect, though, that the predictable structure of the president's speeches is a case of form following function. His rhetorical predictability is linked to a need for a broader predictability in the eyes of international markets. When he says 'there shall be no policy changes', he is not so much talking to us as to international markets. That is the path the ANC has chosen, and that is the path we are stuck with for the next five years. It is what Douglass C North called 'path-dependence' of the worst kind. There will be none of the 'bold, persistent experimentation' that Franklin Roosevelt spoke about when he confronted America's poverty and unemployment in the 1930s.

That's exactly the kind of social experimentation this country needs if we are to confront our social challenges. But I also know I am howling in the wind. That kind of social experimentation would require a different kind of intellectual leadership from the president, away from the Wittgensteinian model to the Socratic model of public engagement. A new social function could perhaps yield a new form of speech, one that speaks to the young people of this country. I'm sure the markets can wait; they might even appreciate it.

This column provoked strongly worded responses from the presidential spokesperson Bheki Khumalo as well as the head of the ANC presidency, Smuts Ngonyama. In a letter to the editor headlined 'Mangcu's song' (Sunday Independent, *19 February 2004), Khumalo wrote:*

Sir:- What to make of Xolela Mangcu? His column, 'Cryptic Mbeki runs risk of losing touch with common people' (12 February) has an undertone of hell having no fury like a columnist spurned. From Mangcu's whimsical opening ('I have never met President Thabo Mbeki') one can see trouble ahead. Wittgenstein could never bring himself to meet with students, wails

Mangcu. You do not have to be a student of psychology to understand the particular axe that Mangcu is grinding. Mangcu decorates his column with big names; it seems that the president's sin is not to play along. How dare the president quote Rian Malan and the tragic heroine Ingrid Jonker, but not the great Mangcu, a legend in his own mind?

Mangcu's columns tend to be overburdened, undigested polymathism, and the present column is an example. In rapid succession, and neatly giving the subeditors the slip, Mangcu has the president citing a non-existent poet 'Yates' (I think the fellow means Yeats) and a further , also non-existent, poet called John Dunne. The fellow means to say John Donne. Mangcu is singing for his supper.

Not long ago, the editor of *Business Day* urged South African conglomerates to shower Mangcu's institute with money. But then comes the irony: Mangcu is not only a trader and entrepreneur in ideas, he is a sectarian advocate of black consciousness. That is why, methinks, he resents the president's citing of Malan and Jonker. Whites must get little or no credit in Mangcu's world – except, of course, when white-run corporates bring gifts to fundraising dinners. In our president's world, nonracialism is the governing principle of true Africanism.'

Ngonyama weighed in as follows (Sunday Independent, *19 February 2004):*

Sir:- Xolela Mangcu's broadside against President Thabo Mbeki and the ANC in his article, 'Cryptic Mbeki runs risk of losing touch with common people' (February 12), betrays a deeply insecure intellectual who chooses conjecture over fact. While he claims never to have met the president, he nevertheless ventures out and casts deep aspersions on his person and integrity. The average reader would assume that his admission that he has never met the president would suggest that he is less than qualified to make the kind of judgement he makes. The fact that he has never met Mbeki is indeed telling, as we are certain numerous opportunities had presented themselves to him, but he failed to oblige.

Selective amnesia has never made a man honourable, and it certainly does not make the writer seem any more intelligent. South Africa is very aware of the very wide range of African writers and artists Mbeki frequently quotes and does not need anyone to point them out, especially in a selective manner that smacks of malice. A substantial number of them are renowned and celebrated African scholars, including S E K Mqhayi, A C Jordan, J J R Jolobe, Wally Serote and Wole Soyinka, to mention but a few.

Mangcu makes an issue out of the president's quotation of Ingrid Jonker and Rian Malan. It is mind-boggling why it should be wrong for the president to acknowledge South Africans like Jonker and Malan. Is he perhaps suggesting they are less South African because they are white? Mbeki is the president of South Africa, a multiracial nation that has acknowledged every one of its citizens across the racial spectrum as an equal citizen.

Mangcu continues his tirade and ridicules the president when he remarks that there are people who refuse to think in our society, and misses the context entirely. It is indeed true that there are many in this country who are fixated to a particular point of view and do not want to look at issues from others' point of view. Those are the people who refuse to think and see the bigger picture. Those are the kind of people who do not make any meaningful contribution to our national discourse.

Mangcu makes the point that the president utilises the term 'some among us' and refers to this as '*ukukwekwa*'. Mangcu's toying with the language is rather strange, and belies his desperate need to find fault where none exists. A reference to 'some among us' hardly qualifies for *'ukukwekwa'* in Xhosa, as the statement simply acknowledges that there are others who share the same point of view. The president does not need to make veiled references to DA leader Tony Leon; at the same time, he is not naïve enough to believe that there are no others who share Leon's point of view, as surreal as it may be.

We believe a person of Mangcu's calibre has an incredible role to play in shaping our future discourse. It is rather unfortunate that he chose not to take up the challenge to play a meaningful role in building our nation. The ANC believes that African scholars like Mangcu can and should become beacons of hope and inspiration to the rest of the nation.

Troubled by the tone and language of these letters, the academic and author Njabulo Ndebele waded in with the following letter to the editor, published a week later (Sunday Independent, *19 February 2004*)

Sir:- I have always found Dr Xolela Mangcu's column thoughtful and insightful. He has consistently come across as a genuinely concerned and candid commentator on a range of public issues, persuading most people who read him that his views deserve serious consideration. In this, he is often provocative and sometimes succeeds in eliciting very robust public reaction.

I do not believe that he, nor anyone else who dares to express considered opinions, deserves the ad hominem attack that presidential spokesman Bheki Khumalo made in his letter (19 February). It is not too much to expect of the presidential spokesman to enhance rather than diminish public discourse. In my view, Mangcu's 'offending' article could have been better viewed as feedback for the president's speech writers who have to understand a complex national environment and then grapple, I suspect, with the search for appropriate and most effective rhetorical strategies to achieve desired effects in the president's speeches.

A response in this regard could have helped the public better understand the challenges of preparing the president's speeches. Instead, righteous indignation has left us in the dark. An opportunity to clarify has been lost.

If anything, Trahar understates the extent of political risk in SA
Business Day, 16 September 2004

I respectfully submit that President Thabo Mbeki had no business getting worked up about the assertion by Tony Trahar, chief executive officer of the Anglo American Corporation, that the 'South African political risk issue is starting to diminish – although I am not saying it has gone'. I have read and re-read this statement many times to find the nuance that could get the president so riled up. I think Trahar completely underestimates the political risk situation in this country, precisely because he does not want to be perceived as negative. But there is nothing negative about telling the truth. And the truth is that political risk in South Africa is far greater than even Trahar makes out, and that this has nothing to do with the colour of our skin. It has everything to do with the country's economic and social policies.

In his column on the ANC website last week, the president posed the question: 'What information does Anglo American have, or projections into the future, which say that there is a persisting political risk in our country, on which it must base its decisions about our country?' The newspaper *ThisDay* followed with an editorial stating that, 'thinly veiled sarcasm aside, the president is justified in posing such questions'.

I don't know how the president and the editors of *ThisDay* could miss the evidence of political risk all around us. If I was sitting in New York and thinking about where to put my money, I would indeed be worried about the risk posed to the productivity of the South African workforce by the scourge of HIV/AIDS. I would be even more worried about what the government is doing, or not doing, about it. I would see risk in the levels of poverty and inequality in this country, with almost half of its people living in poverty. I would be worried by the growing levels of unemployment and inequality. I would be worried about the prospects of returns in a country that has anaemic growth rates. A number of eminent economists – Dani Rodrik, Paul Krugman and Samuel Bowles among them – have pointed out that investors are attracted to countries where the prospects for returns are greatest, even if that means going to communist China.

I remember teaching graduate students at the University of Maryland that this risk-factoring process played a central role in company location decisions, and even decisions about choosing cities within countries. Contrary to the common assumption that business looks for places with cheap labour, what emerged in the literature about local economic development was that the quality of schools, health facilities, security, and other similar types of social facilities played a major role. And the truth is that our social fabric is falling apart because of HIV/AIDS, joblessness, inequality, crime, and sheer hopelessness. If our head of state is going to be so sensitive about everything or anything that anybody says which is remotely unpleasant about the state of affairs in our country, then we are going to end up with a mute nation.

Speaking at the Steve Biko memorial lecture in Cape Town last week, Nelson Mandela cautioned against this hypersensitivity in our leaders. The following day, a journalist called to ask if I thought Mandela was referring to Mbeki, which is what everybody was whispering in any event. I dismissed her by saying that Madiba did not mention anyone's name, and there was therefore no reason to speculate. I even lectured her about how poor our journalism is because of this clairvoyance. But I also knew I was just being defensive. And no sooner had I given that defence than the president came out with this response to Trahar.

There has, of course, been a great deal of damage control in the wake of the president's remark, which is to be welcomed as a great improvement on the tendency for the Presidency to allow things to drag on and on, affecting our collective morale in the process. But the damage control also begs the question of whether the president shares his writings with his advisers before going to print. If he does, and they still allow such outbursts, then they should all be fired.

All in all, not only do I find that Trahar minimised the political risks in this country, but I also have very little sympathy for the president on this one. Those of us who raised our voices to question the London listings by South African corporations were told to shut up because the government knew better. Now, it seems, the government wants to have its cake and eat it as well.

The archbishop and the president: debate or consensus by silence
Business Day, 2 December 2004

The clash of political cultures has come to a head following the public spat between Archbishop Desmond Tutu and President Thabo Mbeki. By political culture, I mean our broad understandings of our relationships with authority. Attitudes to authority are often a function of historical experiences. These attitudes can vary from acquiescent deference to robust engagement with authority.

Tutu gives a fairly anodyne, nuanced speech about the good and the bad in our country, and in the process earns the wrath of Mbeki. COSATU's general secretary, Zwelinzima Vavi, offers a fairly commonplace criticism about black economic empowerment, and is called 'a child' by the ANC's presidential spokesperson, Smuts Ngonyama. In the past, Tutu used his moral authority to speak for a constituency that transcended any single political party, which is probably why he never joined the ANC. Why Tutu's strategically valuable non-membership of the ANC in the past should be used against him in the present is not clear to me at all. What does all of this tell us about our political culture?

As a religious leader, Tutu probably feels he has no earthly superiors, and thus feels free to engage robustly with presidents, whether P W Botha or Thabo Mbeki. The trade union movement has a somewhat similar understanding of authority. Vavi's authority comes from his members, and this informs his approach to authority, whether chief executive officers of large corporations or heads of state. And so, just like the church, the trade union movement – even when it's clearly aligned to a particular political party – has to be conscious that its constituency transcends any singular party.

If the political culture of churches and trade unions is that of robust engagement with earthly authorities, the political culture of political parties is the exact opposite. From their early beginnings, political parties have had a strictly defined authority structure which operates like a machine – hence the use of the term 'political machine' to describe political parties in the 19th century. This applies equally to the ANC, PAC, AZAPO, DA, and the New National Party (NNP). Even when they alternate with each other in power, political parties rarely change the political culture of centralised authority. Instead, they tend to replicate the historical pattern of using political dominance to punish opponents and reward supporters. Add to this the militarist culture of exile, and you have the makings of an even more regimented political culture.

What I have described are thus two historically distinct political cultures. The one typifies what sociologists calls the life world of social movements, churches and trade unions, and the other the systems world of parties and bureaucracies. In the words of the American sociologist Robert Bellah, the life world is characterised by 'argument, even conflict, about the meaning of shared values and goals'. This world, Bellah continued, 'is not about silent consensus; it is a form of intelligent, reflective life, in which there is indeed consensus, but the consensus can be challenged and changed – often gradually and sometimes radically – over time'.

It is this life world that gave us Desmond Tutu in the 1970s and 1980s. The 'systems world', on the other hand, is the world of political parties, ideologies and governments. It is the world of well-defined, regimented authority that for decades was Mbeki's home in exile. The sociological observation is that this political culture rarely brooks criticism, whether of Mbeki or George Bush. In other words, this is nothing personal, Mr President; just a mere sociological observation about the history of political parties and the political cultures they produce.

The spat between the archbishop and the president is therefore less about ideology and more about different sociological understandings of the relationship between individuals and social movements on the one hand, and authority structures on the other. The very identity of the ANC depends on the resolution of this question: will it go the way of the 'life world', or the way of the 'systems world'? Or will it find an accommodation of both?

It has of course been argued that just as Tutu readily metes out criticism, he should also be willing to receive it. I am sure no democrat would disagree with this proposition. But when is it prudent for the head of state to respond to public criticism? This is a matter of political judgment. In exercising that judgement, the leader must weigh what he has to lose and what he has to gain by his responses. The question, then, is this: did the president gain more in the world of local and international public opinion by responding in the manner he did to Tutu, or did he reinforce the very image of a hypersensitive leader that Tutu was describing?

'Elitist' Tutu maybe, but what of 'elitist' Mandela, Mbeki and Biko?
Business Day, 3 February 2005

I find the ANC's revisionism about Archbishop Desmond Tutu quite astounding. I suspect it's because Tutu dared to disagree with our head of state. Ronald Suresh Roberts, who is writing a book about President Thabo Mbeki's intellectual history, penned a rather sardonic article that described Tutu as no more than a manipulable mascot in the hands of Western powers – just like that other intellectual, Jonathan Moyo, has learnt to describe Mugabe's critics as Western agents.

Roberts argues that Tutu is an elite member of society, and therefore protected against the vagaries of persecution. If anything, this rather reflects Roberts's ignorance of the role of social elites in the liberation struggle. By dint of his standing in the community, Tutu was bound to be part of the elite – and so was Pixley ka Seme, John Dube, Sol Plaatje, Nelson Mandela, Robert Sobukwe, Steve Biko, Thabo Mbeki, and many others. The history of the ANC is, for the most part, the history of an elite that assumed the task of leading the struggle for political rights, from 19th century conservative elites such as John Tengo and Don Tengo Jabavu to the radical elites of the ANC Youth League.

A great deal of this elite construction had to do with the missionary education that these young leaders received at Lovedale, Healdtown, St Matthews, St Peters, and Adams College. The challenge was always how elites would use their social positioning to advance broader political, economic and social goals. The historian Noel Mostert argues, for example, that Steve Biko, 'himself missionary educated, represented the last African generation to be beneficiaries of that tradition . . . yet he embodied as well a complete rupture with that tradition'.

Writing about the elite character of the students who started the black consciousness movement, Sam Nolutshungu argues that 'despite their student and middle class background, it was not the leadership's class position that mattered but whether their political aims were disposed to advance the interest of a middle class in opposition to that of the working people'. He concludes that the students 'conjured a strong wind that poorly served the black middle class while increasing the number of those who sought a radical dissolution of the entire economic and social order'.

A broader investigation into why the clergy, educationists, entertainers, sports personalities and other notables were never touched by the apartheid government could save Roberts from the preposterous assertion that 'to touch the head of the Anglican Church, the regime knew, would have inflamed the cultural flames of the Boer War'.

The first point is that a proper assessment of Tutu's role in the liberation struggle must be understood in the context of a longer history of elite consciousness in black society. The second is that I am always intrigued by the contradictory positions of the

ANC on the subject of elites. At various times, the president has strongly rebuked the elite for their crass materialism, at others, he has defended the black elite for their private enterprise, and even called for the creation of a black capitalist class. The understanding of elites is so fluid that some elites are more acceptable than others, depending on how critical they are of government policies.

The irony of the ANC pointing the finger of 'elitism' at others is that I cannot imagine anything more elitist than our economic policies, designed with the active participation of the World Bank, International Monetary Fund, and international investors. I cannot imagine a more horrendous outcome of elite decision-making than the social consequences of these policies.

Put crudely, Tutu's purported 'sucking up' to global elites pales in comparison to the ANC government's disastrous attempts to serve international elite interests over the welfare of the general mass of the population. Only the other day, our minister of finance made bold to say that the idea that this country was going to create jobs was an illusion. He made this extraordinary remark barely eight months after the ANC ran a national election campaign based on the promise of creating jobs for the people. Where is the historic elite consciousness in all of this? Why would this elite disregard for the welfare of the majority of our people be any more acceptable to the ANC than Tutu's critical utterances about HIV/AIDS?

We should be thankful to people like Tutu for constantly pricking our elite collective conscience. In erasing him from our collective memory, we would also erase a big part of who we are, or once were, and the things we once valued.

Will Thabo Mbeki, like Richard Nixon, kick it all away?

Business Day, 24 August 2006

Does the arms deal have the makings of our own Watergate – the American scandal that cost Richard Nixon his presidency? This is a rather foreboding question. The whole arms deal thing is so confusing that, in the midst of accusation and counteraccusation, no one is going to come out clean. I still cannot believe that the ANC has allowed the matter to get this far without brokering a political compromise.

I am, of course, not qualified to comment on whether President Thabo Mbeki committed any wrongdoing. What I am qualified to do, however, is to make historical comparisons between events in our country and events elsewhere in the world. Everywhere I travel, I'm confronted with the same recurring question: 'What's wrong with your president?' Well, I don't know what's wrong with my president – I'm not a psychoanalyst. However, I do know what's wrong with his style of leadership. And it's on those grounds that I compare him with Nixon.

In his book *Eyewitness to Power: The Essence of Leadership from Nixon to Clinton* (2001), David Gergen, who advised several American presidents, including Nixon, Ronald Reagan and Bill Clinton, attributes Nixon's disgrace in the Watergate scandal to a number of paradoxes that I sometimes see in Mbeki. The greatest paradox, Gergen observes, is that 'Nixon had it all, and kicked it away'.

I often feel this way about how history will judge Mbeki. I never imagined that we would be the butt of jokes at international conferences because of Mbeki's prevarication about the deadliest health challenge to humanity, namely HIV/AIDS. There are several other qualities that our president shares with Nixon.

Nixon was the great foreign policy president who opened America's door to China, despite American paranoia and xenophobia. Mbeki is the foreign policy president who similarly opened our door to the rest of the African continent, despite our own xenophobia.

Nixon's great domestic policy achievements were the desegregation of schools and environmental legislation. Mbeki's legacy will be the rhetorical impetus he has given to racial transformation in this country. Nixon had a deep sense of intellectual history, often using historical precedents to explain his policies. Mbeki often appeals to historical texts, including the Scriptures. Nixon said he wanted to 'nudge history'. Mbeki 'nudges' the international community to pay more attention to Africa.

Nixon had a penchant for role models from history, and this is where the two leaders begin to share less than admirable qualities. Nixon admired the French leader Charles de Gaulle for his aloofness, believing that it lent him a certain mystique, which kept his enemies guessing. Nixon did not appreciate that such aloofness would never work in the rough and tumble of American politics. He showed a disdain for the media, indicating that he would rather follow De Gaulle's approach to press conferences: 'Two per year, with a thousand journalists, beneath crystal chandeliers in the *Élysée* Palace'. Similarly, Mbeki often refers to Pixley ka Seme, but perhaps forgets that Seme, the aloof autocrat, lost his battle against the radicals in the ANC in the 1930s. Mbeki's disdain for the media is almost palpable.

Nixon surrounded himself with some of the key thinkers of the 20th century – from Daniel Patrick Moynihan on domestic policy to Henry Kissinger on foreign policy. But he also surrounded himself with thugs who indulged his mean streak – Charles Colson, Bob Haldeman and John Ehrlichman. Similarly, Mbeki is surrounded by an equal mix of brilliant minds and bumbling sycophants who indulge his 'lone warrior' model of leadership. Only someone with a 'lone warrior' model of leadership can stand against the world medical community's opinions on the most devastating health challenge of our times, HIV/AIDS, with the minister of health, Manto Tshabalala-Msimang, happily playing the role of the court jester – except that the joke is on her. There are indeed none so blind as those who will not see. Blind sycophants defended Nixon to the very last minute. Gergen describes this blind defence as follows:

> We held tight to our belief that, whatever the shenanigans of his team, Richard Nixon himself was innocent, and so were the people in his inner circle. In politics there is a will to believe in your man, especially if he is elected to the presidency, and even more so if you are working for him in the White House. It's a natural human tendency, strongest among the young, to idealise your leader, persuaded that you are part of some larger crusade for good and ignoring evidence to the contrary. Your wagon is hitched to a star; you resent those on the outside who tarnish the adventure.

By all indications, the wheels are coming off the wagon of the Mbeki adventure. Opportunists of various stripes are jumping off in time to catch a ride on the Jacob Zuma express. Unfortunately, the political and legal muck that these political wagons leave in their wake is likely to tarnish us all.

III
COMING APART AT
THE SEAMS

ANC can ill afford to let balance of power tilt to the centralists

Business Day, 31 July 2003

I have in the past observed how quickly the ANC has fallen prey to what the sociologist Robert Michels famously called the 'iron law of oligarchy' – a reference to the tendency towards the centralisation of power in political parties. Michels's analysis inspired a whole range of theories of political power, all of which pointed to the power of elites to control society. History is indeed replete with examples of the 'iron law' reaching its limits within liberation movements. This happens because there can never be enough patronage or positions to go around. After a while, the disaffected outsiders may launch a revolt against the small circle of insiders.

The political scientist Benjamin Barber has argued that political parties were created to maintain the precarious balance between the centrifugal (decentralising) and centripetal (centralising) logics of politics. Political parties were meant to be 'the buckle linking governmental authority to the people in whom authority had its theoretic origin, linking elite and mass in a continuum that made voters the ultimate yet passive arbiters and the elite the active but dependent governors of the nation's political life'.

This has been a precarious balance indeed, with most political parties tending towards one side of the scale or the other. The question is whether the ANC will exhibit centripetal or centrifugal tendencies as it goes towards the 2009 elections. Daggers are drawn in what has become a high-stakes battle for political succession within the organisation.

Speculation abounds about why there has suddenly been a spate of leaks implicating senior political leaders in corruption. The most common speculation, and one most consistent with elite theories of power, is that the leaks have been designed to nip the presidential ambitions of people such as Jacob Zuma and Mosiuoa Lekota in the bud. We are told that Zuma's ascendancy to the deputy presidency was supposed to be a temporary measure after Joel Netshitenzhe had declined this position or was shunned by Mbeki. The ANC is thus cleaning up after an organisational mess, so that someone else could take over as deputy president. Who that successor might be is of course a mystery to all of us lesser mortals. All we are left to do is speculate whether it would be Netshitenzhe, Nkosazana Dlamini-Zuma, Jeff Radebe or Charles Nqakula.

Utilising the elite theories of power that seem to inspire the ANC, we would see why a third term for President Thabo Mbeki would not be such an impossibility after all. Mbeki would go into a third term as ANC president with a trusted ally in the Union Buildings. I emphasise though that such a conclusion is only possible if we go along with the assumption of an all-powerful political elite.

But even if people like Zuma or Lekota are permanently removed from the race for succession, there may be others who will see their dreams deferred if they do not seek and get the deputy presidency now. For others still, the deputy presidency may not even be the best way of seeking the leadership of the organisation. They may not want to get muddied by the current battles. Only after a declaration of a third term by Mbeki would they openly challenge him. With their own ambitions permanently foreclosed, they would at that point literally have nothing to lose.

The point of all of this is that in politics there are certain inescapable truisms. One of those is that no amount of political patronage and political control can extend long and wide enough to satisfy everyone. That simple realisation can either lead to a self-destructing jockeying for position, or to open and transparent preparations for democratic succession. This is the choice facing the ANC.

Masters of political diversion do SA's revolution no favours
Business Day, 11 September 2003

Mac Maharaj has been long in the business of calling people 'spies'. According to my sources in the ANC, it was Maharaj who started the vicious rumour that Steve Biko was a spy, and the black consciousness movement a third force sponsored by America's Central Intelligence Agency. When he repeated this allegation to Neville Alexander in Europe, Neville told him where to get off, in language cruder than can be printed here. Good for you, Neville. But this rumour was recycled throughout the 1980s, and often became the basis of the internecine violence that took place between ANC supporters and supporters of the black consciousness movement. Many young people lost their lives in the wake of that rumour.

The question must then be asked: what moral culpability does Maharaj bear for the deaths of those young people? Or is that too much to ask of a communist posing for a CNN advert praising *The Economist*, and invoking Nelson Mandela's name in the process: 'When I was in prison with Nelson Mandela, the only publication we had access to was *The Economist* . . .' He then drones on in one of the most embarrassingly cynical manipulations of Madiba's name.

By the way, I was with Mandela the other day to present the

Kenyan writer Ngugi wa Thiong'o. Madiba spoke of the need to recognise all of our political formations in the liberation movement, particularly AZAPO and the PAC. 'We all contributed to the struggle,' he said with his incorruptible generosity. Ngugi thanked Mandela for his global moral leadership, and for inspiring black people everywhere. No sooner had Mandela stepped down from office, however, than some of the leaders in his own party began to undermine that moral leadership.

The question is why Maharaj would seek to impugn one of the most revered and selfless heroes of the liberation movement, namely Steve Bantu Biko. Biko was getting closer to Oliver Tambo and the nationalists within the ANC in the 1970s. Maharaj and the communists, who had long dominated the ANC, felt threatened by the impending loss of control. Maharaj is thus an old hand at character assassination for the sake of political survival.

This brings me to the question of why the rumours about Bulelani Ngcuka – that he was an apartheid-era spy – are only surfacing now that Maharaj, Deputy President Jacob Zuma, and the Shaik brothers are embroiled in allegations of corruption. If the ANC had this information about Ngcuka, why would they have elevated him to what is effectively our attorney-general? And would it make Maharaj, Zuma and the Shaiks any less corrupt if the allegations were true?

Unfortunately, South Africa's leaders have become masters of the politics of diversion, and attacking the messengers. It is interesting to watch the denials of the existence of racism in the Springbok rugby team. But it is also important that a white South African, Mark Keohane, is the one to reveal this culture, even though he and his boss, Rian Oberholzer, are now being vilified for their actions.

Black South Africans are not any less denialist, putting our heads in the sand because of a supposed white bogey. When are we ever going to stop being schizophrenic about white people, and start behaving like the people in power that we really are? This is not to say that racism does not exist. The rugby case demonstrates very well that this scourge continues to eat away at the fabric of our society. But, for God's sake, racism cannot explain everything, including thuggery among our own people. The question facing us black people is whether we are going to allow the crooks to define who we are, in the name of black solidarity. Are we going to allow rumour-mongering to define and debase our political discourse?

Destructive culture of conspiracy feeds into ANC's denialism
Business Day, 27 November 2003

Mob justice or the rule of law: that is the question. Last Monday I participated in Given Mkhari's talk-show on Radio Metro about the Bulelani Ngcuka spy allegation saga. At the end of it all I was thoroughly depressed by what I had heard from some of the callers. I certainly hope that what I heard is not representative of black political opinion, or the majority of ANC supporters. For if that's the case, we're in big trouble. I have always maintained that our democracy will be made or broken by black political behaviour. We are, after all, the majority.

And so I write this column desperately in need of reassurance from other black people that this democracy is safe in our hands. What did the callers say that drove me to despair? In essence, they were saying that, the specially constituted commission of inquiry notwithstanding, they still suspected that Ngcuka had been an apartheid spy. It did not matter that Mac Maharaj had admitted that he did not know whether Ngcuka was a spy. It did not matter that Mo Shaik could not back his claims and was left to cry crocodile tears, asking Ngcuka to forgive him for scurrilously suggesting that he had betrayed the late Griffiths Mxenge. All Shaik was left with was a mere 'suspicion' that Ngcuka was a spy. He was open to change that opinion if anything to the contrary was put in front of the commission, shifting the onus to Ngcuka. But how is it possible that the callers would deliberately ignore what has transpired at the commission hearings, and hold on to their conspiracy theories nonetheless?

Three explanations suggest themselves. First, some people will believe what they want to believe, and will manufacture endless scenarios and self-fulfilling prophecies to support those scenarios. Many people lost their lives in the 1980s simply because rival neighbours sought to smear them. It is a conspiratorial culture that is deeply rooted in our political history. Maharaj's and Shaik's actions play to that conspiratorial culture. Conveniently, Shaik's source for the allegation that Ngcuka was a spy in Mxenge's office is a deceased Dirk Coetzee. I say, the ANC must expel both Maharaj and Mo Shaik for bringing the organisation into disrepute, and for their complete disdain of the organisation's position on how to deal with the matter of spies, all under the pretence of conscience. It is rather rich for Shaik to pontificate about conscience after acquiring the services of the former apartheid security policeman Gideon Nieuwoudt, whose hands are dripping with the blood of Steve Biko, Sipho Hashe, Champion Galela, Qaqawuli Godolozi and Siphiwo Mthimkhulu. Is there really no sense of honour among these individuals?

The second reason why people are disregarding the evidence, or lack thereof, is that the commission has become a proxy for ethnic battles. For some people, this whole saga is a proxy for tribal wars. Ngcuka's supporters argue that Indians are ganging up against Africans, and that, as a future president, Jacob Zuma would be heavily indebted to those Indians, particularly Schabir Shaik. Zuma's supporters see this as a battle against the so-called 'Xhosa nostra'. No amount of dispassionate evidence before a commission of inquiry will dissuade people wedded to ethnic prejudices. It is apparent that some of the callers to the talk-show have not even followed the commission's proceedings.

The third reason why people are ignoring the commission's proceedings is that it has become a proxy for political battles within the ANC. Even though I believe the ANC should expel Maharaj and Shaik, it is unlikely to do so because of the politics of expediency, especially with elections around the corner. Judging by the nature of the calls to Given Mkhari's show, it seems there is a sizeable number of ANC supporters who back Maharaj and Shaik because they carry Deputy President Jacob Zuma's flag. One of the callers even suggested that the deputy president is popular among young people.

Indeed, the deputy president gets a standing ovation whenever he attends a COSATU congress. COSATU, which is clearly unhappy with President Thabo Mbeki's policies, is throwing in its lot with Zuma. The union federation's logic seems to be, 'my enemy's enemy is my friend'. Has COSATU become so desperate that it is prepared to flout all ethical considerations in deciding whom to support? The commission should wind down so that the ANC can confront its political stalemate independently. However, as one youth leader from my township has put it: 'The problem is that the ANC is in denial.' It is a denialism that leads to endless conspiracy theories, which could in turn come to paralyse the organisation.

Four questions about Zuma's ability to lead

Business Day, 10 March 2005

In a country where the majority of people have been underdogs for centuries, it is easy to see why there would be so much sympathy for Jacob Zuma as a possible successor to Thabo Mbeki. But we should also be warned that the seductive appeal of popular acclamation can lead to the tyranny of the majority. The early crafters of democracy in the 18th century had their own cynical reasons for insisting on the separation of powers among the legislature, the executive and the judiciary. They simply feared and distrusted the masses, and wanted, in James Madison's words, to protect 'the minority of the opulent'.

These cynical origins notwithstanding, the separation of powers has often served a useful purpose by holding power-wielders in check – holding up to their faces the constitutions that they have so fiercely professed to love. That is the beauty of living in a constitutional democracy, as opposed to the thuggery and barbarism we lived under until just over a decade ago. Even as we disagree about the details of what constitutes the good life, we should never forget how this country was pulled kicking and screaming into the civilised world. Thanks to the efforts of the liberation movements, we can also call ourselves democrats. It is precisely because of that democratic legacy that we should let the courts decide Zuma's fate.

If Zuma should enter the ring as a candidate to replace Mbeki, his supporters would have to answer at least four questions. The first is whether Zuma's corruption is congenital – in which case we definitely don't want him as our president – or whether we are dealing with a lapse in judgment. We tend to have a very punitive, unforgiving culture in this country, even though we pride ourselves on reconciliation. This punitive culture often comes into play when the culprits are black: Winnie Mandela, Tony Yengeni, and now Zuma. But when it comes to P W Botha the monster, Hansie Cronje the crook, or Darrel Bristow-Bovey the plagiarist, all we hear from the white community are pleas for forbearance.

If Zuma can in the interim show remorse for his lapse in judgment, we may give him another chance. But any forgiveness would have to be combined with consideration of a second question: would Zuma come out of this gruelling experience a bitter man, ready to take revenge on those who 'persecuted' him? A bitter Zuma would lead to even greater degrees of polarisation than we currently have, both within the ANC and the country at large. Consideration would have to be given to whether Zuma can separate his personal feelings about perceived or real 'enemies' from the intellectual, political and social contributions they could make to his overall agenda.

Zuma's ability to compartmentalise would in turn depend on the answer to a third question: is he a democrat by disposition? We often complain about today's centralised authoritarian political culture. However, just as bad, if not worse, would be a form of decentralised authoritarianism – the kind displayed by some civic movements in the 1980s. Would Zuma be the kind of president who could retain his autonomy from his supporters at the grass roots, or would he be so beholden to them as to be stymied by their demands? The Schabir Shaik trial shows a picture of someone beholden to his financiers, but can he change and overcome that weakness, if it is indeed proven to be a weakness? This is important given the multiple interest groups that, in one way or another, seek access to the highest office in the land.

The fourth question is whether Zuma's lack of formal schooling would lead to insecurity about his ability to lead the nation. Given his record, I see no reason for suspecting such insecurities. He could well use his story of overcoming adversity as a *leitmotif* for inspiring the young and marginalised.

In recent weeks I have been arguing against the idea of a president who is also an intellectual. Such leaders tend to do the thinking for the nation, and produce a nation of hypochondriacs in turn. What we need is a leader who can call on us to think and act together – that's the true meaning of democracy.

We need leaders for all seasons, sensitive to views of others
Business Day, 11 August 2005

Leadership is one of the most vexing questions of our times. Societies will not always have great leaders. Good leaders will do for most of the time. However, given the daily reports of corruption, one begins to fear that we face the danger of lowering the bar of leadership even lower. We may now end up with individuals who are available to lead simply because they haven't done anything wrong. It would then take another generation to move from those leaders by default to good leaders to great leaders.

I don't know whether the ANC has a systematic leadership development programme. Given the party's dominance of our public life, such a replenishment of leadership may be the only line of defence between our illustrious history and the likely prospect of leadership by default. Such a leadership programme would have to examine the causes of present maladies. One answer may well be that the liberation struggle did not prepare them for the demands of a post-liberation era. The Ghanaian writer Ayi Kwei Armah alluded to this when he said that we should not expect our liberators to also be our innovators.

I am not sure I would draw such a stark contrast between

liberators and innovators. Some liberators have indeed been innovative thinkers as well. But the general tendency has been for struggle heroes to fall under the weight of the new challenges presented by the new, post-struggle societies. Defensively, they try to present themselves as technocrats of one sort or another – just to give a sense of being in control. But the challenges are not really technical; they are to be found in the political culture within which political leadership develops, and the adaptations that leadership has to make.

What, then, are some of those challenges? To begin with, just the sheer number of constituencies and publics that have to be addressed has become manifold. It is one thing to issue a command, edict or slogan in the context of a relatively like-minded political movement, but quite another to cultivate consensus among multiple publics, some of whom may be explicitly antagonistic. This antagonism is especially strong in racially and ethnically divided societies. It can even be quite annoying, as evidenced by the new righteousness displayed by some of those who supported and sustained apartheid.

Then there is the glare of the media – yet another public. The media, which are made up of ordinary human beings, may not be interested in the things you think are important as a leader. They may even be ignorant about such matters. But they can also write editorials and articles aimed at yet another finicky public: the anonymous but omnipotent investors. The rules of accountability or lack thereof that pertained in the liberation movement are suddenly unacceptable in a context that emphasises codes of governance. A secretive political culture is followed by requirements for openness. More often than not, good people find themselves making stupid mistakes, and doing so in the context of an unforgiving society, the discourse of racial reconciliation notwithstanding.

Then there are the multiple publics within the political movement itself. Many of them may not even understand what their leaders are talking about. Some of them may find leadership talk distant, and some of them may be opposed to the leadership's agenda. Those who do not have the patience or temperament to deal with these complexities should not make themselves available for public leadership. Or, even better, political parties should not elect such people as leaders. After all, leadership is a mirror of followership. Comrades should know each other better, to be able to say who is likely to be a menace to society with power in their hands. Indeed, the great division of our times are no longer about ideology but about sensibility. There are people who are impatient and intolerant of different views, and they are to be found in every sector of our society. They exist in all political parties, in the media, and in every racial and ethnic group.

The issue of sensibility is not something that can be learnt from a business school textbook. It is what some people call 'break-through leadership' – the ability to understand and break through one's own limitations, and even one's world view, and fully enter the world of others, even for a moment, without necessarily agreeing to its terms. Nelson Mandela was a master at this – but not before he underwent a lifelong process of political socialisation and education. Leadership is biography. It may well be prudent to identify good leaders now. They could well turn out to be great leaders in the making.

SA's leadership must bring down the banners of self-deception
Business Day, 24 November 2005

The ANC's response to its internal troubles reminds me of the greengrocer's store the Czech writer and political leader Václav

Havel wrote about in his essay 'The Power of the Powerless'. Havel describes how the manager of a fruit and vegetable shop wakes up every day to put up, among the carrots and the onions, a banner that reads, 'Workers of the World, Unite'. The store manager does this because 'if he were to refuse, he could be in trouble. He could be reproached for not having the proper "decoration" in his window; someone might even accuse him of disloyalty. He does it because these things must be done if one is to get along in life.'

Through this ritual, human beings are turned into zombies and automatons in a surreal panorama in which 'the banning of independent thought becomes the most scientific of world views'. This is a world in which, Havel writes, people literally and actively 'divest themselves of their innermost identity' by convincing themselves that the truth is the lie, and the lie the truth. This is possible because 'each person succumbs to a profane trivialisation of his or her inherent humanity, and to utilitarianism. In everyone there is some willingness to merge with the anonymous crowd and to flow comfortably along with it down the river of a pseudo-life. This is much more than a simple conflict between two identities. It is something far worse: it is a challenge to the very notion of identity itself.'

As befits a rainbow nation, our banners of self-deception are even more varied and colourful: HIV does not cause AIDS, corruption is a figment of the racist imagination, rape charges against Jacob Zuma are part of a conspiracy, there are no divisions in the ANC, and so on. We hold up these banners because we know nothing better than the ANC – even if it means we must 'flow comfortably along the river of a pseudo-life'. In quick succession, we have moved from romantic idealism to an age of cynicism. Could anyone have thought this could happen to us, smart and revolutionary as we were? We were extremely naïve in our South

African exceptionalism. We thought we were older than history. But history has shown us to be mere children – technocratic wizards, but political clowns. At this rate we will be handing out miniature banners to the little ones, turning them into little cynics as well.

It is indeed difficult to believe that only a few years ago the people who are running the country were the leaders of our dreams. It will be even more difficult for our children to believe. The poet-politician Jeremy Cronin has said it all, and said it well: the ANC needs a revival. I would not be surprised if the cynics pulled out the race card to shut him up. I would also not be surprised if he quickly apologised and furled his banner, as he did the last time he was reprimanded.

The genie is out of the bottle for the ANC leadership. In the same essay, Havel speaks of a store manager who wakes up one day not to put up the banner. He stops speaking in hushed tones, and finds his real voice in the din of the anonymous crowd. Friends initially look the other way or cross the street when he comes along. He becomes a social outcast, the disloyal one. But he persists in telling the truth.

A number of individuals and social movements have played this role, most notably around the issue of HIV/AIDS. But where is the political leadership? The search for leadership has become nothing more than a process of elimination. Jacob Zuma has shown himself to be lacking in judgment, Mosiuoa Lekota suffers a heart attack, and several others are implicated in one scandal or the other.

Bring the banners of self-deception down, folks. But then again, being politicians, you will not listen. In the end you will always court disaster. It would not matter if this was simply your disaster but, as has been proven over and over again, the self-deception invariably turns to embarrass us all.

Mbeki should rather issue a call to hope – and then just let go
Business Day, 9 February 2006

Over the years, I have consistently followed President Thabo Mbeki's State of the Nation Addresses. Sometimes I have applauded, and sometimes I have criticised. I wasn't planning to write anything about this year's address until Mbeki started talking about the 'age of hope'.

This assertion confirmed my cynicism about politicians. How could the president say such a thing, given the abundance of suffering and hopelessness that still afflicts most people in this country, especially among the youth? Every day I run into qualified, well-educated young people begging for jobs, with tears in their eyes. We must know we have a crisis when the best and brightest of our kids see no future in our society.

There was indeed a time when our hopes rode on Mbeki's brilliant idea of an African Renaissance. As young black cultural nationalists, we embraced and celebrated the age of the African Renaissance as our age of hope. We hollered for the president to listen to our voices. He dismissed us as upstarts who thought they were smarter than everybody else. His advisors suggested that we did all of this because we wanted to meet the president – confusing their own sycophancy with our desire to make a contribution to a worthy national ideal.

The lowest point came when the president called black intellectuals 'foot-lickers' of the white man for daring to ask him to get back to the basics of our political morality. That political morality still requires us to confront the HIV/AIDS pandemic, the economic inequality and joblessness in our country, the corruption so extant among our leaders, and a Robert Mugabe bent on undoing the collective achievements of his people.

Our spirits began to wane, and our resolve wavered. Cynicism replaced hope, not only among intellectuals and in our public institutions, but also in our communities. Now, communities all over the country are up in arms in protest against corrupt politicians, and the ANC is split into factions. Just the other day, a young man from my township, Ginsberg, sent me the following SMS: 'Ginsberg in chaos!!! All has broken loose. Remember 1985 riots?' This does not sound like a hopeful people to me at all.

I must also say there are very few things that I find more sickening than politicians doing the rounds at election time, promising us the heavens. And so, instead of asserting an age of hope, as if he can will it into existence, Mbeki should rather issue a call to hope. Then the question would be: who among the ANC's potential leaders would be best placed to bring such a politics into existence?

Such a discussion would inevitably involve an assessment of what went right and what went wrong under Mbeki. But that cannot happen while he is still head of the ANC. I am glad he has assured us he will not be seeking a third term as president, something that would leave our children with a terrible and horrifying precedent of leaders for life. But I also think he should let go of the ANC. That may well be the best way of reflecting on his mistakes while still building on the positive aspects of his legacy, which is mostly about a greater African consciousness for all South Africans. Tanzania's Julius Nyerere comes to mind as an example of such a reflective leader.

Counter-intuitively, letting go would be the best way for Mbeki to ensure a balanced reflection on his leadership. There are still many things a person of his calibre can do for this country and this continent. Some leaders have achieved more greatness after they left office. Jimmy Carter comes to mind as an example. In fact, there are now initiatives to think seriously about how to find a dignified exit for our leaders. My bias is always towards giving them distinguished endowed fellowships at universities, so they can share and reflect on their experiences with future leaders.

Boston University runs a programme for retired African leaders, and a professor at the Harvard Business School recently told me about a leadership initiative there, focusing on retired American leaders – in politics, media and business. Such initiatives enable societies to build on their institutional memories, and to prepare the next generation of leaders. There is no reason why our universities should not provide such reflective spaces.

Zuma affair a sordid symptom of a failure in our political culture
Business Day, 9 June 2005

The chickens are coming home to roost. For me, what has been described as a legal problem of corruption is ultimately a problem of political culture. The people rallying to Jacob Zuma's support do so as a desperate, last-ditch opportunity to identify with someone they see as an alternative to Mbeki's style of leadership – which they see as distant and generally unsympathetic to their concerns.

For the past five years, the ANC has run the country from the centre with very little of the politics of identification and mass involvement that kept it intact over the decades. Naturally, a party in power cannot wholly operate as a liberation movement. But surely the distance from the rest of its constituencies can still be moderated. Instead, whatever sense of identification existed within the party has been eroded by a series of public policy faux pas characterised by a culture of centralised unilateralism. This, in turn, has bred a defensive culture of denial. Faced with this denialism, it is hardly surprising that the ANC's own constituencies have taken to the streets to demand inclusion.

This is what the TAC said about the government's position on HIV/AIDS. Through court action, the TAC was able to get the government to provide medication to people carrying the virus. This is what the trade unions and civil society organisations have been saying about the role of the state in economic development. Communities are up in arms over desperate social conditions, and all the ANC can do is look for a 'third force' to explain the troubles away, just like the apartheid government used to do.

The ANC is coming apart at the seams because it dismissed early critics of the arms deal as nothing more than what President Thabo Mbeki called the 'fishers of corrupt men'. If the organisation had indeed listened to the critics of the arms deal, it would probably not have found itself where it is right now. All I am saying is that the Zuma affair is a sordid manifestation of a failure in the ANC's political culture. My professor at Massachusetts Institute of Technology (MIT), the late Donald A Schön, once made a useful distinction between what he called single-loop learning and double-loop learning. Single-loop learning consists of easy solutions such as, in this case, calls for Zuma to be charged. Of course he must be charged if there is enough evidence of corruption. However, double-loop learning would urge us to look beyond the person of Jacob Zuma to the structuring of opportunities in our society, and how individuals in search of instant treasures align themselves with powerful politicians.

This is not a problem limited to government, but pervades the whole political culture of our society. Merit means nothing in such a culture. The children of so-and-so will eternally be at an advantage over the children of so-and-so. That is how the elective oligarchy transmutes and extends itself into a social oligarchy. The masses, on the other hand, will in their desperation rally behind any demagogue that comes around. That is how a baser form of nationalism develops.

The president may indeed return to announce a new deputy president – say, Nkosazana Dlamini-Zuma – but this would do nothing to deal with the underlying structural problem of an elective and social oligarchy organised around opportunities and resources while the rest of the people eat cake. In short, neither the Mbeki elective oligarchy backed by the rule of law nor the Zuma elective oligarchy backed by desperate masses will take us out of this political miasma. The ANC needs a new life breathed into it by a unifying leader who is likely to bring a psychological revolution within the organisation, rebuild the connection between the oligarchy and the masses, open up the political decision-making processes, separate the link between political connections and life chances, and thus prevent the current travesty from happening again.

In a previous column, I suggested that in choosing such a unifying leader the ANC will ultimately have to choose between 'organisational' people such as Kgalema Motlanthe, Nkosazana Dlamini-Zuma and Joel Netshitenzhe, and 'public' people such as Mosiuoa Lekota, Cyril Ramaphosa and Tokyo Sexwale – or at least someone comfortable in both identities. In making such a decision the ANC could do well to heed the words of the Harvard University leadership guru Abe Zaleznik: 'The task of a leader is identification. The job of a leader is to get people to identify with him or her so that the leader becomes a presence in their minds and in their thinking. Leaders need to be so aware of themselves and so comfortable with the power they possess that they're willing to let people use them as objects of identification – as totems, almost. This creates enormous cohesion in the organisation.' I cannot imagine anything more important for the ANC, and by extension our society. Bring back the glow, folks.

Questions we must start asking to bring SA back from the brink
Business Day, 15 March 2007

One of my friends has complained that I was extravagant in my characterisation of our political society as 'sick to the core'. However, the ink on the column had hardly dried when there were revelations of yet another corruption scandal involving the ANC. This time, the allegations are that the ANC received R24 million from the notorious fraudster Brett Kebble. The ANC has been accused of selling time to business people, and not too long ago the party's secretary-general, Kgalema Motlanthe, said the rot was across the board in the ANC. I frankly don't think we have seen the last of these allegations, as party leaders and public servants continue to pilfer public resources.

In their book *The Criminalization of the State in Africa* (1999), Jean-Francois Bayart and his colleagues describe corruption as 'the privatisation of public resources'. This is happening on a grand scale in our country. You know that a problem is endemic when it begins to assume all kinds of colloquial descriptions in everyday life. Wherever I go, people talk about 'the loot'.

Some years ago, I wrote a column arguing that the problem with patronage is that it is impossible to satisfy everyone, and those who feel left out will join whatever movement emerges to challenge the status quo. In other words, once you start out on a particular path, there is no way of turning back. The question is: when does a society reach that point of no return? And having reached that point, how does it turn itself around? Before answering those questions, I would like to quote extensively from a column I wrote on 7 November 1999, entitled 'In a time of Mbeki-led stability we must prepare for change'. This is what I said:

President Thabo Mbeki has been so brilliant in shaping the public discourse we are tempted to think that all that could be said has been said. We take the immediacy of our experience and generalise for all time: 'This is how things always were and always will be,' we say. Yet it is not outside the realm of possibility that new political movements and ideological currents will emerge to shake our most fundamental political assumptions. I then asked whether we had the cultural glue that would hold us together through those changes. Could we build a long-term political culture, identity and framework based on an abiding tolerance for change? 'We'll see in 2010 – if we can think that far ahead.'

Well, 2010 is upon us, and the ANC is divided right down the middle. Now the very same people who said I was crazy in thinking about new political and ideological currents that would challenge Mbeki are the same people who think I am crazy when I say that our political society is sick to the core. But, as the 19th century French intellectual Ernest Renan once said: 'The best way of being right in the future is, in certain periods, to know how to resign oneself to being out of fashion.' Is this a self-congratulatory pat on the back for my prescience? Not at all – if only for the reason that observations about the inevitability of change would have been obvious to anyone who has studied the history of political parties.

I am currently reading a wonderful but difficult book by Alain Badiou entitled *Metapolitics* (2005). He explains why political parties betray their people by first asking the question that has preoccupied many of us over the past few years: 'We must ask the question that, without a doubt, constitutes the great enigma of the century. Why do the most heroic popular uprisings, the most persistent wars of liberation, the most indisputable mobilisations in the name of justice and liberty end in opaque statist constructions, wherein none of the factors that gave meaning and possibility to their historical genesis is decipherable?'

His answer is what he calls 'political unbinding'. He says political representation is a fiction through which politicians pretend to represent the interests of others. This fiction necessarily leads to an unbinding of the political party as some gain and others lose out in the processes of patronage.

The ANC is without a doubt in a process of such un-binding, the denials notwithstanding. Badiou welcomes such unbinding because it is what makes collective intellectual work possible. Before things get worse, we must seriously start self-critical public conversations about whether our political system and our leaders constitute just the type of representative fiction which Badiou describes, and what it is that we all, collectively, need to do to pull this country back from the brink. One can see this political unbinding in the government's nonchalant response to the beating of Morgan Tsvangirai and other opposition leaders in Zimbabwe.

IV
THE ROAD NOT TAKEN

Echoes of Kennedy in 1960 as Sexwale arrives on the scene
Business Day, 17 May 2007

Tokyo Sexwale's re-emergence on the national political scene is the most exciting political development of our times. There is something about it that is reminiscent of John F Kennedy's emergence as the candidate for the United States presidency in 1960.

Kennedy inherited a Democratic Party run by a corrupt political machine. Before Kennedy, the Democrats chose their leaders through backroom dealing. After Kennedy, they chose leaders through open competitive primaries. Kennedy was able to do this because he was not beholden to party bosses. The scion of the Kennedy dynasty, he was also wealthy, and therefore independent. I watched Sexwale's interview on BBC's 'Hard Talk' and found myself saying: 'Wow, this could be our very own Camelot.'

I have previously argued that the ANC needs to reinvent itself into a truly public organisation led by public leaders. Public leaders are different from organisational leaders. Organisational leaders are driven by survival, scheming, conformity and loyalty. Most of them turn out to be dour securocrats and dictators. Public leaders are aware that the best ideas are often to be found outside the limited circles of their organisations, and that they are accountable to a mission bigger than their organisation. They inspire hope among young and old. During John F Kennedy's presidential campaign, little girls wore buttons saying: 'If I were 21, I'd vote for Kennedy.'

I often wonder what this country would look like if its leaders reflected all of its intellectual diversity. Over the past five years of President Thabo Mbeki's rule, we have been bogged down by a narrow racial nativism that is leading us into a dead end. Borrowing from Es'kia Mphahlele, I have elsewhere called it 'a burning lava of hate' that uses race as the lens through which to see everything. But, as Mikhail Gorbachev said about breaking up the Soviet system: 'We do not have to live like this.'

Imagine with me, if you will, an ANC NEC that sets aside a quota of seats for some of the best thinkers in this country: people such as Eddie Webster, Njabulo Ndebele, William Makgoba, Zackie Achmat, Barney Pityana, Elinor Sisulu, Mamphela Ramphele, Francis Wilson, Nadine Gordimer, Lebo Mashile, Mcebisi Ndletyana, Pumla Gqola, and so on. A public organisation would use the media as allies, not protagonists. Kennedy was the first American president to incorporate the news conference into his philosophy of governance. Imagine with me a president who wakes up every day to inform the South African people about the latest developments in government.

Some people, including the ANC's Kgalema Motlanthe, have complained about Sexwale's presence in the media. The truth is that no contemporary leader can make it in the world without a command of television, the internet, and the latest communications technologies. Sexwale's BBC interview was watched by millions of people around the world. This country needs that kind of presence, after so many years of being battered by the international media about Mbeki's position on HIV/AIDS, Zimbabwe, crime and corruption.

Here's another similarity between Kennedy and Sexwale's potential candidacy. Kennedy appeared on the American political stage at a difficult time for that country. It had just emerged from World War Two, and was on the brink of a nuclear war with the Soviet Union. Kennedy made some blunders. I am sure Sexwale will make some too – and I will be the first to point those out.

But Kennedy is also the one who said: 'And so, my fellow Americans, ask not what your country can do for you, ask what you can do for your country.' It is true that Ted Sorenson penned that line, and that Kennedy took the credit. That is what happens when leaders surround themselves with what David Halberstam divined as 'the best and the brightest'.

Kennedy also promised that, by the end of the 1960s, the United States would put a person on the moon. We need a fresh vision for this society, based on the best traditions of our liberation movements. I suppose that is what Sexwale means by 'the Mandela way'. Over the past few years, this country's leaders have rubbished Nelson Mandela's legacy. Mbeki appeals to the Xhosas and Zuma to the Zulus, and we all sit quietly and say nothing. Kennedy was the first Catholic president of a deeply Protestant United States. Perhaps Sexwale, who belongs to neither group, would be the first leader to take us beyond the logjam of racial nativism and ethnic chauvinism that is threatening to tear this country apart.

We need to reinvigorate the sense of common belonging and creativity that Mandela epitomised. Sexwale may turn out to be the best approximation we have to that. He presents us with a choice outside of Mbeki's aloofness, and Zuma's militarism. The question is whether the ANC has the common sense to recognise this, and bring us back from the brink.

We deserve public virtuosity from those who would lead SA
Business Day, 14 June 2007

The writing is on the wall for President Thabo Mbeki. By all indications, the idea of a third term as ANC president is not flying. Last weekend, five provinces repudiated the scenario favoured by

Mbeki's supporters – that of two centres of power. According to this arrangement, Mbeki would remain ANC president and make way for his own stooge to become leader of the country. More provinces are likely to follow suit in rejecting Mbeki's third party-presidential candidacy. In many ways, Mbeki is reaping what he has sowed in the provinces. Throughout his presidency, he has taken it upon himself to appoint premiers of his own choosing, while alienating popularly elected leaders.

The rejection of two centres of power has as much to do with provincial politics as it does with Mbeki's role in entrenching those divisions. Mbeki's leadership has been characterised by an inexplicable intransigence, from how he has dealt with HIV/AIDS to the current labour strikes. Thus, I would not be surprised if Mbeki were not bothered with what is happening around him. And yet, the longer he remains in the race, the more energised his opponents will become, particularly those in the Jacob Zuma camp. I have no doubt that Zuma would beat Mbeki hands down in an open contest between the two. But Zuma would have a more difficult time competing with Tokyo Sexwale or Cyril Ramaphosa. Someone said to me that while Mbeki and Zuma are candidates of the past, Sexwale and Ramaphosa are candidates of the future – in their youthfulness, and in what the political philosopher Hannah Arendt called 'public virtuosity'.

In her essay 'Truth and Politics', the philosopher Hannah Arendt wrote about 'the joy and gratification that arise out of being in company with our peers, out of acting together and appearing in public, out of inserting ourselves into the world by word and deed, thus acquiring and sustaining our personal identity and beginning something entirely new'. If the attendance of Sexwale's public lecture at Wits University last week is anything to go by, this country is yearning for something entirely new. It was a dazzling performance to a packed hall but, more importantly, the man showed the courage to expose himself to the kind of public grilling that goes with public leadership. As Arendt put it: 'It requires courage to even leave the protective security of our four walls and enter the public realm.' We have not seen that kind of public virtuosity from any of the other candidates. Unfortunately, this prevents us from properly gauging Sexwale's public virtuosity against them, as routinely happens in other countries.

This then brings me to the question: if Ramaphosa is indeed also a candidate of the future, should he also not join in 'the joy and gratification' of appearing in public with all of us? Does he not owe us elements of his vision for a future South Africa? We are surely entitled to ask: 'Are you interested, Mr Ramaphosa? And if you are, should you not come out and share your vision with us?'

Let me now venture into the domain of a woman deputy president. The idea of politics as public virtuosity must also be applied to the suggestion of a woman deputy president. I would like to see greater openness and competition around the deputy presidency. A bad choice could have long-term ramifications. At the root of the Mbeki–Zuma fight is the question of whether the deputy president of the ANC should automatically become the president. My view is that the election of a deputy president should provide no guaranteed path to the presidency. However, given the expectations that this position plants in the public mind, we ought to think carefully about the person that we elevate to this position.

I hear through the rumour mill that Nkosazana Dlamini-Zuma is the consensus candidate for this position. But on what basis has this consensus been reached? Is her candidacy also a product of party intrigue? Does that make her a candidate of the past? Is it acceptable for us to call for public deliberation around the male candidates and not demand the same for a female deputy president? And what about Lindiwe Sisulu? Would she not be qualified to assume the role of deputy president? After all, she possesses all the struggle credentials that have become the criteria for leadership selection in the ANC. And she would represent the arrival of a new generation of leaders – the 1976 generation.

The succession debate must not be just about the replacement of individuals by others. It must also be about making the transition from one generation of leaders to another. The women in the ANC must open up the debate about which female leaders we deserve.

Hounding of Zuma recalls an old duel
Business Day, 30 August 2007

Why can't the state just leave Jacob Zuma alone? I have read so many stories of what he did in the course of the liberation struggle that I ask: what treachery has this guy committed that you should hound him so much? Just the other day, you pardoned the former apartheid minister of police, Adriaan Vlok, by giving him a suspended sentence. Is it because he kissed the feet of one of your own, Nelson Mandela? Why can't you cut a deal with your own comrade?

For years now you have been trying to nail Zuma, and every time you have failed. Bulelani Ngcuka said there was no prima facie evidence against him. And because we are a country of laws, Zuma stood before a court of law on rape charges, and was acquitted. He did not defy our courts or do anything of the sort. Judge Herbert Msimang threw his case out of court. Soon after that, Judge Hilary Squires denied that he had ever said there was a generally corrupt relationship between Schabir Shaik and Zuma. The media was left with egg on its face. Now we are told by the state's own attorney, Wim Trengove, that the state cannot prosecute Zuma just on the strength of the Schaik verdict.

I hold no brief for Zuma, but why is he being prosecuted and persecuted in this way when there are people who have done more dastardly things? The only answer is that he is a political threat. The philosopher John Rawls once wrote about how 'the priority of the right' takes precedence over 'the priority of the good'. In other words, far more important than the outcome of a case against Zuma is the process followed.

I have often been asked whom I would choose between Mbeki and Zuma. The assumption has always been shot through with tribal and intellectual presumptions. Mbeki is an intellectual and a Xhosa, and so am I. He therefore should be my man. My answer has always been, 'intellectual and Xhosa, my foot'. I have spent my entire life fighting such tribalism. I don't think Zuma should be our president, but neither do I think Mbeki should continue to be our president any longer. We have much more eminent candidates. In some ways, though, the Mbeki-Zuma duel recalls the duel between the *amakholwa* (Christian believers) and *amaqaba* (those who resisted Christianity) in early African history, a duel that came to be defined politically as one between 'the educated elite' and 'the people'. I think if Mbeki stood for re-election, he would set himself up for humiliation by someone whom he regards as *iqaba,* and therefore beneath him.

The trouble is that African people respected *amaqaba* because they are the only ones who ever stood for *inyani* (the truth) about our condition. *Amaqaba* would never write secret letters to people such as Nicolas Sarkozy: 'What you said in Dakar, Mr President, has indicated to me that we are fortunate to count you as a citizen of Africa, as a partner in the long struggle for a true African renaissance.' As it turns out, Mbeki's hero, Sarkozy, borrowed straight from Karl Marx's observations about the French peasant in his essay 'The Eighteenth Brumaire of Louis Bonaparte': 'The small-holding peasants form a vast mass, the members of which live in similar conditions but without entering into manifold relations with one another. Their mode of production isolates them from one another instead of bringing them into a mutual intercourse.' Marx continued:

> In so far as millions of families live under economic conditions of existence that separate their mode of life, their interests and their culture from those of the other classes, and put them in a hostile position to the latter, they form a class. In so far as there is merely a local interconnection among these small-holding peasants, and the identity of their interests begets no community, no national bond and no political organisation among them, they do not form a class. They are consequently incapable of enforcing their class interests in their own name, whether through a parliament or through a convention. They cannot represent themselves, they must be represented.

There is a certain disdain for community that runs through from Marx to Sarkozy to Mbeki. Zuma is a historical response to that arrogance: the sub-optimal president. People such as Tokyo Sexwale and Cyril Ramaphosa should be the real leaders of this country. We all know that. Why can't we just be honest with ourselves?

A solution to the ANC's presidency battle
The Weekender, 8 September 2007

The solution is staring the ANC in the face. If you think about it, there is really only a handful of serious candidates for the presidency of the party: Thabo Mbeki, Jacob Zuma, Cyril Ramaphosa, Tokyo Sexwale and Kgalema Motlanthe. Through a process of elimination, it's fairly easy to reach a compromise. Mbeki's leadership has been nothing short of disastrous, leaving the country socially devastated and the ANC irreparably divided. Zuma's militarism is frightening, to put it mildly. Mosiuoa Lekota is absolutely right: *izinto zokudlala zinamavili* (these are not things to be played with).

Ramaphosa has once again told us he does not want the job. I don't know why we keep saying he wants the job when he says he doesn't want it. I'm now taking the man at his word – until he indicates otherwise. He is most likely to go down in history as the greatest president we never had. I remember how Americans genuflected in front of the popular New York governor Mario Cuomo. The same thing happened with Colin Powell, but apparently his wife, Alma, would have none of it. Whenever would-be presidents try to re-enter the race, the window of opportunity has passed. That is also what happened to Senator Bill Bradley, the famous ex-Rhodes scholar and National Basketball Association star.

With Mbeki, Zuma and Cyril out for all those different reasons, we would then be left with two viable candidates: Sexwale and Motlanthe. Now, instead of fighting a bruising battle over the next three months, why can't these two comrades form a team, with Sexwale as president and Motlanthe as deputy president? Sexwale would mostly attend to the business of being the face and voice of the nation, and Motlanthe to the business of maintaining relations with the party and the tripartite alliance.

Seeing that the ANC has been talking about creating the position of prime minister, why can't they offer that position to Zuma? You have to give him something if you want him to stand down from running for the presidency. And then offer the position of deputy prime minister to Lindiwe Sisulu. Now there's a future prime minister. In one fell swoop, the ANC would have satisfied the radicals, the business elite, the various ethnic nationalists, and the gender lobby, as it used to do with its omnibus politics in the old days.

In the long term, we could move to a new system in which the prime minister and deputy prime minister are elected by parliament, and the president and deputy president by the general public. Not everyone would be happy. Political parties are always riven by factions. The leadership challenge will always be how to manage them. Politics is about give and take. The ANC started to learn this under Mandela before quickly giving way to Mbeki's style of holding no prisoners. With Mbeki, you are in or you are out. Unfortunately, he is now likely to be the victim of the very culture he inaugurated. The natives are at the gate and they are restless, baying for his blood.

The ANC's chickens come home to roost
The Weekender, 15–17 September 2007

I must confess to being thoroughly bored with the leadership succession debate in the ANC. I can't wait for its national conference in December. Everything is being held in abeyance. Bring on Jacob Zuma if you must, but please spare us Thabo Mbeki. I say this because there is a hallowed principle involved here. We should never get into the habit of over-relying on any individual.

Just imagine the prospect of having to live with Ronald Suresh Roberts as presidential spokesman and Christine Qunta at the helm of the South African Broadcasting Corporation for the next five years or more. That would be the first time I would consider leaving the country – just to get a breather elsewhere. I am suffocating, badly.

I can hear you say: 'You see, that's the problem with intellectuals – they run away when the going gets tough.' Look, between me and you, I don't have another struggle in me any more. Been there, done that, got the t-shirt. I never liked it anyway. I remember being *klapped* so hard by one cop that one of my comrades, Lunga Lefume, jumped at him and threw him against a wall. That cop never touched me again. That was the difference with those black consciousness guys – they fought back. But I digress.

The reason so many of our continent's leaders have been able to hold on to power is their stamina, and their insatiable appetite for power. The battle between Mbeki and Zuma is becoming a matter of stamina. Guys like Tokyo Sexwale and Cyril Ramaphosa may not be afraid so much as they may just not have the stamina. That is why so many countries tend to end up with mediocre leaders. Who needs great leadership qualities if stamina is all you need?

Politics can be a dirty business indeed. The ANC is coming apart at the seams because of what many of us have been saying for a long time – no single individual can ever successfully micromanage a society, let alone an organisation, without disastrous consequences for that society, the organisation and himself.

Just reading allegations about plots and counter-revolutions in the ANC sends a chill down one's spine. Where does it leave lesser mortals like us when the head of the government's intelligence services, Billy Masetlha, resigns to 'save myself and my family'? If it is true that Masetlha made this decision after a late-night meeting with the president? And if it is, what did the president say to him that frightened him so much? Does the public have a right to know, or is this material too dangerous for us to handle?

Masetlha says he submitted a report to the president, and that 'everything in it has seen the light of day'. Stop speaking in riddles, comrade. As Malcolm X would say: 'Make it plain.' What exactly is going down?

143

Eating your words . . . and your shoes

The Weekender, 22–23 September 2007

Thabo Mbeki and Jacob Zuma are taking us on a road to nowhere. Think about it for a moment. If Zuma wins the ANC leadership race, he is still likely to be prosecuted, and could even be convicted on those corruption charges. In that eventuality, his victory will become Pyrrhic. The same holds for Mbeki. Far too much is made of the influence he will have in choosing his successor as president of the country in 2009. Baloney. Mbeki's power derives from the fact that he is the head of the government, and one of the greatest dispensers of patronage in living memory. Those who support him do so in anticipation that he may still be of use to them over the next two years.

The truth is that Mbeki will lose his power the moment he walks out of the Union Buildings in 2009. Everyone will be repositioning themselves with the next president. I cannot understand why we have assumed that as president of the ANC he would wield so much power that he would pick the country's next president. He will certainly not have the power to punish and reward that he now wields as head of state. The lobbying for the country's presidency will be so intense that to hang it on one individual is simply ridiculous.

So what's the fuss of going through the motions with these two individuals who are leading us into a dead end? What's the logic in all of this, if there is any at all? The whole thing just boggles the mind.

I remember entering a wager with ANC veteran Frene Ginwala in a *Sunday Times* panel discussion at the beginning of the year. As ANC members are wont to do, she said I would eat my shoes in public because the ANC would ultimately emerge with a consensus candidate. I then wagered that this was a runaway process, and that Zuma would be its biggest beneficiary. Well, I am still waiting. To be perfectly honest, this is one wager I would like to lose, for two reasons. First, I pray every day that the ANC will spare us the dead end of a Mbeki or Zuma presidency. Sadly, the process may be out of control, and Zuma may emerge as ANC president. Second, I really dread the prospect of having to ask you to eat your shoes in public, Madame Speaker. I was taught to respect my elders. You might get away with just buying me dinner. Nothing hectic there. So here's to hoping you win.

While on the subject of wagers, one of my best friends called the other day to warn me about something more important than eating shoes: '*Ek sê*, Joe, do you realise you may have to leave the country if u-Zizi (Mbeki) wins?' Damn – I thought this was all about the small matter of eating shoes.

Nation in fear cries out for the voice of Mandela
Business Day, 16 October 2007

Dear Tata:- I hope this letter finds you well. I am not well. Tears came to my eyes as I read news of the imminent arrest of *Sunday Times* editor Mondli Makhanya and deputy managing editor Jocelyn Maker. I am not exactly sure whether I was crying for Mondli or for myself or for our country, or for you in particular. I was probably crying for all those things, and more.

You see, Tata, the foundations of our democracy have never been shakier, the credibility of our justice system never more suspect, the institutions of state never more compromised, and our public culture never more hateful as it is now, under your successor, Thabo Mbeki. He has single-handedly taken this country to its most perilous moment. He has become a god unto himself, accountable to no one but himself. He fires, suspends and punishes those who stand in his way. Everywhere I go, people are shaking their heads in disbelief. 'What has gone wrong with this man?' they ask.

I will not presume to comment on the legalities of the cases and the dismissals of high-level ANC cadres such as Jacob Zuma, Nozizwe Madlala-Routledge, Billy Masetlha, Vusi Pikoli, and now Makhanya. These are just the state's most public victims. That is what dictatorial regimes do: they isolate individuals and punish them in public in order to demonstrate that they will not tolerate dissent.

You know from your experience, Tata, that power knows no limits. Stalin showed us that not even the most loyal comrades were beyond the gulag. Power jails, power silences, power banishes and power ultimately kills those who are a threat to it. Power is conscious of itself, but power is most dangerous when it is unconscious of its actions or when it is on autopilot (actions take on a certain automation). The reflexive instinct to punish takes over all faculties. Public perceptions and consequences be damned.

For a while, there have been rumours that the wolves are circling around Makhanya. I do not think there is a journalist more hated by Mbeki's regime than him. This is because he has dared to expose the depravity at the heart of Mbeki's government. Now we hear that Makhanya's and Maker's cellphones had been tapped. When news broke that the SABC had a blacklist of certain commentators, I said any state that blacklisted its citizens was only a step away from assassinating them. Someone called me the other day under the guise of a journalist seeking commentary about the leadership succession race in the ANC. But I could immediately sense that I was talking into a tape. Maybe I am being paranoid. But how could I not be paranoid when there are allegations of links between the highest offices in our land and the criminal underworld? The very things that were done to us by our former oppressors – the reflexive instinct to punish through imprisonment – have become the order of the day in this land, right at its birth. To paraphrase the scholar Achille Mbembe, we have forgotten that this democracy was born at the edge of the grave.

I have read the journalist Justice Malala's plea in the *Sunday Times* for ordinary South Africans to stand up and express their outrage. But it is his conclusion that scared me so much: 'When, one day, we open our eyes and our mouths, our children will not have a country to live in. This country will be a Zimbabwe because we allowed Mbeki and his cronies to rape it.' Those of us who can run will, of course, run before the wolves get to us. And, writing in *The Weekender*, Jacob Dlamini has described Mbeki as 'one of the pettiest presidents South Africa is likely ever to know'. This is based on the view that Mbeki uses state institutions to persecute anyone who mildly disagrees with him.

In the short space of time since you stepped down from the presidency, Tata, the state itself has become indistinguishable from the individual leader. This is a disgrace for a country that was held aloft as the beacon of freedom, democracy and justice just a decade ago. But how did we fall so quickly from grace? Where are the good men and women of the ANC? How could they allow their senses to be deadened this way? How could they connive in the dismemberment of the very project everyone gave up so much for? How could people who were so brave under apartheid just cower under one man? What is it that they know that we do not know?

I am writing this letter, Tata, to say you are our last hope, our only chance. You cannot watch silently while your successor deliberately pulls apart everything you and your departed comrades so carefully put together. Your voice would reverberate across this land, across this continent and across the world. Your voice,

Tata, could help avert evils that are certainly going to be visited on the people of this country by a power-mad bunch in the Union Buildings. Your voice could pull this country from certain ruination. Your voice could save our lives.

Voices of struggle few and far between
Business Day, 1 November 2007

We may well be approaching the peak of what Karl Polanyi called the 'double movement'. Author of the classic *The Great Transformation* (1944), Polanyi was writing about how societies protect themselves against the ravages of market capitalism. Trade unions are a classic example of the double movement. And so it is with politics. Human societies will, in one way or another, protect themselves against the vicissitudes of tyranny. Polanyi warned that we could not tell whether the double movement would ultimately save or destroy societies.

And so it is with the succession debate in the ANC – will it destroy or save us? I was reminded of Polanyi's double movement by a colleague who said that in my lamentations about our political culture, I had lost sight of the fact that there are countermovements. Her phrase was 'political maturity'. The idea is that people are slowly finding their feet, and coming into their own. For example, just as there are attempts to gag the media, there are people such as Nelson Mandela speaking for media freedom; just as Mosiuoa Lekota bumbles around trying to gag public discussion of the ANC leadership race, an influential ANC branch nominates Cyril Ramaphosa for presidency of the ANC, and Kader Asmal wastes no time in taking to the airwaves to explain the decision. No sooner does the ANC branch nominate Ramaphosa than the minister of arts and culture, Pallo Jordan, calls for a generational change in the leadership of the ANC, beyond Thabo Mbeki and Jacob Zuma. And, in the most public expression of the political double movement, Tokyo Sexwale declares that HIV causes AIDS, and asks which tyrant will tell him that this is not so. Then there is Zwelinzima Vavi launching a frontal challenge to Mbeki, blaming him for destroying the tripartite alliance.

What do these voices add up to? There can be no ready-made answer to that question, because politics is not an exact science. In fact, I found an interesting parallel between what Polanyi was saying about the double movement and Jordan's observations about political struggles as 'cyclical movements' in his edited book *OR Tambo Remembered* (2007). I am sure Jordan was not even thinking about Polanyi when he described processes of political change as follows: 'Because there are at least two forces, reverses, partial victories, defeats and even grave setbacks are inevitable. Any struggle consequently is a cyclical movement, with moments of high activity followed by inactivity and quiescence.'

Some people in the ANC are slowly passing from the phase of 'inactivity and quiescence' to some level of activity. Jordan argues that it is the task of leaders to give positive direction to the double-movement or the cyclical movements: 'To sustain the continuity between the previous phases of struggle, the present and future ones by acting as the custodian of the best traditions and the political experience of the people in struggle.'

To be sure, Polanyi was writing about the history of struggle against laissez faire capitalism, and Jordan about the history of the struggle against apartheid. Nonetheless, the principle of the logic of movements and countermovements is basically the same. ANC leaders will ultimately make a difference if we are to manage these movements and countermovements in ways that will restore South Africa to what Jordan calls 'the best traditions and the political experience of the people in struggle'.

I have suggested in numerous columns that both Mbeki and Zuma are taking us towards interminable conflict, and that Lekota is doing his bit in fanning the fires. I have suggested that the ANC is like a bunch of people going over a cliff with their eyes wide open. But at least some of them are beginning to speak. The problem is that they are few and far between, and my biggest fear is that it may well be too late. In the final analysis, the jury is out on whether the double movement of these lone voices will be destroyed by the age of political immaturity of the Mbeki-Zuma stalemate, or whether they will bring us closer to the much-anticipated new era of political maturity.

Handed the holy standards by Tambo
The Weekender, 3–4 November 2007

President Thabo Mbeki is truly a piece of work – the master of the art of campaigning without campaigning. For lack of a better phrase, let's call it political ventriloquism. In other words, it is not he who wants the presidency, but other people who want it on his behalf. Nonetheless, it remains his responsibility to announce what these other people are thinking through the public broadcaster, which is always on hand for such announcements. I've actually lost count of how many times the SABC has staged these announcements for Mbeki. Nothing is better than television to show how pained the president is by the print media. They can only mean bad, and only he can mean good.

In fact, it is not simply that he is the only source of good intentions; he also happens to be the carrier of wisdom as delivered exclusively to him by Oliver Reginald Tambo on his deathbed. It's something like the Biblical story of Moses receiving the Ten Commandments after a conversation with God. In the recently published book *Oliver Tambo Remembered* (2007), edited by Pallo Jordan, Mbeki recounts how he was prevented from going back to the country to confront the apartheid regime by comrades Govan Mbeki and Tambo. This appeal to memory and militarism is obviously an effort at dispelling those who might want to question his revolutionary credentials. Charming indeed, I must say.

Then the helpless young man was conscripted, kicking and screaming, to work at Tambo's feet 'preparing the drafts of OR's public speeches and the major public documents of our movement'. Just in case the movement should think of handing its reigns to an uneducated populist such as Jacob Zuma, Mbeki reminds us that 'this work demanded intimate understanding of the strategic and tactical tasks of the movement, the contemporary balance of forces at home and abroad, our objective challenges at all moments, and what the leader of the ANC, Tambo, would have to say publicly, bearing in mind our domestic and international tasks and audiences, in order to sustain the advance of our struggle'.

I don't know if you can make that out. I certainly can't. But wait, here's the clincher. Mbeki describes how Tambo, almost by divine intervention, tasked him with the leadership of the ANC: 'He then communicated another mission, the most challenging since I first met him in Dar-es-Salaam 27 years earlier: look after the ANC and make sure we succeed. You will know what needs to be done.' Tambo authorised him to make contact with Nelson Mandela because he knew that 'I would not make mistakes that would compromise the advance of our revolution and struggle'.

Now how much more authentic does it get, really? However, Mbeki seems acutely aware of how inappropriate this kind of writing is for a commemorative book on Tambo: 'It might appear to the casual reader of this contribution to this book of tribute to Tambo, on what would have been his 90th birthday, that this

151

humble piece is more about myself rather than the immortal hero of our struggle.' Well, I would have been led to think so myself, Mr President.

Ten reasons why Mbeki should reject calls for a third term at the ANC helm
Business Day, 7 December 2007

Here are ten reasons why Thabo Mbeki should reject calls from certain sections of the ANC in the Eastern Cape that he should serve a third term as party president. First, such a development would take the ANC closer to the edge of the slippery slope of one-person rule. The ANC would be veering dangerously close to changing the constitution to extend Mbeki's stay as leader of the country as a whole. I may have been brought up differently, but there is something quite unseemly about a whole group of adults being so obsessed with one individual that they would mortgage their futures in this way.

Second, we know the horrors of one-person rule from the experience of other African countries, with Zimbabwe being the latest example. I once had the privilege of hosting the late Mwalimu Julius Nyerere at a workshop. He used himself as an example of the dangers of the big-man syndrome in Africa. 'You either supported me, or you shut up,' he recalled. 'No one could come out and oppose me, because he would be a traitor. If you were working for government, you did not want to lose your job and so you shut up. Occasionally, you might even secretly come to me and give me some facts.' There are indeed plenty of examples of government mandarins who go around issuing political expletives just to please the 'Great Leader'.

Third, the call for a third term for Mbeki could lead us to a tribal conflagration such as we have not seen in our democracy. The call could be interpreted by all sorts of ethnic entrepreneurs as yet another attempt by the Xhosas to hold on to power. Mbeki and Jacob Zuma should avoid taking us to a tribal Armageddon by gracefully exiting from the political stage. It is outrageous for people to suggest that the ANC lacks leaders. What about Cyril Ramaphosa, Tokyo Sexwale, Mosiuoa Lekota, Kgalema Motlanthe, and many others?

Fourth, a third term for Mbeki at the helm of the ruling party would mean more of the same in terms of public policy. For years, Mbeki has refused calls to become a champion in the battle against HIV/AIDS – the most devastating public policy problem of our times. We would probably also see more of the same in respect of the government's economic policy, leading to endless battles with the other members of the tripartite alliance.

Fifth, such battles would bring forward the prospects of a split in the ANC. An emboldened Mbeki might be tempted to ostracise the ANC's alliance partners even further. Currently, the other alliance partners do not have a political champion. Such a champion could emerge from within the ANC were Mbeki to be re-elected. The development of such a left-wing opposition could augur well for our democracy but I doubt Mbeki would want to go down in history as the person under whose leadership the ANC split.

Sixth, the call for a third term is a political gambit that could backfire with increasing vocal opposition from within the ANC in other provinces, and could ultimately leave the president with egg on his face. Already, delegates at the Eastern Cape conference give different accounts of what really transpired, putting into doubt the authenticity of the call. It is important to bear in mind that the Mbeki faction won by the smallest of margins, meaning that the Eastern Cape will be going to the December 2007 leadership conference with a divided delegation.

153

Seventh, even if Mbeki were to adopt a conciliatory approach to his opponents within the movement, he would be hobbled to act against powerful individuals by the desire to hold the party together, and to get backing for his preferred successor. It could well be that Mbeki's inaction against police commissioner Jackie Selebi has more to do with issues relating to the ANC's internal balance of forces than with the absence of wrongdoing by the commissioner. After all, Jacob Zuma was dismissed for something far less sinister than what is being alleged against Selebi.

Eighth, as the political analyst Thabo Rapoo has put it, as the former head of state, Mbeki might be tempted to intervene in the processes of government from behind the scenes, leading to confusion about where the buck really stops. Ninth, growing perceptions of tribal, political and criminal instability would put South Africa's prospects of hosting the World Cup in further jeopardy. And tenth, this country needs a changing of the guard – a fresh face, a fresh soul, a fresh voice and a new image. That would send a powerfully evocative message to the world – a leadership change without a gunshot being fired.

Nelson Mandela left us such a wonderful legacy when he stepped down from both the leadership of the ANC and government after one term in office. Two terms as ANC leader must be enough for Mbeki, surely?

This country is way ahead of both of them – but if you put a gun to my head, I'd have to go with Zuma
Sunday Times, 9 December 2007

I have never understood the idea of President Thabo Mbeki as an enigma. Mbeki is just like any other African leader who cannot resist the lure of power. I always thought I was alone in that observation, but by the looks of things the majority of ANC branches seem to be feeling the same way. The president must have been shocked by the drubbing he received at the hands of his comrades during the nominations for the ANC presidency. I suspect he will get an even bigger thrashing should he proceed to oppose Jacob Zuma in three weeks' time; the ANC conference would go down as the biggest repudiation of any sitting president in ANC history.

It is indeed ironic that this should be the repudiation of a man who saw himself as the only rightful heir of the ANC's leadership mantle. In that self-perception, Mbeki committed one fatal political error: he acted like an oligarch in a country with strong democratic traditions. He took members of his own party for granted; some might even say he abused them. His stay in power is littered with all manner of political corpses – with only one that refuses to die. With each and every stab, Zuma seems to rise from the dead. My purpose here is to make a few observations about how important the nominations process has been for South Africa, and how better to analyse the prospects for democracy under a Zuma presidency.

First, in a society where one party is as dominant as the ANC, it vital for democracy to be cultivated within the party. Political plurality is now the ANC leadership challenge, as never before. Second, the nomination process demonstrated the power of ordinary people when they are well-mobilised – even against a strong state-backed candidate. Mbeki has been the beneficiary of all kinds of propaganda – SABC nightly news, pro-third-term newspapers – and all manner of biographies that came out on the eve of the leadership elections. The ANC-in-government has to find a way of keeping its base in the branches energised if it is to keep communities engaged with policy processes. An energised base will also provide a ready bulwark should Zuma start behaving like Mbeki.

Third, in the long-term interests of our democracy, Mbeki campaigners should respect the decisions of legitimately constituted electoral and judicial processes. Zuma was acquitted on rape charges, and has yet to be found guilty of corruption by a court of law. Democracy requires that our passions should never substitute for respect for the law. It would be ironic if it were to be Mbeki who undermined the decisions of our courts by constantly speaking of 'rapists and criminals' in his political rhetoric. Even though Mbeki has denied that this is a reference to Zuma, the rhetorical style is classic Mbeki. He has long relied on a form of political argumentation by indirect allusion and never through direct engagement. Hence his constant references to those he disapproves of as 'some among us', without referring to them directly.

Another example of this form of argumentation comes from the HIV/AIDS controversy. The president typically does this by posing a rhetorical question about whether it is really possible for a virus (HIV) to ever cause a syndrome (AIDS). This enables his defenders to deny that he ever denied the HIV/AIDS link thus: 'where is the exact sentence where the president ever said HIV does not cause AIDS'. Yet the denial is there in the rhetorical question itself.

Similarly, it is hard to believe that the references to rapists and criminals are not directed at Zuma. These rather self-indulgent and rhetorical games may make a philosophy seminar a little more interesting, but they can never fool an adult citizenry all of the time. At least, that is what the ANC nominations outcomes seem to be suggesting. The consequences of this fake intellectual formalism are deadly, whether we are talking about HIV/AIDS victims or the integrity of our justice system.

The Zuma affair raises an interesting question about the relationship between the private morality and public morality of elected officials. My own view is that while a leader's private morality may compromise his or her ability to lead, a leader's public morality may not always be reduced to his or her private morality. An example of a leader whose private morality affected his public duties is the 19th- century American president Martin van Buren. Van Buren was known to disappear from work for weeks on end on account of his drinking. Equally there are leaders – Franklin Roosevelt, John F Kennedy, Francois Mitterand, Bill Clinton – whose questionable extramarital relationships never detracted from their public achievements, or what Hannah Arendt would call their 'public virtuosity'.

The question to ask is whether Zuma is so incapacitated by the scandals of his personal life that he cannot lead the country effectively. But even if we think that to be the case, we must still respect the outcomes of democratic processes. Failure to do so would be the real precedent for mob rule.

SA on the threshold once more
Sunday Times, 16 December 2007

The old is dying, and the new is struggling to be born. South Africa is on the brink of yet another transition from one generation of rulers to another. The time could not be more propitious for a planned transition. No one has the guns cocked at our heads, and there are no tanks to run us over. We are a free people, and yet this ability to plan our future seems more and more elusive.

There's a sense of purposelessness all around. It is an incredible turn of events for a people who were the toast of the world barely a decade ago. We are held back by fear, mutual suspicion, and acrimony among the very people who are supposed to provide societal guidance and vision. Our dreams have been turned into nightmares by selfish and grubby politicians who seek to make our country their private kingdom, and all of our collective sacrifice futile.

By virtue of the time they spent in exile and prison, they have arrogated unto themselves the exclusive power to govern. They have patented the revolution under familiar struggle names. That ultimate social quality called leadership has become a matter of inheritance. Thabo Mbeki writes about how a dying Oliver Tambo handed over the movement to him, and Jacob Zuma claims it is now his turn. None of them will spare a thought for us – the people who actually elect these dudes into power.

One of my friends have complained about the perceived fact that I've attributed the shift in the political culture of the ANC to Sexwale instead of Zuma. In response, I said Zuma and Sexwale opened up ANC culture in radically different ways. Zuma was forced to defend himself against what he sees as political persecution. Had it not been for that, he would have kept quiet as a matter of old-fashioned solidarity.

Sexwale displayed a different kind of courage. This is courage in the manner described by the great political philosopher Hannah Arendt, 'it requires courage to even leave the protective security of our four walls and enter the public realm'. To enter the public realm at a time when no one dares to enter can be an unnerving act of self-exposure – exposure to ridicule, scorn, rejection, and assaults on one's dignity.

Some have said Sexwale could be courageous because of his independence and wealth. But no amount of money can protect an individual from the vulnerability of the public stage, the humiliation that comes with rejection, and the attack on one's integrity by the questioning of one's motives. Courage is the only political virtue that makes it possible for an individual to disregard all of that and enter the public realm anyway. This is why Winston Churchill described courage as the first among all political virtues.

I do not mean that Zuma lacks courage. His reputation speaks for himself in that regard, and he was Sexwale's military commander to boot. But a different courage is now demanded of Zuma. In my forthcoming book *To The Brink: The State of Democracy in South Africa*, I describe Zuma as a transitional figure in South African political history. I suggest he can play this transitional leadership role in one of two ways.

First, whether Zuma would seek one or two terms as president, he would be well into his seventies at the end of his rule. The same goes for all the members of the 'class of 1942'. I cannot imagine the ANC electing another seventy-something to lead it in 2012 or in 2017. To be sure, Nelson Mandela was in his seventies when he was president, and many countries have had old and successful presidents such as Ronald Reagan.

The problem is that many of our 'old timers' come from a culture of exile secrecy, solidarity and vertical hierarchy. However, the world we live in demands openness, accountability and horizontal networks. It's a new world with new policy challenges – ranging from energy security to climate change to changing geopolitical realities characterised by the emergence of China and India.

Zuma would do well to take seriously Pallo Jordan's call for the ANC to identify the next generation of leaders. He must never take the country to the brink in the manner Mbeki has done over the years, which was to make the matter of his successor his personal prerogative. If we cannot vote directly for our leaders, let us at least talk publicly about who will have our fate in their hands.

The second manner in which Zuma can play this transitional

role would be in his role as party leader. Even though he has said he would step down if he were found guilty of the corruption charges against him, Zuma's task is likely to be difficult even if he is acquitted. He has won the ANC presidency on the strength of a deep and widely held sense of resentment against Mbeki in the ANC. But he will no longer have Mbeki as the anti-type against which to mobilise. He would have to do extraordinarily well to overcome the sense of foreboding that his state presidency portends in the minds of the public – at home and abroad.

Zuma would do well to step aside for a younger leader drawn from a different political culture. Sexwale is at ease in the public realm because he came of political age at a time when black political culture was open and public. It is time for the leaders of that generation to leave the protective security of their four walls, and revive that culture of free, open and public deliberation that once made us such a proud people.

We need a leadership renaissance in South Africa, desperately. But we should never let our guard down even with those new leaders. The lesson of history, including the most recent history of the ANC, is that we do the greatest damage to ourselves and our societies under the leaders we love the most.

V
THE ZUMA SURGE

Mbeki a far bigger threat than Zuma
Business Day, 22 November 2007

If it's going to take Jacob Zuma to rid us of Thabo Mbeki, then so be it. To be sure, I would have preferred someone else to lead the ANC, and subsequently the country. But in a democracy, columnists and pundits don't have their way. They have to deal with the wishes of the majority. According to the minister of arts and culture, Pallo Jordan, 'the ANC would not prefer Mbeki to continue as president of the ANC. That is the view of the majority.'

It is this principle, articulated by Jordan, which leads me to the conclusion that even Zuma would be better. Jordan says this about Mbeki: 'It is not desirable for one president to lead, especially in a young democracy like ours, for such a long time.' Decade after decade, African politics have been bedevilled by political leaders who do not want to leave office, which is exactly what Mbeki wants to replicate here. I cannot for the life of me understand how a people so smart, so sophisticated and so steeped in struggle could allow one man to even suggest the prolongation of his term in office – by any means necessary.

Zuma does not present such a threat. Yes, he has embarrassed us in so many ways. But his shenanigans pale in comparison to the damage Mbeki has inflicted on this society. Zuma's ridiculous statement that he would take a shower to protect himself against contracting HIV/AIDS pales in comparison to the deaths that have occurred because Mbeki and his government would not provide medicines that could have saved those lives. Even if we were to assume that Zuma solicited a R500 000 bribe from a French arms company, this pales in comparison to the allegations that the president of our country is protecting from prosecution the police commissioner, Jackie Selebi, who is said to be a mobster.

It may well be that Zuma is not an intellectual. But Mbeki has demonstrated that the idea of the 'intellectual president' is overrated and dangerous. If the ANC policy chief Joel Netshitenzhe's submission that the ANC is paralysed by the succession debate is anything to go by, then of course the buck must stop with the leader of the party. There should have been no succession battle in the first place, and Mbeki should long have given way to one of the many other able leaders in the ANC.

To wit, we have a society that is demoralised, and a ruling party that is paralysed, because of one individual. If anything, we should measure Mbeki by his record (what political scientist Robert Mattes calls 'retrospective evaluation'), and Zuma by his potential (what I call 'prospective evaluation'). By either of those measures, I cannot imagine how Zuma could be worse than Mbeki.

Having said all of that, I wish Zuma would be content with just being ANC president. In writing about some of the candidates for the presidency of the ANC, I once drew a distinction between what the former Cornell University academic William Whyte called 'organisational man', and the City University of New York academic Richard Sennett called 'public man'. I suggested that the ANC needed the latter, and at the top of my list were Mosiuoa Lekota (who has since become a factionalist in all of this); Cyril Ramaphosa (who chickened out when his country needed him most); and Tokyo Sexwale (who has been brave enough to nail his colours to the mast).

Zuma is both 'organisational man' and 'public man.' He can get the party to rally behind him like no other ANC leader, and he can relate to the public like no other ANC leader. However, his identity as a 'public man' has been dented by his personal

164

travails. It is perhaps time for him to retain the role of 'organisational man' as president of the ANC and give over the role of 'public man' to Sexwale. It is perhaps time for Sexwale to relinquish the idea of 'organisational man' and take on the role of 'public man', either as deputy president or chairman of the party.

Sexwale would bring enormous credibility to the Zuma team. His presence would allay all those who are fearful of a Zuma presidency, including international observers and markets. These two individuals and other senior ANC leaders need to get into a huddle soon, before Mbeki takes us down the ignominious path of so many other African countries. In short, this is a desperate, last-minute plea for some measure of sanity in the ANC – for the sake of all that we fought and gave up so much for.

Rainbow, renaissance – what will Zuma add?
The Weekender, 1–2 December 2007

I am not afraid of Jacob Zuma. That is why I invited him to come and give a talk at the Platform for Public Deliberation at the University of Johannesburg. I invited him also because I would like to engage him on a different set of questions from the ones we have been fixated on for the past few years. I gave a talk at the launch of the Open Society Foundation's Afrimap project in which I argued that the fixation on things such as Zuma's shower after sex prevents us from asking more political questions about him. We have spent so much time talking about Zuma's sexual morality that we have spent no time at all engaging with his political morality.

Three hundred years ago, the French philosopher Jean-Jacques Rousseau coined the concept of the civil religion. Rousseau's argument was that religious morality and political morality were two separate things. While members of a society would always hold on to different moral positions, what was needed to hold a society together was a civil religion, or what he called sentiments of sociability that keep a people together. We have spent many years in this country grappling with different versions of our civil religion.

First we had the idea of the rainbow nation championed by and embodied by Nelson Mandela and Desmond Tutu. Then there was the idea of the African Renaissance articulated most brilliantly by President Thabo Mbeki in Parliament in 1996 – before he proceeded to undo every aspect of it by his turn to racial nativism. What caused that turnaround will be the subject of historians for ages to come.

What I want to know from Zuma is this: what is your animating idea, Mr President? Just give us one big idea from which we can find meaning again. Zuma has not done himself a favour by always insisting that he stands for whatever the party says. Still, that is not an entirely bad thing. With Mbeki, we have seen what happens when a society depends on just one individual for its direction. Mbeki's biggest mistake was to be his own person with his own odd ideas.

The party ultimately responded by taking back those powers, and rejecting him. In our system, we vote for the party. It is therefore vital that Zuma should represent the views of the party. This has several implications for the relationship between the party and the public. This relationship requires that the ANC should stop behaving like a secretive, Stalinist organisation. It is that culture of secrecy which landed us in the arms deal and saddled us with HIV/AIDS, desperate levels of unemployment and poverty, and young people who are disconnected from the political system.

At the heart of the transformation of the ANC must therefore be the transformation of its national executive committee. The committee must be more open in its deliberations, and must be made up of a wide variety of what David Halberstam called 'the best and the brightest', or was described as 'Camelot' in Kennedy's time, drawing on the ancient idea of people attending a public court to discuss the matters of the day.

This is for you Zuma: presidential etiquette 101
The Weekender, 15–16 December 2007

The ANC leader Mathews Phosa is absolutely right, and so are Jacob Zuma and Tokyo Sexwale: never again should we put ourselves in the thrall of one individual leader. As Phosa reportedly put it: 'We should, in the name of democratic principles that we have fought for, resist the temptation to personalise political parties into private kingdoms.'

Phosa speaks from experience. Thabo Mbeki replaced him with the unmemorable former homeland apparatchik Ndaweni Mahlangu. Does anybody remember him – he of 'politicians lie' fame, or is it infamy? Mbeki did the same thing in almost every province, replacing popular leaders with some really funny characters. But I am tired of writing about Mbeki now. I cannot wait to pose to Zuma the same questions I have been posing to Mbeki – at least, that should take care of Kader Asmal's crazy idea that I have a vendetta against Mbeki. I will have a vendetta against Zuma if he should seek to make this country his private kingdom.

So how can Zuma avoid the nasty barbs of do-nothing journalists and columnists? The answer seems so obvious that one wonders how it escaped Mbeki for so long. In other words, Zuma should study Mbeki, and do the exact opposite of what he did.

First, speak to journalists on a regular basis, for God's sake. Second, don't take their criticism personally, and don't think of them as enemies. They mean well, and if you're smart about it, you can use them to feel the pulse of your society. As Renée Bonorchis put it in a brilliant column in *Business Day* the other day: 'Rightly or wrongly, the way the press perceives the Presidency is what makes it into the papers and what goes on to shape public opinion'. She suggests that even if you personally don't like the media, find people who like the media to work for you.

Establishing a media tribunal is a no-brainer. Perish the thought. And banish the word 'conspiracy' from your vocabulary. It worked for your campaign, but there is nothing as unseemly as a president who keeps complaining of conspiracies. Banish further the thought that there are racial conspiracies with racists behind every desk, and 'coconuts' ready to do their bidding. It's just a nasty way of constructing the world – the 'us and them' mentality. Don't do it. Otherwise you will find yourself debilitated.

Oh, and never fall into the trap of thinking that your advisers are always telling you the truth about the world. Find contrary voices, and listen to them closely. Much of your support comes from the working poor, but you know as well as I do that they are not the sum total of society. Managing plurality is going to be your biggest challenge.

By plurality, I also mean the plurality of perceptions. It will take some doing to be liked by everyone. But, as Bonorchis puts it, if you engage with the media, your 'previously tainted image will continue to be reworked and refashioned into something that many will find favourable'. That's if you escape prison. Good luck.

Zuma's choices and our own
Business Day, 21 December 2007

The most puzzling thing about Thabo Mbeki is how someone purporting to be an intellectual could be so oblivious to the one historical principle that has proven true over and over again. I used to go around reciting it as a little boy in my home town of Ginsberg in the Eastern Cape, having read it in one of Steve Biko's essays: 'The limits of tyrants are prescribed by the endurance of those whom they oppress.'

Mbeki was not yet an oppressive tyrant, but with the passage of time he could easily have transmogrified into one. The signs were there for all to see. But I would not be surprised if Mbeki still insists that ANC members suffer from false consciousness: 'I can see that this is all a machination of racists, liberals and coconut intellectuals.' The man's ability to deny is unparalleled. He is truly tiresome in that way. But enough about Mbeki. He is a man of the past. Our gaze must turn to Jacob Zuma. In my forthcoming book *To The Brink: The State of Democracy in South Africa*, I argue that Zuma is likely to be a transitional figure in at least three ways. The first scenario would not be so much of a scenario were it not for its social consequences. I have always argued that we should have found a political solution to Zuma's woes.

Mbeki took us to the brink pursuing Zuma, and was ultimately left with egg on his face when he was defeated by Zuma for the ANC presidency. But Mbeki still remains president of the country, and might be tempted to retaliate through the legal process. That would simply escalate the tension. We may look to our most recent history for a precedent. The state could do with the Zuma matter what it did with the former apartheid minister of police, Adriaan Vlok, who received a suspended sentence for apartheid atrocities. Zuma could also be pardoned by an incoming presi-

169

dent – the way Gerald Ford did with Richard Nixon during Watergate. The quid pro quo would be that Zuma should exit gracefully into the sunset.

The second scenario would be one in which Zuma is acquitted and elected president of the country. He would be 71 at the end of his first term, and 76 at the end of the second. The same goes for all the members of the so-called 'Class of 1942' of ANC leaders. I cannot imagine the ANC electing another seventy-something to lead it in 2014 or in 2019. Granted, Nelson Mandela was in his seventies when he was president, and other countries have had old and successful presidents. America's Ronald Reagan comes to mind. The difference is that many of our 'old-timers', Zuma included, come from a culture of exile, secrecy, hierarchy, and quaint notions of old-fashioned solidarity. The world we live in demands openness, accountability, and horizontal networks.

On a cautionary note, Zuma should avoid the triumphalism that goes with what the American presidential scholar Richard Neustadt called 'newness': 'Everywhere there is a sense of a page turning, a new chapter in the country's history, a new chance too. And with it, irresistibly, there comes the sense, "they" couldn't, wouldn't, didn't, but "we" will. We can because we won.' This can be dangerous, particularly in the sensitive and closely watched areas of economic and foreign policy.

The third scenario is my most preferred – for Zuma to give way to someone such as Kgalema Motlanthe or Tokyo Sexwale. I would prefer Sexwale over Motlanthe because the latter is more of an organisational leader, and the former more of a public leader. Either one of them would give us a breather. We need it, desperately.

Zuma won on the strength of a deep and widely-held anti-Mbeki sentiment in the ANC. Now that he has won, he will no longer have Mbeki as his foil and anti-type. All eyes will now be on him. He pulled us back from the brink of tyranny, but will he have the presence of mind to save us from himself? Surely he would also agree that there would be too much 'stuff' around him, and that would distract him from being an effective leader of his country. As party leader and elder statesman, he could still play an active and influential role in guiding the ANC. The country would be forever grateful to him, and history would remember him kindly for such a statesmanlike act.

Whether Zuma chooses to go down in ignominy in a jail cell somewhere, bear the burden of the state presidency, or be remembered as a party leader and statesman who pulled his country from the brink of tyranny is entirely his gambit. The challenge for us and future generations is different. It goes beyond Mbeki and Zuma to Neustadt's celebrated admonition: 'Choose your president carefully, because at the end of the day no one can save him from himself.'

'Ngcu-boy, you guys must be celebrating'
The Weekender, 12–13 January 2008

If you ask me, I'd rather still be in bed recovering from the holidays. A holiday is rather a misnomer when I go home. I spent the holidays partying, hanging out at the beach, playing golf, drinking at my friend Viwe's shebeen in Ginsberg. I also went around the Eastern Cape with my other buddy Ben Jonas, winning golf tournaments. To be sure, he did the winning and I did most of the enjoyment. One of the prizes we won was a whole lot of meat at the King William's Town Golf Club. He is still sulking and not talking to me because I braaied and ate the meat with other friends without his knowledge. Sweet revenge, I say. The guy had been helping himself to my whisky without my knowledge, and now he's crying.

That's the same guy who sent me a message saying: 'Best wishes for the new year to you and JZ.' He was not the only one to accuse me so. About half a dozen others made the same accusation. Someone would walk into the shebeen, buy a beer, quaff it a little bit, sit quietly for a while, and then say: 'Ah, Ngcu-boy, you guys must be celebrating; your man has won.' I simply refused to be drawn into any political discussion. But after a few helpings of good Scotch, the inhibitions went away and I was all agog about how great it was that the country was now relieved of Mbeki.

I returned from an overseas trip to receiver an SMS from another friend: 'Free at last, ma Jola. That's the country you return to post-Polokwane. A victory you helped usher with your pen and prose. You helped demystify the age of arrogance and intellectual thuggery. We have a reason to celebrate. Freedom from denialism, delusion and intellectual pretensions. Happy holidays.'

I try to explain to my buddies that I would have preferred Tokyo Sexwale or Kgalema Motlanthe or anybody else as ANC president to either Mbeki or Zuma. In the final analysis, I came to support Zuma as Mbeki was the greater danger to our society. So much for trying to be nuanced at one in the morning after a good helping of Scotch, with music blaring in the background and everyone hollering at you. There's no Doctor Mangcu here. It's Ngcu-boy, arguing endlessly with his childhood friends.

I should also say that some of these dudes have had varied experiences with the law, to put it mildly. Some of them have been on the wrong side of the law for so long that they have a pretty intimate knowledge of the functioning of the criminal justice system. I'm afraid what they have to say will come as cold comfort to Zuma. They asked me to take with me a message to my 'friend JZ'. In their respective experiences, it is unheard of for anyone to escape 18 charges. They tell me while he might have won the battle for the ANC presidency, he will certainly lose the war for the South African one.

The beauty of all of this is that these buddies of mine are Mbeki-ites and we can still break bread together. There's a lesson there for both Mbeki-ites and Zuma-ites in the ANC. Kiss and make up, which is exactly what I have to do with the friend whose meat I ate. Hard, but necessary.

Finding our voices again after Mbeki
Business Day, 15 May 2008

There is now near-universal consensus that President Thabo Mbeki has been an unmitigated disaster for this country. His erstwhile defenders are nowhere to be seen or heard. There is a part of me that feels vindicated by this sudden realisation, and a part that is angered by it. Naturally, I support calls for Mbeki to resign or be recalled by the ANC. The man has become an embarrassment and a vexation. But how long should a people take to wake up and speak truth to power? This question will be as relevant under the new group of leaders as it was under Mbeki. For years people watched as his depredations worsened.

There is now a qualitative difference between Mbeki's grave policy blunders and what he is being accused of lately. In all of my critical writings about his policy faux pas, I never questioned the man's integrity. I just thought he was highly overrated as an intellectual and a political leader. What concerns me about the latest revelations is the possibility that the president may have been deliberately dishonest. It is one thing to be egregiously wrong about public policy, but it is simply unforgivable to betray the trust of your people. One reason why Richard Nixon will forever stay in ignominy is that he lied to the American people.

Allegations that Mbeki suppressed a critical report about the 2002 Zimbabwe elections; ordered a shipment of arms through to Zimbabwe; intervened to protect Jackie Selebi from being prosecuted; claimed that he knew nothing about the allegations against Selebi; or may have improperly benefited from the arms deal are just of a different order of magnitude from anything I may have written about the man. That is why not too long ago I wrote one of the most difficult columns of my writing career, in response to Barney Pityana's criticism of Jacob Zuma as immoral while at the same time exonerating Mbeki. I felt like I was writing in public against my own parent, which is what Pityana has always been to me.

But in all honesty, this is no time to be comparing which leader is more morally deficient. That exercise in itself is a demonstration of how low we have sunk over the past decade. The strategic question is how we get ourselves out of this mess. Some people have been calling for a new political party as a way out, and others have called for changes to our electoral system to loosen the ANC's grip on our society. We are in this mess because we cannot directly elect our leaders. What the ANC decides is what we all have to live with. It's as if they are holding us by the scruff of our necks, and we can barely breathe. Something's got to give – either society will suffocate to death, or the ANC will have to be kicked out of power, unless it reimagines itself as a democratic organisation.

That is the great challenge of the new leadership: how to rediscover its voice after a decade of connivance and collusion with Mbeki. The challenge of the citizenry is similar: finding individual voices after conniving and colluding by remaining silent during the most foreboding moments of the Mbeki years. Ours is as much of a political challenge as it is a civic one. As Wole Soyinka put it in his memoir *You Must Set Forth at Dawn* (2007), 'to be robbed of the seemingly intangible – such as a civic voice – is to be diminished as a citizen'.

We must also find our voices against the despicable thugs who have been killing and maiming fellow Africans in Alexandra township. These are our brothers and sisters, forced to flee their land because our own government and some of its influential citizens could not find their voice on the crisis in Zimbabwe. As citizens we need to stand up and be heard, not only in our own country but right across our region.

The challenge is to look beyond crude dichotomies
Business Day, 2 October 2008

Some people write about former president Thabo Mbeki's departure from our national life as if their lives depended on him staying. In some instances this is indeed true. The chief is gone and, with that, their bread and butter. All of these people happily cheered Mbeki along as he violated the rights of almost everyone, including the right to life of the citizens of this country through his cruel stance on HIV/AIDS. No one dared utter a word of criticism without being blacklisted and labelled. The most elegant label came from the 'chief' himself and it was that his critics were 'foot-lickers of the white man'. The less elegant phrases were left to the henchmen, who called us coconuts and askaris.

As if plucked out of a Ngugi wa Thiong'o novel, these characters grinned from ear to ear in Mbeki's presence, as if he were an emperor. Their badge of honour was about who could say 'hail to the chief' the loudest. And now they have discovered their inner voices and mouth platitudes about tolerance and the dignity of others. There is nothing quite like self-interest to rouse people's courage.

However, there are those who have been roused to raise their voices out of concern about the long-term implications for our political culture of Mbeki's removal. The distinguished scholar Achille Mbembe is one of these. Mbembe sees the rebellion against Mbeki as part of a lumpen radicalism that is driven by a primitive religion: 'A fundamental phenomenon of primitive religion is to bring mass hysteria to a high pitch and to hurl the spirit of the mob onto one totemic individual who is then turned into a surrogate victim.' Now this is entirely in keeping with Mbembe's penchant for reducing politics to the metaphysical. What is disappointing is that it is simply an inversion of Mbembe's earlier analysis of Jacob Zuma as *u-mprofethi* (a messiah) who, like Nongqause, the Xhosa prophetess who caused the cattle killing, is supported by a mob.

In Mbembe's framework, politics is reduced to a Manichean game with a uniform delusional mob behind Zuma on the one hand, and a rational mob defending Mbeki on the other. But if things were so black and white, we would have a difficult time explaining the rational moderates who wanted Mbeki fired, and the mob mentality of the cabinet ministers who resigned because they did not want him fired. The point is that if you scratch the surface, there is enough rationality and mob mentality all around in the ANC, and in life in general.

This brings me to the problem of the interpretation of political events. There will never be a time when analysts, or anybody for that matter, will see the events the same way. That is because of the irreducible plurality of politics. The challenge is not to wish away the voices we disagree with, or to lump them together as simply irrational. The challenge is to put our arguments out there in the hope that they will be persuasive. And this extends to political leaders. Mbeki did not even try to persuade us; he lorded over us. Or as Mbembe puts it, 'he made enemies of people who could have been his friends and of those he could have easily won over by charm, persuasion, or simply by carefully listening to them'.

Mbembe says Mbeki made these enemies because 'he never really achieved the kind of inner peace and inner joy that could have set him on the path towards authentic freedom – freedom from past wounds, pettiness, paranoia, vindictiveness and lack of generosity'. The way in which Mbeki was removed is the way in which leaders with much kinder personalities have been removed elsewhere. I hope our new president will take our goodwill for what it is, and not with the kind of cynicism Mbeki did. We seek neither position nor patronage when we say, we would like to help rebuild our country. We want to do so because it is our country, and we love it. We want to be happy and inspired again.

Give Zuma a chance after the intolerance of the Mbeki regime
Business Day, 12 March 2009

Over the past decade, we were called terrible names by Thabo Mbeki and his bloodhounds: 'foot-lickers of the white man', 'coconuts', 'native assistants', 'askaris'. We were banished from the public broadcaster, and disinvited from many a conference. We were hounded out of our jobs because we marched to a different drum. We were called unpatriotic, and plotters against Mbeki. His commandos put us down as wannabes who were only interested in meeting the president. So bloated was Mbeki's sense of self-importance that his acolytes actually believed this gibberish. You would have been forgiven for thinking the whole squadron was in a state of delirium. The delirium inoculated them from the reality that there were other people with minds of their own out there.

But, as Malcolm Gladwell puts it in his brilliant book *Outliers: The Story of Success* (2008), 'knowledge of a clever boy's IQ is of little help if you are faced with a formful of clever boys'. The trouble with Mbeki was that he was faced with not just a formful but a nation of clever boys and girls. For reasons that lurk in 'the private lair of his skull', he could not bear that reality. How else do you explain the terrible insults and the name-calling?

I don't know if people will ever realise how hellish life was for some of us under Mbeki's nightmarish reign. The thought that it might be extended for another five or ten more years was truly frightening. And so Polokwane came to us as a rescue. As soon as they were toppled, Mbeki's cast of characters migrated en masse in search of a fix for the delirium. They found it in something called the Congress of the People (COPE). I see my editor, Peter Bruce, has a difficult time choosing between the DA and COPE. All I can say, Peter, is that I would be damned if I would bring those people back to power after all they did to us over these past ten years. How can we forget so easily?

I don't know if Jacob Zuma will be any different, but I am pleased with what he has been saying. I recently attended a meeting with 100 other academics at the University of Johannesburg in which Zuma gave a clear commitment to academic freedom. Mbeki had made me so cynical about these things that I kept pinching myself. This could not be real, the cynical little voice in my head kept telling me. I then realised how abnormal our public discourse has been over the past decade. Because of Mbeki's arrogance, there was an estrangement between the government and the intellectual community in a manner I have not seen anywhere else in the democratic world. Mbeki would rather import HIV/AIDS dissidents than listen to 'the formful of clever boys and girls' in his own country.

In the United States, the government draws its ideas from institutions as different in outlook as the liberal Brookings Institution and the conservative Heritage Foundation. The Kennedy School of Government at Harvard is the training ground for public leadership and policy innovation. These institutions are no less independent for their public policy function. Besides, if academics feel that their academic freedom is being compromised by their association with government then they can always resign – as I did from the Human Sciences Research Council. Or could it be that we do not trust our own courage to walk away?

And so, I am going to give Zuma the same benefit of the doubt I gave Mbeki in the late 1990s. If he should squander that goodwill, then I would be the first to let him know. What this country needs is a wellspring of ideas that come from within its academic institutions – inspired by the experience of its people, and enriched by the formful of other 'clever boys and girls' in the land.

At graduate school I used to watch wistfully as my classmates from India, Brazil, Indonesia, and China went back to play a meaningful role in the development of their countries. I used to watch Bill Clinton cross the land engaging America's best academics on all manner of public policies. There was none of the cynicism we have seen here over the past ten years. All we need is the creation of an inclusive dynamic by a self-confident leader – and a formful of magnanimity.

True test of democracy as the baton is passed to the 'outlaws'
Business Day, 16 April 2009

We have inherited some truly terrible things from both the era of NP rule and the past decade under the ANC. One of those is the instinctive dismissal of our political interlocutors as something other than what they claim. In the 1980s, the Nationalists came up with the idea of the 'total onslaught' to shut out democratic voices. If the label stuck, no amount of rational argument would persuade the other side to listen to what you had to say. It was the intellectual equivalent of the 'guilty until proven innocent' idea that is now in vogue in our media. Thabo Mbeki perfected this form of instinctive dismissal into a science.

Just the other day, Fikile Mbalula laid out a detailed indictment of Mbeki's legacy. The charge sheet is not anything different from a similar letter I previously wrote to Nelson Mandela. But I would not be surprised if the contents of Mbalula's letter were to be caricatured or simply ignored.

Over the past five years, I have made one consistent argument on the Jacob Zuma matter, which is that even though he was not my political preference, I would nevertheless defend his legal rights to the death. I have held on to that belief without waiver. And somehow this is taken to mean an oath of loyalty to the man. Somehow one is expected to look away from injustice lest one be seen to be sucking up. What kind of existence is that?

I am still dismayed by the silence about the evidence of a power grab involving Mbeki among so-called democrats and guardians of the rule of law. Here we are faced with the most brazen abuse of power in the history of our democracy, and no one dares to say a word about it. I cannot help but conclude that the only reason for this silence is that these guardians of the rule of law hate Zuma more than they love the rule of law. The irony is that it takes the 'outlaws' of our social imagination to protect this hallowed rule of law and expose the gangsterism of the westernised leaders. But we will not dare listen to these outlaws in the SACP or COSATU because of who they are and not because of what they say. It is not just a figure of speech to say, therefore, that our public discourse is tragically vacuous. Hence the resort to cartoons and caricature. But how does one enter into a proper political discussion with cartoons – the worst form of caricature?

It may well be that we have exhausted our own imagination as guardians of democracy and the rule of law. That is the only conclusion one can reach when we look the other way in the face of such gross abuse of power as we have been presented with over the past few weeks. I suspect that to find relevance we have to venture into the spaces where people live and understand why their behaviour is so much at odds with our vacuous exhortations. We may seek to comfort ourselves in the 'truth' of our ideas by describing the people supporting Zuma as anti-modern, irrational or millenarian. But the fact that their way of looking at the world does not correspond with ours does not make it any less legitimate and valid. That would be the height of moral, political and intellectual arrogance.

Next week's national and provincial elections are interesting not simply because we have passed yet another test of democracy. They are different from any other election precisely because it is a form of cultural insurgency. It may be the biggest test of democracy precisely because the baton has passed to people whose language, mannerisms and social behaviour we do not understand. The pluralisation and heterogeneity of our society has finally caught up with politics, thereby depriving us of a language of address. It has often been said that Zuma will be the new dictator. As the real test of our own courage, I say: Bring him on.

How to maintain independence in Zuma's exciting new world
Business Day, 23 April 2009

I arrived at Ellis Park Stadium at 9 am last Sunday for the ANC's Siyanqoba Rally, its last major show of force before the 2009 general and provincial elections. The place was not even a quarter full when I arrived. I assured a friend that there was no way the ANC was going to fill that stadium.

As early morning gave way to mid-morning, the empty red seats also gave way to a sight of endless yellow t-shirts. Then the whole place broke into a thunderous roar when Nelson Mandela made his appearance. The sheer force of the numbers, the goosebumps-inducing symbolism of Madiba, and the dignity of the proceedings would have led anyone to believe this was not a party event but a national event. It was certainly the most amazing political experience of the past 15 years.

I choose to look at the event as some form of humanistic revival after the long nightmare of the Thabo Mbeki years, particularly the delusional presumption that the ANC could never survive his departure. But these people were repudiating much of what goes for political analysis among the chattering classes. They were rebelling against being put down every day of their lives by the Zapiros of this world. To Zapiro, these ordinary men and women, and the extraordinary Nelson Mandela, could not possibly be sensible because they had come out to support the great anti-Christ, Jacob Zuma. It is this arrogance that makes it impossible for some in the media to see Zuma as a sociological representation of something new in our history.

In last week's column, I argued that what distinguishes this election from all others is that it is a cultural insurgency. Not only has the profile of the leader changed, but also that of the follower. The 'great unwashed' have changed the very meaning of politics. In the past we used to go to rallies to get the message, but now people go to rallies as a ritual of collective identification – as if to try to restore their integrity in the face of a relentless onslaught through cartoons and various types of stereotyping. I suspect these men and women join Zuma in singing 'umshini wam' ('bring me my machine gun') not for the entertainment or the militarism. This song and dance is an affirmation of life and youthfulness. What distinguished this campaign was in fact its youthfulness, which gives one hope that our politics will survive the present generation of leaders.

At the end of the rally, though, I whispered to my friend that I was so glad I was not a member of the ANC – mass rallies scare me. For all of my defence of Zuma, I did not vote for his party in the elections. I voted for AZAPO, for reasons that have less to do with Zuma than my own historical loyalties and identity.

Between now and the next election, the role of independent intellectual will be twofold. On the one hand, it is to guard against mass adulation turning into a personality cult developing around Zuma. The new president will not stand outside of history. He will be just as susceptible to the 'iron law of oligarchy' as politicians have been throughout history. On the other hand, it is to guard against cynicism that sees no democratic possibility in Zuma's victory. This will require going against the instinctive cultural prejudices that have characterised media analysis of the Zuma affair. To stand between the Charybdis of mass adulation and the Scylla of a crippling cynicism requires the development of an ambidextrous intellectual quality.

And here it may be important to describe 'independence' as less of an assumed posture than a quality of the mind. It is a quality that examines ideas on their own merit. It is time to take to heart the great sociologist C Wright Mills's argument that an activist intellectual is the one who simultaneously educates and receives education from struggling people in society. We have done a great deal of the former, including insulting and degrading other people. What we have lacked is the humility required for the latter. After all, how can you learn from people you don't respect?

As a result of our arrogance, we find ourselves despised by the very society we are meant to engage. The great folly is to mistake the arrogance for intellectual independence. We need a deeper understanding of intellectual independence as a guard against both political oligarchy and the cynicism that holds us back from democratic participation in the life of our own country.

Why living in hope is crucial as SA begins a new political era
Business Day, 7 May 2009

For the first time in more than a decade, I feel a sense of excitement about this country's public policy possibilities. I am sure there will be mishaps, failures and acts of arrogance by the new government. But to live in perpetual anticipation of failure is to lead a cynical existence.

The role of the critic is to live in hope. In his book *Restoring Hope* (1997), Cornel West argues that hope is neither optimism nor pessimism. Optimism and pessimism assume that people are spectators who survey the landscape, and infer on the basis of the evidence around them that things will get better or worse. But hope assumes that people are participants who act in and on the world. Over the past decade, we were reduced to what the Indian scholar Charta Pattharjee has called 'empirical objects of government policy, not citizens who participate in the sovereignty of the state'. Hope as activism springs eternal in South Africa, and things have changed because of that spirit.

So what are my hopes going into the future? Actually, they have not changed from those I expressed in the *Mail & Guardian* in 1998. First, I suggested we should develop a national consensus – or a sense of purpose – in the full knowledge that criticism is the life blood of a democratic society. Second, I suggested that we needed to develop community-based institutes and forums for public deliberation – in our universities, the media and, most importantly, in our communities. Third, I said we needed to nurture the next generation of black public intellectuals. Unless we did that, there would be no one left to combat the racist stereotypes that saturate our public discourse. Fourth, I argued that 'all of this could be one way of fostering a deliberative culture'.

Eleven years later, I am still banging this public deliberation drum, and none of my hopes have been actualised. Fortunately, we now have a president who seems genuinely happy just being around people. I will not judge him by how much he can split hairs about public policy issues, but by how much he can get all of us to collectively split hairs about those issues. He must not think for us, but think with us. He could take a lesson from the former United States president Ronald Reagan. Reagan did not see his job as the technical mastery of public policy – that's what ministers, bureaucrats and advisers were paid to do. Reagan, like Theodore Roosevelt long before him, saw the presidency as a 'bully pulpit' for bringing forth hope among the American people.

The great Brazilian intellectual Paolo Freire explained why he wrote *Pedagogy of Hope* (1994) as a sequel to his famous *Pedagogy of the Oppressed* (1986): 'We are surrounded by a pragmatic discourse that would have us adapt to the facts of reality. Dream and utopia are called not only useless, but positively impeding . . . It may seem strange then that I should write a book called *Pedagogy of Hope: Pedagogy of the Oppressed Revisited.*' Freire then warned that 'the attempt to do without hope in the struggle to improve the world, as if that struggle could be reduced to calculated acts alone, or a purely scientific approach, is a frivolous illusion.'

All around us in South Africa there is evidence of the devastating consequences of the 'frivolous illusion' that led our president to split hairs while children died. It is time to make a change by adopting what Franklin Delano Roosevelt called 'bold, persistent experimentation'. In doing so, we must bear in mind that governance is not a technical science in which you lock yourself in your laboratory or study and experiment on your own, deep into the night. That's how Frankensteins are created. Governance is founded on what Steve Biko called a feedback system: 'a discussion, in other words, between those who formulate policy and those who must perceive, accept or reject policy'.

I suggest, Mr President, that you take that line and frame it next to your mirror. For, as Cornel West has put it, a politically rich life 'has to do with what you see when you get up in the morning and look in the mirror and ask yourself whether you are simply wasting your time on the planet or spending it in an enriching manner'. Enriching us, as we enrich you. That should be your bargain with history, or what India's first prime minister, Jawaharlal Nehru, would have called your 'tryst with destiny'. Use it or lose it, Mr President.

Listening to each other over the sound of our own interests
Business Day, 18 June 2009

Almost everywhere in the world, people vote for leaders or parties that represent their interests. But no sooner are those leaders sworn in than they tend to their own interests. Societies have thus come up with all manner of institutions to curtail such self-seeking leadership. We give the name 'civil society' to the constellation of those institutions outside the state. But they are not immune from self-seeking behaviour.

In his book *Who Are We?: The Challenges to America's National Identity* (2004), the renowned political scientist Samuel Huntington argued that a society able to generate a sense of identity was then able to generate the ordering of interests consistent with that identity. Most interest groups operate by generalising from their self-identities to the national identity, and thus turn their claims into national responsibilities. If big business wants a certain set of policy priorities to prevail, then it must generate a discourse that helps people imagine society to be irrevocably that way. Remember how Francis Fukuyama literally told us that we had come to the 'end of history' in a book with the same title – before that project fell flat on its face? Similarly, socialists will not stop to remind us that South Africa's struggle was always Marxist-inspired, despite all of the evidence to the contrary.

Some scholars would celebrate the contestation over interests as 'interest group pluralism', and therefore yet another variation on democracy in the manner laid out by theorists of democracy such as Robert Dahl. But there is a danger to this romantic view of interest group pluralism. It can also descend into 'a tragedy of the commons' as each group tries to take as much out of society as possible without putting anything in. The public philosophy of interest group pluralism is often 'gimme, gimme, gimme', without attention to the needs of others and the needs of society as a whole.

In *City and Regime in the American Republic* (1987), Stephen Elkin demonstrated how business groups in the United States often attempted to define the country as a commercial republic.

But this was always countered by arguments about civic virtue and the creation of community as the alternative story line. Most importantly, these debates took place at the local level. Citizens would then extend their expectations to national political leaders. They would also do something John Locke predicted a long time ago: they will generalise their local-level skills to the national level.

This is not just democracy from below, but also an exercise in public reason-giving. Group interests are neither foisted nor dismissed as less deserving. And, perhaps more importantly, interests are not presented as mutually exclusive. Unfortunately, what makes people think their interests are mutually exclusive is the very language of identity in which pluralist discourse is often conducted.

While the National Economic Development and Labour Council (NEDLAC) is meant to be a negotiating forum for business and labour, it is even more crucial that this culture of public reason-giving takes place in our communities. That would help us transcend our identities as a way of negotiating our interests – first at the local level, and ultimately at the national level.

To be sure, there are inequalities in the public square that make some better able to justify their claims than others. Sometimes these are business leaders who have better access to means of communications. Equally, when teachers go on strike, children are not as well placed to argue why they deserve to be educated. It is then that leaders must intervene on the side of the weak.

I look forward to seeing President Jacob Zuma apply his much-vaunted mediating skills. But we should not make the mistake of getting him to do our work for us – which is to talk directly with each other across the divides of identity and interests.

Zuma must beware the booby-trapped calls for 'leadership'
Business Day, 25 June 2009

This is a plea to Jacob Zuma to please ignore the hypochondriacs. Those are the people who are so dependent on the idea of the leader as the 'big man' that they are now having withdrawal symptoms. This reliance on the big man – or what Afrikaners call *'die hoofleier'*, or 'the chief' – lies deep in the history of this country. It's a political culture we inherited from Jan van Riebeeck right through to all those vainglorious 19th century colonial governors. The history of the 20th century is littered with these big men, and they were all men – Paul Kruger, Louis Botha, Jan Smuts, D F Malan, Hendrik Verwoerd, John Vorster, P W Botha and F W de Klerk.

I may have missed some of these unlikable characters, but I'm sure you get the drift. Dan O'Meara illustrates this culture brilliantly in his book *Forty Lost Years*: *The Apartheid State and the Politics of the National Party, 1948–1994* (1996), the best thing written about the history of the NP. O'Meara also makes the observation, first made by Steve Biko in the 1970s, that people such as Verwoerd went beyond just Afrikaner nationalism to the construction of an overarching culture of white supremacy that included English-speaking whites.

The columnist Steven Friedman has described how the pervasiveness of white supremacist thinking produced a culture that always treats black people as suspect, and gives the benefit of the doubt to the worst white people. Indeed, how does an unreconstructed racist such as the columnist David Bullard achieve the status of a superstar in the white community? Well, in the same way that a white person with a Standard Four could spit in the face of a black doctor or lawyer and be decorated as a hero.

189

Just as this society and its institutions have taken white mediocrity to be the standard, we have inherited the reliance on '*die hoofleier*' or 'the chief' in the democratic era. Our evolution over the past ten years was shepherded by two very different big men: Nelson Mandela and Thabo Mbeki. I shall resist the temptation to elaborate on the differences between them. Let's just say one was tall and one was short – literally and figuratively.

The absurdity of the 'big man' logic is that Zuma is expected to solve every major problem we otherwise cannot solve. And if he should fail, then he would have failed as a leader, which would then confirm what the Bullard has secretly wished for in the first place, so that all manner of racist stereotypes could then be confirmed. While the pleas for 'leadership' may sound the most reasonable thing for citizens to ask of a president, they are actually not that innocent. In reality, these are pleas not just for Zuma to intervene, but to intervene on the side of those who make the pleas. Clever. But don't take the bait, Mr President. Instead, provide the platform for us to work out our problems.

If all the legacy you left was a nation in conversation with itself in search of solutions for its problems, then you would have done more than most presidents in history. There will be times when you have to make decisive interventions. But even as you do that, avoid the trap of seeming to have answers for everything. That would make you a pretender. People don't like pretenders. If you don't believe me, ask your predecessor.

If I were to advise you on one thing, it would be to recommend one of the best pieces I have ever read on political leadership. It's a chapter titled 'Neither leaders nor followers' in Benjamin Barber's *A Passion for Democracy: American Essays* (2000). He warns us about the idea of the leader as the big man thus: 'Public officials displaying an omnicompetent mastery of their public responsibilities unburden private men and women of their responsibilities.'

He then warns that 'the people are apt to cry "what will we do without him?" and doubt whether they can go on. What is really only a departure is experienced as a loss and an incapacitation.'

Frankly, this is the stuff that makes presidents think they are indispensable, and gets them conspiring to extend their stay in office by any means necessary. Who can blame them when we build them into the dictators we later decry? But if we cannot learn from our most recent history, then what shall be our guide?

Towards a political architecture that helps voices to be heard
Business Day, 30 June 2009

The world community is at yet another epistemological turning point. Old certitudes are coming under critical scrutiny. The global financial crisis has occasioned lively debates about financial institutions. The electoral victories of presidents Barack Obama and Jacob Zuma were inspired by a spirit of political rebellion against elite rule. But the economic and political rethink has not been matched by anything similar in the domain of government institutions.

In his book *Beyond the Stable State* (1973), Donald Schön suggested ways of rethinking government so as to bridge the gap between the centre and periphery – between those who make decisions at the centre, and those who are supposed to implement them on the periphery. Alas! For the most part, institutions of modern government still operate according to the same centre–periphery logic. A cabinet sits at the apex of the institutional architecture of government. Its decisions are meant to cascade right down through the rest of society, and be implemented by people far and wide.

To have this kind of co-ordinated action is an incredible achievement in human history. But the enormity of the co-ordinative challenge also explains why policy directives are not often implemented by the variety of actors who, even though belonging to the same party, nonetheless remain individual human beings with their respective strengths, weakness and issues. If you think about it, the system of government we have now was invented 300 years ago – based on principles such as the separation and balance of powers. Throw in the media and civil society, but the structure of governmental decision-making remains the same.

I am overstating the case, of course. This is how David Kennedy described the achievements of the New Deal: 'Into the years of the New Deal was crowded more social and institutional change than in virtually any comparable compass of time in the nation's past.' Even then, what he is in fact saying is that the United States had not undertaken any major institutional change since the 1780s. For six decades, the New Deal structured modern American life. At its core was the idea of providing security to all Americans – rich and poor – until Ronald Reagan began to pull that social consensus apart in the 1980s. But, as Kennedy argues, the New Deal did nothing to either alter the principle of private ownership of the means of production, or to broaden participatory decision-making in government.

There are reasons why both private and public institutions take so long to change – a point made brilliantly by Karl Polanyi in his book *The Great Transformation: The Political and Economic Origins of our Time* (2001). Institutions provide the very foundation of our everyday existence, beyond politics and the economy. If there was no change in the basic institutional structure of the American governmental system, it is also interesting to see how different presidents improvised to meet the challenges of their times or their own personal temperament.

Andrew Jackson opened up the bureaucracy to ordinary people; Abraham Lincoln enjoyed public debate, if the Lincoln–Douglas debates are anything to go by; Teddy Roosevelt introduced the idea of the presidency as a bully pulpit; Franklin Delano Roosevelt came up with the idea of the fireside chat; Harry Truman created the National Security Council; John F Kennedy created the Peace Corps; Bill Clinton thrived in town hall meetings; and Obama is the first Internet president.

By now, I hope you see where I am going with this. Zuma is unlikely to alter the structure of our institutions. However, what he can do is to leave behind an institutional innovation that reflects his temperament. Zuma has been extolled for being a great listener. But that is a human trait that will go with him when he retires. That personal trait needs to be given an institutional reality. I am not exactly sure what it would be, which is exactly the reason any society needs a deliberative culture, to get as many opinions as possible. But what I know for sure is that the service delivery argument is woefully inadequate in helping us think of institutional solutions for citizen participation in decision-making.

But, more importantly, it should be an institutional innovation that goes beyond instrumental economic and political purposes. It must have intellectual character – if we understand that to mean a place for exchange of ideas between the leaders and the people. Maybe the National Planning Commission is meant to be that institution, or maybe it's something more decentralised. But the task of successfully thinking outside the box, and creating institutions of public deliberation, cannot be beyond a nation with our history and talent.

VI
TRIUMPHALISM AND ITS DISCONTENTS

The new ANC and the iron law of oligarchy
Business Day, 24 January 2008

I'm starting my first column of the year with a wager. I suggest that you cut it out, file it away, and pull it out five years down the line. The wager is simple: the incoming crop of ANC leaders are likely to behave in ways that are not radically different from their predecessors.

While the reassertion of the political party is in some ways a good thing for democracy, one of the most enduring observations about political parties is the one articulated by Robert Michels in his study of German political parties almost 100 years ago. This is the idea that political parties tend towards the 'iron law of oligarchy'. They tend to be centralised, insular, defensive and intolerant, whoever the incumbents are. The sociologist Alvin Gouldner described this organisational condition as 'metaphysical pathos'. However, Gouldner was also quick to suggest that political agency within organisations can lead to their democratisation. This is what we saw with the rebellion against Thabo Mbeki. Other scholars have suggested that we need to look far beyond political parties for our democracies to survive. Whether oligarchy or democracy will prevail in the new ANC is anyone's guess.

My own sense is that there is no getting around the oligarchy. There can be no greater illustration of this than the ANC leadership's most recent behaviour. Jacob Zuma's depiction of the media as an enemy is unfortunate, counterproductive, and ultimately futile. The ANC can set up a media tribunal if it likes, but it will soon find, like so many authoritarian governments have

197

found out before, that you cannot control what people say or write without running into enforcement difficulties and without inviting international opprobrium. The challenge of leadership is not so much to set yourself up against the media as it is to leverage the media in all of its complexity to share your vision, solicit ideas, and generate public debates about public policy. Any leader worth his or her name will use the media to tap into the collective genius of a society.

Political parties would rather create non-existent enemies so they can keep themselves internally mobilised, and their leaders internally buffeted. But they should be warned that political power is not the same thing as social and cultural power. The new leaders in the ANC may have won the battle against their political rivals in their own party, but they will lose in the bigger war for social and cultural power in society at large if they behave like bullies. Mbeki tried his hand at bullying through intellectual pretence, and the present group are trying it through militarism.

Take as yet another example the reaction to Deputy Chief Justice Dikgang Moseneke's assertion that he was not in court to serve the ANC. ANC secretary-general Gwede Mantashe came out guns blazing, attacking Moseneke for his remarks. While the attack may have been a display of political brawn and militarism, it dissipates the ANC's social and cultural power. And if the ANC deputy president, Kgalema Motlanthe, is going to spend his precious time running around putting out fires started by his own comrades, he is going to be burnt out before he realises it.

And then the splits will happen. They will happen also for reasons that have to do with the operation of populist movements. As the Argentinian political theorist philosopher Ernesto Laclau argued in *On Populist Reason* (2005), the different factions that provided the populist frontier begin to vie for their individual and factional interests. The trouble is that there are never enough positions, and there is never enough patronage to go around. There is no reason why the populist coalition should not come under similar strains.

By the way, there is an interesting entry on populism in Wikipedia. It should come in handy in discussions of populism as a political category and not a venting of prejudice against political opponents. Anyway, my point is it cannot be that the ANC's *raison d'etre* at this historical juncture is simply that of protecting one individual. After all, the ANC is voted into power by millions of people so that it can implement its electoral promises. The individualisation of the movement around Zuma is likely to be no different from the individualisation of the party under Mbeki, with ghastly consequences for society as a whole.

In my book *To The Brink: The State of Democracy in South Africa* (2008), I argue that future generations will look back on the present crop of leaders as transitional. They performed an important role in getting rid of a would-be dictator, but when their turn came, they were found to be no different. In short: tread carefully, comrades, and beware of the triumphalism that comes with newness.

New ANC leadership starts out on an old path
Business Day, 31 January 2008

In a previous column, I made two observations which have since materialised. First, I suggested that the incoming group of ANC leaders was unlikely to be radically different from its predecessors. Political parties, I argued, tend to be 'centralised, insular, defensive and downright intolerant, whoever the incumbents are'. The ink had hardly dried when the ANC's new treasurer-general, Mathews Phosa warned that those party leaders who did not toe the party line would be given 'marching orders'. Even the much-reviled Thabo Mbeki was more subtle than that.

I have received an e-mail from someone who compared Phosa's tirade to a form of mental enslavement of parliamentarians, provincial and local leaders. Drawing on Bob Marley and Steve Biko's work on psychological liberation, the writer said: 'This thought comes to mind when thinking of the slaves of Luthuli House, who will shortly stand to attention when parliament resumes in Cape Town. The masters of the slaves of Luthuli House boast that ANC members of parliament are "deployed" into parliament and can be "deployed" out again at their own whim or say-so. They can be "deployed" wherever they are told to go. They have no individual moral agency, they are not answerable to their own conscience so long as they remain ANC MPs, and they are not answerable either to any local community of electors, who can hold them to account for their conduct in and out of parliament, and deprive them of their seat, if necessary. Deploy is a military term. It means that the person who is deployed is subject to military discipline by his superior officers, which he cannot disobey except (in the military sense) at risk of court martial. For this term to apply to MPs is to negate the nature of parliament, and to confuse military order with civic responsibility. It imposes a form of order of a dictatorial kind in what should be a forum of civic debate.'

Need I say more? The operative phrase here is 'individual moral agency'. For decades, we Africans have watched helplessly as nationalist leaders demanded we should suspend our moral agency on account of racial and political loyalties, with Robert Mugabe and Thabo Mbeki being the latest examples. The results have been calamitous. I truly never understand why political leaders always go down political dead-ends. Should it not be obvious in this day and age that uniformity of thinking is a dangerous pipe dream enforceable only through genocide, if at all? I had hoped the ANC would find a new leadership culture that was more about managing plurality than enforcing uniformity.

My second observation was that 'the splits in the ANC will happen . . . for reasons that have to do with the operation of populist movements. . . . the trouble is that there are never enough positions, and there is never enough patronage to go around'. Once again, the ink had hardly dried when it emerged that Jacob Zuma had been banging the table at a meeting of the ANC's national executive committee, saying how angry he was that some were pushing Kgalema Motlanthe for president and Phosa for deputy president. The NEC then issued a statement that Zuma would be their candidate next year. Now, is this not what Zuma was made to do by Mbeki when it emerged that he might be harbouring presidential aspirations? If all of this is true, then Zuma would have learned well from the master.

Now, rumour also has it that Phosa and Motlanthe may be vying against each other for the presidency. I use the word 'rumour' deliberately, simply to highlight that the ANC is going to be devoured by the very culture of secrecy and back-room dealing it cherishes so much. People naturally resort to guesswork, rumour-mongering and rebellion when they don't know what's cooking behind those closed doors. No number of threats and ultimatums can ever stop that. It would seem, therefore, that nothing short of a wholesale change in the organisation's leadership culture can save the party.

And so, here's a word of advice for Luthuli House: get rid of your fears, stop the threats and the ultimatums, and open up your party to future generations before they pass harsh judgment on you. Time is running out.

We must act to prevent party remaking nation in its image
Business Day, 7 February 2008

I would like to add another dimension to discussions about the behaviour of the new leadership of the ANC. Many people have expressed legitimate concerns about the ANC's assertion that the party is the centre of power in our democracy. Of course the party cannot be the centre of power. The real centre of power is our constitution, which is not an ANC but a South African constitution.

But it seems to me that we cannot even begin to address the conflation of party and state without resolving an underlying problem: the even more dangerous conflation of party and nation. In its behaviour and utterances, the ANC interprets its electoral dominance as an entitlement to remake our national identity in its own image. Hence the desire to have everyone march to the same beat – the party's beat. In this image, the ANC is South Africa, and South Africa is the ANC. The problem is that our history has always been much more plural. Difference has always been at the heart of black political and intellectual life, which explains the rich tapestry of black political movements and intellectual currents, including the All Africa Convention of D D T Jabavu, the PAC of Robert Sobukwe, and the black consciousness movement of Steve Biko, let alone the women's, youth and trade union movements that existed outside the ANC.

This political plurality points to the folly of any single party thinking it can take the national identity upon itself without precipitating resistance and, ultimately, violence. The political plurality is compounded by the social plurality of our society. Our identities – across race, ethnicity, culture and gender – are varied, and yet deeply intertwined. As Frantz Fanon wrote in his seminal treatise on the impacts of colonialism, *The Wretched of the Earth*

(1961): 'The colonised, after encountering the full weight of the colonial culture, cannot return to any authentic and unspoilt past.' Fanon thus argued that the colonised then always occupy 'a zone of occult instability'. It is how they respond to this sense of immanent instability and plurality that will tell us whether the colonised, once in power, will become democrats or will in their turn become postcolonial autocrats.

There is nothing to prevent the violence between rival political parties in Kenya from happening here. After all, many people died in our communities precisely because the ANC and its proxies sought to impose ideological hegemony in our communities in the 1980s. In the belligerence of the ANC leadership, I sometimes sense a mix of the militarism of exile and the civic authoritarianism of the 1980s, and it scares me.

And then there is the matter of generational change. However much we may resist it, our children will never see the world the way we see it. We are the products of apartheid. They are not. Let us give them the freedom to imagine themselves differently – as the children of a free and democratic society. In short, let us stop holding them ransom to history.

I suggest, therefore, that we find political and institutional ways of resisting the temptation to think about the party as the nation. There are a number of things we can do to come to terms with our political and social plurality. First, we need to give greater voice and protection to those who think differently. Second, we need to change our political and electoral system and make the party secondary to the citizen. Third, a movement needs to get under way to change the constitution so we can stop our marginalisation from political life. We need to have greater participation in the election of our national, provincial and local leaders. Fourth, we need to listen more to what opposition parties and civil society organisations have to say.

This is the only way in which we can build a national identity beyond individual leaders and political parties. Political parties and individual leaders are too dangerous and unreliable to serve as crutches on which to hang the identity of a nation. Citizens are a far better bet.

Phosa's call still puts the party first
Business Day, 6 March 2008

I've just read an article by the ANC's new treasurer-general, Mathews Phosa, in which he asks members of the public to stop being armchair critics and to present their views to the party instead. On the face of it, this is a departure from the aloofness we have come to associate with our leadership. Now we are being invited to become part of the project of national renewal by a senior and influential member of the ruling party.

But for some reason there was something about Phosa's call that made me feel uneasy. Then it dawned on me that while his opening up was a departure from the ways of Thabo Mbeki's administration, it was not that radically different, at least in its epistemology. It is also rooted in the idea that the people must come to the party, and not the party to the people. In Mbeki's case, authority pivoted around the person of the president, and in Phosa's case authority pivots around the party collective.

There are several examples of how the party can adapt to conditions facing the people – a process described brilliantly by Myron Weiner in *Party Building in a New Nation* (1967). The case I am most familiar with is Harold Washington's leadership of the city of Chicago in the 1980s, most astutely described in Pierre Clavel and Wim Wiewel's work *Harold Washington and the Neighbourhoods* (1991). Also relevant is Donald Schön's seminal *Beyond the*

Stable State (1973), Michael Lipsky's work on street-level bureau-crats, and what Saul Alinsky described as 'resident leadership' in his classic *Reveille for Radicals* (1946).

In short, we are not short of models for how to turn the gov-ernment-community relationship inside out. One way of reversing this relationship would be to change the electoral system so that we could directly elect and recall those resident leaders who do not represent community interests. To be sure, the constituency system is just as susceptible to influence by lobbyists as the cur-rent system is dependent on party patronage. It would not be a substitute for greater transparency in the political and electoral system, which brings me to the role of the social critic in society.

In the course of his call, Phosa castigates 'armchair critics'. This phrase was often used by members of the ANC as an epi-thet against members of the black consciousness movement in the 1980s because they supposedly spoke too much and did too little. The irony is that black consciousness leaders did not pay any less costly a price, including their lives. The greater irony is that the ANC adopted the very ideas of those armchair critics, and vulgarised them to near extinction. But the broader point is that critics are not doers, and that does not make their role in society any less important. The African-American philosopher Cornel West has described the critic as that 'person who stays attuned to the best of what the mainstream has to offer – its paradigms, viewpoints and methods – yet maintains a ground-ing in affirming and enabling subcultures of criticism'.

A critic who remains locked in the mainstream is easily a con-formist, and yet a critic locked in subcultures of criticism is easily a perpetual grumbler. In my home town of Ginsberg, we call such people '*oo-Nozikhalazo*' (people who are always complaining about one issue or another). The socially relevant critic is able to do these things from his or her armchair. But that does not mean that their ideas cannot be used by governments and political parties. Instead of looking at criticism as a threat, ANC leaders are better advised to look at the social intelligence that flows from criticism – in newspapers, and so on.

Fire has come to a leaderless country
Business Day, 22 May 2008

My book is entitled *To the Brink: The State of Democracy in South Africa* (2008), and I have repeatedly been warning about 'the fire next time'. Does that make me a doomsday prophet? You bet it does. We are skidding on the road to nowhere with our eyes wide open. In the short space of a decade, we have become rudderless and leaderless.

All manner of theories have been propounded for the xenophobic violence that began recently in Alexandra. We would not have had this refugee problem if President Thabo Mbeki and his acolytes had acted early enough to prevent the meltdown in Zimbabwe. His government has reproduced apartheid urban geography a million times over, ghettoising and warehousing the black and poor in areas where they can only lash out at each other in the most violent ways. Their dismal record on every social indicator has been there for everyone to see. Only this time, the evidence had to take the form of an inferno. And the leaders dithered and cowered for days on end as the thugs took over the streets. If anything, this is the most dramatic display of the lack of political authority in this country. If the ANC thinks it rules this country, it is deluding itself.

As for Mbeki, he is president only in name. Nobody respects him anymore – not his party and not the marauding gangs. I came of political age when leaders would confront such gangs and tell them to lay down their weapons. I am thinking of the courageous leadership of people such as the late Muntu Myeza, Don Mattera, Ishmael Mkhabela and Desmond Tutu. I can imagine Chris Hani and Nelson Mandela putting on their tracksuits, going from community to community to calm the situation. Can you imagine Mbeki doing that?

But the violence is the leadership's own creation in one other important way. Long before we had xenophobia, the leadership of the liberation movements planted a violent culture in our communities in the 1980s. They legitimised violence as the mode of political practice in the townships in the name of organisational and ideological hegemony. There is something about this violence reminiscent of that period. This is the *impi*-like organisation, the open brandishing of weapons, the dancing around burning people. The criminals who were recruited into the revolution are now in control of the state.

The past is making its presence felt in a frighteningly ferocious way. That is because the brutalisation of any group of people is not a tap the leadership can turn on and off as it pleases. Now, they are afraid of their own political Frankensteins. What we have been experiencing has been as much about xenophobia as it has been a demonstration that we do not have a government in this country. We do not have a leadership that can attend to the wounded and brutalised soul of this nation.

But what about you and me? Aren't we also implicated in this tragedy? You and I, the social and economic elites, hide inside our gated communities and air-conditioned offices, repeating the lie among whites that the past never was, and among blacks that the government or the movement is in control. Well, catch a wake-up, folks. No one is in charge. This is the fire next time, and it's raging furiously to a neighbourhood near you. Pretending there's a solution only adds to the civic complacency. We need to reclaim traditions of leadership that existed before the Mbeki era.

In the meantime, Mbeki and his ditherers must go. We need an early election, and an open and inclusive national conversation led by someone that even the angriest members of our communities can respect.

For SA's sake, nip home-grown Pol Pots in the bud
Business Day 19 June 2008

Only two weeks ago I wrote that ANC Youth League leaders should abandon the oft-repeated assertion that the youth are entitled to say whatever they want. 'We may not have cared about what they said in the past,' I wrote, 'because they helped stoke our passions in fighting our oppressors. However, we now watch every Youth League leader's utterances to sift out potential leaders among them. The new measure is not who is the most revolutionary but who is likely to handle power with care.'

I misspoke. Even back in the 1980s, I was one of those who spoke out against purveyors of death. We did so at great peril. These times are no less perilous, with the leader of the ANC Youth League, Julius Malema, claiming to have battalions that will kill counter-revolutionaries, or kill if the case against Jacob Zuma goes ahead. Speaking at the same meeting, Zuma reportedly vowed to rid the ANC of hooliganism and criminality. Where I was raised, it does not get any more criminal and hooligan than inciting murder. It is one thing to be militant and radical, but quite another to be outright stupid. We should not give respectability to stupidity in the name of the revolution. If we did, we would be dishonouring the legacy of so many young militants and radicals of our struggle, from Anton Lembede to Nelson Mandela to Steve Biko.

The ANC should insist that Malema retract his statement and apologise to the nation, or risk validating the assertion the organisation has lost all political morality. A retraction will not mean that Malema is a coward. Instead, it will be part of the process of learning how to lead – taking responsibility for one's words and actions. I don't know whether Malema can recover, but as a general principle, politicians who apologise for mistakes grow in stature.

One of the biggest surprises for the ANC will be the day it does not get 50 per cent of the vote. With leaders like Malema, that day is not far off. Perhaps the sooner that happens, the better it will be for this country. On that day we will see if the ANC would be willing to hand over the reins of power or whether, like Robert Mugabe's Zanu-PF, leaders like Malema will say they cannot be made to relinquish power by a cross on a piece of paper.

The other day, Moeletsi Mbeki chaired a discussion of my book at the Cape Town Book Fair. He said a violent conflagration in South Africa could perhaps no longer be avoided. All great nations – Britain, France, the United States – were forged in civil wars. Malema may well be the harbinger of our own civil war. It may be that with the transition from Thabo Mbeki to Zuma we have moved from the pot to the fire.

Perhaps in time a leader will emerge, but not before we have all been torched and scorched by the Pol Pots of our times. The onus is on the new ANC leadership to demonstrate otherwise. Zuma is to be commended for his rather belated renunciation of Malema's words. No amount of covering up or trying to explain those evil words will suffice.

I wonder how Nelson Mandela must be feeling these days. How could a people who sacrificed so much for their freedom attack the very principles on which their struggle was based? How could one of the greatest political movements of the 20th century preside over such collective decline? Could it be that the cause was worthier than those who pursued it, and that many of its leaders were nothing but thugs and murderers?

It is such a terrible thing to have been part of that dream, only to see it transmogrify into such evil. Better off are those who were never part of the dream. At least they cannot know the meaning of betrayal.

So, let's see, who are those who are to be killed?
Business Day, 26 June 2008

I cannot say I know how to kill. Therefore, I've been wracking my brain trying to imagine what lurks in the minds of the would-be killers Julius Malema, leader of the ANC Youth League, and Zwelinzima Vavi, secretary-general of COSATU. Both have threatened to 'kill' those who stand in the way of Jacob Zuma's ascent to ANC and national leadership. I presume the first order of business would be to identify who is to be killed. We can, of course, speculate about the targets. It's really easy, actually. We can do a sectoral analysis of who the enemies of the revolution might be: the same as the enemies of Jacob Zuma.

Given that this is grave business, I would not dare to mention names, but the targets are all those who have been deemed to be persecuting Zuma. I think it is also fair to speculate that a couple of judges, including judges of the Constitutional Court, would be strong candidates. Then I am sure there are those members of the media who have been writing all those nasty op-ed pieces and columns about Zuma.

Folks, you had better start going through your writings to see whether this is not the time to issue apologia. As for me, I'm not sure. Sometimes I've defended the man and sometimes I've excoriated him. But for those in the business of killing, there is no time for 'on the one hand he was with us; on the other hand he was against us'.

Then there are all those women who marched against Zuma during the rape trial. They know who you are, and they will be coming for you in the dark of night. I am sure the list of possible victims is inexhaustible. Let us then move on to consider the method of death. Will Vavi, Malema and their gang of warriors shoot the enemies in the head even as they plead for their lives? Or will they dismember them in full view of the world to teach others a lesson? Will they set them ablaze in the manner of Ernesto Nhamuave?

And will they laugh around the burning bodies while singing revolutionary songs? Or will they simply do what many leaders did during the 1980s, which was simply to issue orders to the foot soldiers? In those days, the leaders could still go around sipping champagne at society gatherings, knowing full well that the killing machines were in full swing in the townships. Like Liberia's Charles Taylor, the leaders can now still go about their business knowing full well of the death and destruction. Occasionally the cellphone will ring and they will politely ask to be excused from the dinner table so they can get progress reports from the killing fields.

But then again, I don't know what it's like to snuff out someone's life, whether in defence of the revolution or of a friend or a comrade, or for any reason for that matter. I suspect I was never much of a revolutionary in that sense. To be sure, oppression has forced groups of people to take up arms because they had no choice. But there is something fundamentally sick about a so-called democratic society in which so-called leaders speak so casually and brazenly about the ready availability of death as a method of settling political and legal disputes.

Our leaders have over the years shown us how to be immune to death. People have been dying every day in our communities – from the scourge of HIV/AIDS to the brutality of Zimbabwe and the xenophobic violence that has seen people dancing around the burning bodies of foreign nationals. So when we die at the hands of the revolutionaries, there will really be nothing usual about it – and it will be just another day on the job for them. If they play golf, which I suspect they do, it will be par for the course.

You know what? There is a part of me that says, the sooner they bring the death, the better. Maybe that will be our baptism as yet another African country that could not resist the post-colonial propensity for violence. A baptism by fire for sure, but a baptism nonetheless. But the question will linger: how did a once proud freedom movement become a party of death?

Will democracy prove to be the ANC's undoing?
Business Day, 3 July 2008

I am ashamed of this government. On Zimbabwe, it has come to be associated with evil. President Thabo Mbeki defends that country's leader at every opportunity, while countries such as Senegal, Nigeria and Botswana have seen fit to proclaim the Mugabe government as illegitimate.

I suspect that many more African countries are going to show more courage, but not South Africa. Not only are we the pariah of the world – as we were during the apartheid years – but we are likely to be the laughing stock of Africa. I can hear other Africans saying, look at those uppity South Africans who walked on to the world stage pretending they were better than the rest of the continent. I can hear them using the barbarism of the xeno-phobic attacks as a stick to beat us.

And who can blame them when our leader mollycoddles one of the worst dictators in the history of our continent? Can any-one believe that only a few years ago it was Mbeki who was beat-ing the drum of the African Renaissance, arguing against the recognition of dictatorial regimes? Can anyone believe that these were his words: 'The call for Africa's renewal, for an African renaissance, is a call to rebellion. We must rebel against the tyrants and the dictators, those who seek to corrupt our societies and steal the wealth that belongs to the people?' All Mbeki does these days is sing platitudes to the dictators. What a hard and precipitous fall from grace, integrity and credibility. Is it any wonder that the African Union is now talking about having a special envoy to Zimbabwe?

But this is not just a fall from grace of a single individual. This is the fall from grace of a movement and a country. The victors at Polokwane increasingly look like a congregation of fascists – and I use the term in its deeply historical sense, which is when intol-erance becomes the source of its own inspiration and validation through violence. Fascism emerged in a context that is not widely different from ours: a globalising economy and the massification of politics in Europe. Fascists spoke to the disaffected, and it really did not matter whether the disaffected were on the left or the right of the political spectrum. The fascist thrill came not from any ideological programme. Instead, it came from the sensation of domination in the name of the people or the race or the leader.

Shortly before Benito Mussolini became Italy's prime minis-ter, one of his critics asked him about the content of his pro-gramme. He then declared: 'The democrats of *Il Mondo* want to know our programme. It is to break the bones of the democrats of *Il Mondo*. And the sooner the better.' He then added: 'The fist is the synthesis of our theory.' The German critic Walter Benjamin has observed that by replacing reason with the sensual experience of domination, fascism transformed politics into aesthetics. And as Achille Mbembe has observed with respect to Africa, with the satisfaction came a sensation of vulgarity.

Just a few months after their Polokwane victory, Zuma's supporters have become more occupied with protecting their leader from the criminal justice system than with any programme for the nation. To paraphrase Mussolini, the gun is the synthesis of their theory. In the end, we can no longer walk the capitals of the world with our heads held high. If in the past we sought attention in an almost narcissistic way, we now avoid international audiences like the plague. What programme can we proudly share with the world? Having won the long fight, the party realised it had no national vision to speak of, except for the fetish of the gun.

A hundred years is a long time in the life of any party. The struggle helped it hold together, but democracy is likely to be its undoing. The rise of the fascists within its ranks is therefore not without reason or precedent. Fascism gained roots – in France, in the United States, in the Weimar Republic – as a backlash against democracy. Why should we be any different?

New ANC brass joins an ugly tradition of bullies
Business Day, 10 July 2008

Welcome to gangland, folks. We've seen it in Africa over and over again – opposition movements ride the wave of popular protest only to repeat the excesses of their predecessors. It happened in Malawi with Frank Chiluba, and in Kenya with Mwai Kibaki. The new ANC leaders elected at Polokwane are attacking the pillars of our democratic system with an unprecedented and brazen ferocity.

A friend in Ginsberg mocked me recently by saying I would live to miss Thabo Mbeki once the present lot had finished destroying all our democratic institutions. Indeed, their language is even more ferocious than it was under Mbeki. Look at Gwede Mantashe, a senior member of the party, telling us that judges are not sacrosanct. That's what Mbeki and Co said all the time about the media. But saying the same thing about one of the central pillars of the democratic state is even more ominous.

I am always wary of politicians who seek to demonstrate that they are clever – using words to win political points as if their identities depended on it, hiding their real intentions behind convoluted logic. I am disappointed with Mantashe. I thought he would be more sensitive to the challenges of leadership. The fact of the matter is that the judiciary has been the only bulwark against corruption in South Africa. And what, may I ask, would he say if the judiciary ruled in his man's favour? Would he do a *mea culpa*? And what about the damage already done?

The executive has been drunk with power, and parliament nothing more than a rubber-stamp of executive decisions. Now, the only state institution that has shown the courage to take on the powerful without fear or favour is under attack – if only to save the skin of one individual politician, Jacob Zuma.

And we still have the gumption to call this a democracy? No, there is nothing democratic about the rantings of the new ANC leadership. Instead, they suffer from an acute case of what Nicanor Perlas calls 'Rust' – the Residue of Unresolved Statism. RUST has nothing to do with society and everything to do with state capture, by any means necessary. RUST can manifest itself in violent and vile language because of what is at stake: power and resources. Perlas describes RUST's operation as follows: 'The word "statism" means state-centred. It comes from an era when activists and others had a respectful awe . . . of all-powerful states like the state of Bismarck, Germany, or the totalitarian states of many countries today. The state had the power to achieve its ends through legal or illegal coercion.' Coercion becomes central to RUST because politics is a war of substituting one group of autocrats with another.

This has been the history of South Africa, with the rule of Nelson Mandela being an exception in a long line of rule by political bullies. Sometimes I wonder what we did to be saddled with such leadership – from the heydays of apartheid to the heydays of postcolonial buffoonery. The cynicism of the language makes the cynicism of the Mbeki years pale into significance. The only difference now is that 'enemies' are no longer called 'coconuts' or 'askaris'. They are now simply 'counter-revolutionaries', fit for the guillotine, the gun or the knife, whichever instrument is handy. This is the state of our political culture.

But perhaps there is a value to having a time lag between the ANC's leadership conference and the country's general elections. At least this gives the would-be leaders a long rope with which to hang themselves, and the citizenry an opportunity to assess whether we can trust these people with power for the next two decades. Call me a counter-revolutionary, but I do think we need a counter-revolution, a peaceful one staged by the ordinary men and women of this country at the ballot box next year. I cannot imagine anything healthier for this country's democratic prospects than voting the ANC out of power.

From Mandela to Malema in three simple steps
Business Day, 17 July 2008

Our criticism of the ANC Youth League leader Julius Malema is misplaced. Societies are by their nature diverse. They throw up all sorts of people – the good, the bad, the nonviolent, the violent, and so on. Much has been made of the fact that Malema did not finish matric. But neither did millions of our young people. The real issue is that we have a political system that makes it possible for such people to assume the leadership of our land.

This is a result of what I once described as a leadership tailspin in the ANC. In 1990 the ANC had its best leadership collective. This consisted of the wisdom of the generation that graduated from places such as Fort Hare in the 1930s and 1940s (Govan Mbeki, Nelson Mandela, Walter Sisulu, Oliver Tambo); the intellectual brilliance of the exile returnees (Thabo Mbeki, Pallo Jordan, Chris Hani, Zola Skweyiya); and the political brinkmanship of the mass democratic movement of the 1980s (Cyril Ramaphosa, Trevor Manuel, Jay Naidoo). So formidable was this eclectic leadership collective that it left the National Party negotiators reeling.

However, a tailspin then took place in three stages. First, the wisdom of the older generation was replaced by the showmanship of the exile returnees. The returnees seemed more interested in showing how clever they were than with connecting with the experiences of the people. Thus, under their leadership, the life expectancy of the population fell by a whopping 15 per cent. Second, those who had been in the mass democratic movement were recruited to become part of this charade (Trevor Manuel, Mosiuoa Lekota), or disappeared from the public stage, with Ramaphosa being the most prominent example. Third, the intellectual pretenders were themselves kicked out at Polokwane by the foot soldiers of the revolution of Jacob Zuma.

Now, it would be just a matter of time before the foot soldiers would find common cause with the *lumpenproletariat* (the 'comrade tsotsis', as we called them in the 1980s). There is much that brings the foot soldier and the proletariat together – but mainly it is a strong sense of being underdogs. Lacking in the wisdom of the older generation, the intellectual sophistication of the returnees and the sense of community of the mass democratic movement, they employ their only comparative advantage, namely violence.

Nothing gives this group greater satisfaction than seeing members of polite society cringe when it speaks of killing. In his masterpiece *The Wretched of the Earth* (1968), Frantz Fanon describes how the *lumpenproletariat* enter and occupy the centre of the historical scene: 'So the pimps, the hooligans, the unemployed, and the petty criminals throw themselves into struggle like stout working men. These classless idlers will by militant and decisive action discover the path that leads to nationhood.'

Not only that, they will, in our case, take over the leadership of the nation, wielding the language of violence. From there it is a short jump to either the left-wing populism of the Pol Pot variety or the right-wing populism of the fascist variety. Nowhere in their discourse is there any of the democratic populism we had hoped for in urging them to save us from Mbeki.

So what should be the role of intellectuals at such perilous times? Our experience with Mbeki teaches us that it is precisely when politicians are at their most powerful that we should develop a critical distance from them, for our sake and, more importantly, for theirs.

A time of no leaders in SA, only heads of factions
Business Day, 7 August 2008

Who are these people who have inherited the leadership of this country? And if we had really known them, would we still have elected them? Yes and no. Yes, because we know Jacob Zuma well. There is little this country does not know about Zuma. And we know that he is surrounded by some really violent people – judging by the pronouncements of some of his supporters. This does not matter, because this violent streak, despite our howls of protest, is not new. Despite our penchant for glorifying our history, a great deal of blood was spilled in the townships under the spell of what I once described as civic authoritarianism.

There is something of an unintended irony in the argument that I and other journalists have been making about Zuma's popularity, namely that he is so popular because he is so fallible, and that people see in him an 'everyman' to whom they can relate. Our attraction to leaders has never been due to their fallibility, but because they were infallible. Admittedly, in the latter instance we idealised the leaders and created unrealistic expectations, as we often do with Nelson Mandela. But at least that is how high we set the bar: better the virtuous leader with flaws than the flawed leader with some virtues. Now, if Zuma is 'a virtuous leader with some flaws', we should give him a chance and hope that the people around him will protect him against his worst instincts. However, if he is 'a flawed leader with some virtues', he should not come anywhere near the Union Buildings.

Karima Brown argues that there is no one who can stop Zuma from becoming president, and that is because we are a nation of flawed people – 'the ANC,' she writes, 'seems to have calculated the risk for itself as a party. If voters get behind Zuma, it could suggest that they too believe the country can afford Zuma, with his legal woes, as its next president.' This points to the limits of majoritarianism in leadership. In the literature on leadership, there has always been the empirical idea of the leader as the person who stands in front and commands others to do as he or she wishes, because 'the party has decided for itself'. But there has always been the normative idea of the leader as the person who cultivates the will of the people. The former rules through power, the latter through authority.

If all that matters to the ANC is that it wins elections, without any attention to the normative values that have always informed its leadership, then it will find itself ruling with neither authority nor legitimacy. That is what I said shortly after Thabo Mbeki was inaugurated, and look at the mess that followed. I see no reason to change with respect to Zuma.

Speaking of Mbeki, unlike Zuma, he walked on to the political stage as a person of virtue until allegations of corruption started surfacing, culminating in the allegation by the *Sunday Times* that he took R30 million from one of the arms deal bidders. If we knew he was corrupt, I suspect we would not have elected him. He would have come too soon after Nelson Mandela, who despite his flaws still remains the bar by which we measure our leaders.

Benjamin Barber might as well have had Mbeki and Zuma in mind when he wrote:

There are today no leaders, only heads of factions; there is no leadership of ideas, only a competition of ideologies; there is no consensus, only an unstable balance of opposing interests. Adversaries are soon construed as enemies, assassins have their work cut out for them, and finally the prosecution-persecution of enemies is elevated into presidential business. The leaders no longer seem certain of what to expect of themselves, and we in turn no longer expect anything at all of our leaders. It is an occasion of deep national gratitude when a president is willing to be honest.

Malema tending a garden planted in Mbeki years
Business Day, 20 November 2008

Like other South Africans, I was outraged by the ANC Youth League leader Julius Malema's disrespectful utterances concerning Mbhazima Shilowa's past as a security guard, and his failure to provide for his children.

This came close on the heels of Malema's equally discourteous utterances to Northern Cape Premier Dipuo Peters, while Jacob Zuma sat silently instead of standing up to grab the microphone from the young man. I have found myself asking the question: 'How is it possible that a group of adults can sit around the table while someone young enough to be their child spews this venom in the name of their organisation? Is there no self-respect, pride or honour left in the ANC at all?' Then it occurred to me that I had asked a similar question of the ANC several times before.

At the height of Thabo Mbeki's AIDS denialism in 2002, I asked in a column: 'Has the ANC national executive committee become such an elective oligarchy that not a single member, other than Mandela, has the courage and integrity to speak out openly on such a defining issue for our children and our nation?'

It has since emerged, at least according to a Harvard University study, that more than 300 000 grown people and 35 000 infants died while Mbeki was busy denying the existence of the disease. Pallo Jordan informed us at a Platform for Public Deliberation event that we had all got it wrong, and that Mbeki was challenged within the organisation. That is hardly comforting to the families of the dead.

Similarly, it may well be that Malema is being rapped over the knuckles behind closed doors, but once he steps out he finds the glare of the cameras irresistible. In that sense he is unstoppable, unless the ANC takes more drastic action – such as suspending him for bringing the organisation into disrepute. That will no doubt divide the ANC, but it will not lead to a split. In fact, Malema could be the vehicle for the moderates within the ANC, if they can muster the courage, to mount a fight-back against the hoodlum elements in the organisation.

I still believe what I argued last year, that the ANC needs the 'third way' of the likes of Tokyo Sexwale, Cyril Ramaphosa and Kgalema Motlanthe. These are the people who need to bring the ANC closer to the sensibilities of the millions of ordinary men and women who are appalled by Malema's vulgarity.

Having said all of that, I am equally appalled by the hypocrisy that informs the responses to Malema. Malema is tending the same garden of vulgarity cultivated by Mbeki's supporters. For years, these people have openly been saying they cannot be ruled by an uneducated man – in the same way that Malema says he cannot be ruled by a security guard. When Shilowa protests that Malema holds security guards in contempt, Malema can turn around to say Zuma's critics hold the uneducated people of this country in contempt.

People who should know better about the rule of law have been calling Zuma a rapist, despite the fact that he was acquitted by a court of law. Malema's comments become mild when compared to that. The point is that Malema is a child of the very vulgar parents who are chastising him now. For years, they went about calling people 'askaris', 'sell-outs' and 'coconuts'. Repulsed as we are by Malema's utterances, we need to remind ourselves of this ugly chapter of our history, and ask why insults uttered by one group are any more acceptable than those uttered by another.

Some people celebrate COPE's formation as a sign of the democratisation of our political culture. I see things differently. In Xhosa, I would say, *'Sijekeleza endaweni enye'* – 'we are running in one spot'. We are all caught up in the unending Mbeki–Zuma epic, now in a new guise, and the vulgarity that has defined the political culture of both sides. There are no angels here.

Coming of age in an age of looting
City Press, 31 July 2011

ANC Youth League leader Julius Malema has come face to face with the realities of power in all its dimensions – the power of money, the power of the media, the power of political opponents, as well as the power of the legal system. The question is whether he will buckle or prevail under the ensuing pressure. If Malema were to face the full might of the law, which he must if there is any wrongdoing on his part, then I would feel sad for him in the same way I feel for many a child transgressor. For, in political terms, Malema is still a novice, despite the power accorded to him.

And it is an absolute tragedy that the adults in the ANC have abdicated their leadership while filling Malema's head with delusions of grandeur. How could we expect him to avoid the seduction of money and power when that same judgment has eluded his own leaders in the ruling party? And has it really helped that he has been compared to a 'Mandela in the making' or touted as a 'future president' by his political elders? What can that do to a young mind other than make him feel unassailable?

Malema may have been hoisted on his own petard, but if he is found guilty of any wrongdoing he would have been the victim of a corrupt culture created by his own elders in the ANC. He came of age in an age of looting. Just the other day, a friend was telling me about a nephew who asked why he should go to school if he could get rich by getting government tenders. A country in which the young see no value in education, and where the educated are not valued, is a country already in the abyss. Or as one of my friends put it: 'The cancer of corruption has spread too far to be arrested.'

The people who would have been expected to clean up the mess – the politicians – are the ones who benefit from it. We thus find ourselves in the vicious cycle of a dominant party that seems unable to cleanse itself of corruption because that is what oils its cogs. The problem is that not everybody's cogs are oiled equally in the race for party leadership, which may mean we are already into the season of leaks, whether what they contain is true or not. As I argued in my previous book *The Democratic Moment* (2009), law is politics and politics is law in South Africa. In some ways the chickens have come home to roost, not only for Malema but also for the ruling party.

If Malema goes down, he is unlikely to go down alone. He will most likely go down with the adults who allowed a young man with very little political experience to rule the roost, while they repeatedly and insatiably dipped into the public trough, with or without his connivance. Ngugi wa Thiong'o could not have asked for a better script for his novel *Devil on the Cross* than present-day South Africa.

Dealing with Malema will prove far easier than rescuing this country from the morass in which its current leaders have taken it. Whether he is guilty or not, I hope the Malema saga will demonstrate once again that this country is in dire need of new institutional foundations that go beyond the fate of charismatic figures.

The wheels on the bus go round and round . . .
City Press, 3 September 2011

The goings-on outside Luthuli House during the ANC's disciplinary proceedings against ANC Youth Leage president Julius

Malema bring to mind the nursery rhyme: 'The wheels on the bus go round and round, round and round, round and round! The wheels on the bus go round and round, all day long!' The mayhem has all the hallmarks of Polokwane written all over it: like Zuma a few years ago, Malema has become the underdog; there is a massive show of support by the underdog's supporters outside the hearings; then there is the blessings from charismatic priests; the burning of t-shirts bearing the 'traitors' face; and, most ominously for the ruling party, the possibility of yet another split down the middle going into 2012 and 2014. And just as ANC secretary-general Gwede Mantashe describes as anti-ANC those burning t-shirts with Zuma's face, I hear Thabo Mbeki saying: 'Where were you when I needed you most, Mr Mantashe?'

As Karl Marx put it, history repeats itself, first as tragedy and then as farce, except here you have farce and tragedy combined in one historical serving. After all, there was no talk of disciplining Malema when he was threatening to kill people in the name of Zuma, chasing a journalist out of a news conference, or insulting the senior cabinet minister Naledi Pandor, a woman old enough to be his mother, for speaking with a foreign accent. For me, there is therefore no logically consistent explanation for the disciplinary hearing other than that the shoe is now on the other foot. Feeling the pinch, Zuma and his comrades must do all they can to rid themselves of what Fiona Forde called 'this inconvenient youth', just as Mbeki had to do with inconvenient Zuma a few years ago.

The reality is that the politics of intrigue that began under Mbeki may just be continued by Zuma, whom we wrongly thought would be different. The only piece of advice I would have for Zuma's enforcers would be that they should not leave behind tapes with former national prosecutors claiming: 'I am a Zuma man.' The past is always prologue.

While these things are connected, there are also differences between Polokwane and what I would call 'the Luthuli House Moment'. Unlike Zuma's march to Polokwane, Malema's march to Luthuli House did not have the groundswell of organisational support from COSATU, the SACP, the MK Veterans Association, the ANC Women's League, and moles working for him in the National Intelligence Agency. Without that kind of organisational support, Malema will most likely buckle in the face of the political and legal juggernaut coming his way. However, that will come at a cost to the ANC. While the Luthuli House protests may not be our Arab Spring, they are the beginning of a long 'winter of discontent' for the ANC going into 2012 and 2014, especially in the light of increasing voter apathy and declining electoral support under Jacob Zuma.

The wheels on the bus may not just be turning; they may be coming off. Just like Mbeki had to realise how difficult it is to hold on to power, Zuma will then realise that it's damn hard to keep the wheels of these sorts of movements turning round and round forever. At some point, historians will look back to the Luthuli House Moment as the moment the hegemony of the ruling party began to disintegrate – just as historians have had to do that in India, Mexico, and all other societies once governed by dominant political parties.

Time for Zuma and his pirates to go
Sunday Times, 24 April 2011

In 1999, I suggested that then President Thabo Mbeki's rule would not last long because he could not possibly satisfy the political and material ambitions of everyone in the ANC. Indeed, it was only a matter of time before those who were left out or who had been Mbeki's victims started mobilising against him, culminating in his dethroning as president of the ANC in December 2007 and of the Republic in September 2008. I use the word 'dethrone' because any leader who clings to power has assumed for himself the role of a monarch.

In a Harold Wolpe memorial lecture in June 2007, I suggested that Jacob Zuma's populist coalition would dissemble the moment they reached their 'rendezvous with victory'. I went on to say that this was because the populist frontier – from BEE wannabes and ethnic entrepreneurs to fugitives from the law and the ever dodgy *lumpenproletariat* – was not ideologically coherent. 'Wait until Zuma has won, and see the infighting that will emerge,' I said.

The limits of patronage-based politics lie in the fact that there is never enough patronage to go round, whether in terms of material resources or positions. Indeed, there can be only twenty-odd cabinet positions, 400-odd members of parliament, and so many ward councillors at one time. And there can be only so many corrupt government contracts before the state becomes nothing more than a collective piracy. This will be as true for the next leader of the ANC as it was for Zuma and Mbeki. This suggests the need for a discourse about leadership that avoids the pitfalls of our recent past. I suggest three ways for such a discussion.

First, as members of the public, we are not bound by the hush-hush culture of leadership discussions in the ANC. As the American president Woodrow Wilson put it a century ago: 'The state exists for the sake of society, not society for the sake of the state.' As things now stand, we in South Africa exist for the sake of the state, simply spectators as public officials feed at the trough. To paraphrase Steve Biko, what right do we then have to protest if we continue to be bystanders in a game we should be playing as citizens?

The one thing that we share across all of our social divisions is the right to vote – to punish the bad guys, and reward the good. The forthcoming local government elections present a golden opportunity for a more assertive voting public. In fact, the internecine contestation for local government lists should be neither here nor there for voters. The ultimate test should be whether the many people who are adversely affected by corruption can muster the courage to challenge the few people who benefit from it, thanks to their holding public office.

Second, our experience with Mbeki and Zuma demonstrates that the election of leaders on the basis of patronage networks and personal allegiances is unsustainable. In his modern classic *Leadership* (2012), James MacGregor Burns argues that transitional societies are often too eager to provide mass support for heroic leaders 'through votes, applause, letters, shaking hands, rather than through intermediaries or institutions'. We need to shift from focusing on individual leaders, as has been our wont – myself included – to institutional leadership. The test of leadership should be the extent to which those in authority bring integrity to our public institutions, from the local to the national level.

Third, there is a need for a new political dynamic in South Africa. This is simply because, once a society sets itself on the path of corruption, it soon reaches a tipping point and cannot reverse the process for centuries. In his book *Making Democracy Work* (1993), the Harvard scholar Robert Putnam argues that the difference between the more prosperous northern Italy and the corrupt south is a result of the institutionalisation of autocratic rule in 1100 AD and centuries of gangster rule after that. Right now, we are on the fast lane to southern Italy.

No matter how long the ANC may want to delay the leadership issue, at some point they will have to face the elephant in the room: the fact that the state has become a collective piracy. There are too many government and business contracts going to individuals directly linked to the president. There are too many allegations of impropriety linked to the president's cabinet ministers. Whether the president is in the know doesn't matter; these things are happening on his watch.

Inasmuch as I called for Mbeki's replacement as president at the height of his arrogant use of power, I now feel compelled to ask for the ANC to provide this country with alternative leadership and a new political dynamic – or face the prospect of living under a government that has irreversibly become a kleptocracy. The vote, both within and outside political parties, gives us an occasional opportunity to save ourselves from ourselves and build anew our public institutions. Whether the ruling party and the public will muster the courage to do so is, of course, a different matter. I am no soothsayer, but we cannot continue to put our heads in the sand while all is collapsing around us.

We can either manage change, or change will rudely be forced on us, as it has been throughout human history – often at great social and human cost. The changes in North Africa are merely the latest instalment in the tragedy that befalls societies that do not plan for change. It is our collective duty to make sure that our children do not one day wake up to a bare and barren future because we allowed public looting to go on during our watch.

How can we rescue ourselves from this mess: democratic processes, not political parties, create true democracy
City Press, 25 September 2011

The Americans call it 'Monday morning quarterbacking'. This comes from the practice of criticising a weekend football game with the benefit of hindsight. Given Jacob Zuma's disastrous presidency, many of my friends are longing for the 'stable' days of Thabo Mbeki's. Some even suggest that Mbeki should return as the 'knight in shining armour' to save us from the anarchy all around us. The problem with Monday morning quarterbacking is that it requires a heavy dose of revisionism. In the context of the difficulties of the present, the past is always golden.

Having just published a book about the archive and memory in democratic societies, I take the liberty to remind us of how we got here, and what it will take to avoid going down the same path again. First, I was one of those who argued insistently that there was something fundamentally wrong about a nation that mortgaged its future to two highly flawed individuals – Mbeki and Zuma. I argued that this country was way ahead of both of them. I still believe that had the ANC opted for the 'third way' represented by Tokyo Sexwale's failed candidacy, we would not have found ourselves in the depths of anarchy, mediocrity and corruption we find ourselves in now. Even if you were to assume Sexwale turning out to be a bad president, I just can't imagine him being worse than Zuma.

Unfortunately, the 'third way' lost steam, and threw in its lot with Zuma – more out of hope than conviction. Even if you put a gun to my head, I argued, I would choose Zuma to avoid Mbeki's precedent-setting grab for power. To argue that this was a ringing endorsement of Zuma is part of the revisionism that afflicts memory with the passage of time. In understanding and even tempering our frustrations about Zuma's presidency, we should always remember that he came to power less because he was loved and more because Mbeki was hated.

The good thing about writing things down is that they become an archive we can use to jog our collective memories. While I was happy that we avoided Mbeki's power grab, I also posed the following question about Zuma in my book *The Democratic Moment:*

South Africa's Prospects under Jacob Zuma (2009): 'The question at the end of the day is whether the new leadership under Jacob Zuma has the emotional temperament, the ethical–moral commitment, the political willingness, and the institutional resources needed for the revival of democracy. If they do not, then we will be in no better position than we were under Mbeki. In fact we might even be in worse shape. In the end Mbeki's autocratic behaviour might simply be replaced by anarchy under Zuma. The democratic moment would have been just that – a passing moment.' I further cautioned that future generations might look at the Zuma generation as transitional leaders who performed an important role in ridding us of a would-be dictator but that 'when their turn came, they were found not to be any different'.

It is precisely because Zuma was found wanting in all the aspects mentioned above that there are now efforts in the ANC to ensure that his rule was indeed 'a passing moment' in our elusive quest for leadership. But the flight from anarchy cannot mean a return to autocracy. The test of democratic maturity is precisely the gamble that comes with choosing our leaders, not the false security of sticking with one leader just in case things turn out badly under his successor. That would be returning to the political blackmail that has kept our continent in the doldrums for the past six decades.

Americans did not know Richard Nixon would lead them towards Watergate when they chose him over Hubert Humphrey. And as soon as they discovered how flawed Nixon was, they got rid of him. They did not seek to recycle retired presidents, but continued to experiment with lacklustre leaders such as Gerald Ford and Jimmy Carter. It took them a decade to find an inspiring leader in Ronald Reagan, whose policies turned out to be just as distasteful in the end. They continued the elusive search for leadership precisely because they had developed the institutional mechanisms that would cushion them against leadership failures.

231

If their president turned out to be a disaster, they could rely on Congress, the Supreme Court, and competitive elections to make a correction. That is how they came to elect a 'fresher' or novice such as Barack Obama instead of sticking with the false security of the tried-and-tested war hero John McCain. Democracy is a continuous process of course correction, or what Franklin Delano Roosevelt called 'bold, persistent experimentation'.

It is about time for us as South Africans not only to outgrow the tired Mbeki–Zuma discourse, but also to wean ourselves from our dependence on individual leaders. Thanks to these two leaders, we are on our way to becoming the only country on the African continent to have won the country and returned it the former rulers. In any event, the ruling party's downward spiral happens to all dominant parties, sooner or later.

How then can we rediscover our own political agency, and rescue ourselves as a society? Change the political system, for crying out loud. We have a political system that not only lends itself to racial appeals. If the recent local government elections are anything to go by, black people voted for the ANC and white people voted for the DA. Because of the present system, we find ourselves stuck with the autocrats and anarchists those parties throw up. And yet, the parties might present us with different characters if they knew the public was going to vote directly and choose between their candidates and those of opposing parties.

If that were to happen, South Africans would express what they want in an individual leader, and start down a path of discovering the values they have in common beyond race, and beyond the false debates about Mbeki's autocracy and Zuma's anarchy. That space between autocracy and anarchy is what we call democracy. The elusive quest for democratic leadership must therefore continue, not with one eye looking to a golden past that never was.

VII
REALIGN OR PERISH

Dumping Malema is like tossing chairs off the deck of the Titanic
Business Day, 2 March 2012

A few years ago, I invited the ANC intellectual Pallo Jordan to a discussion of the COPE breakaway. Jordan argued that it reflected the extent to which material interests had taken over the ANC. Fast-forward to ANC Deputy President Kgalema Motlanthe's speech at the University of South Africa a few weeks ago. Motlanthe spoke in similar terms about a culture of 'material acquisitiveness that has enveloped the outlook of society – including some of us in the ANC today'. He argued that the ANC would have to renew itself by re-emphasising its traditions and core values, and by 'preventing its quintessence from being corroded by sins of incumbency that have plagued post-colonial liberation movements elsewhere before'.

A number of considerations suggest that it may well be too late to halt the downward spiral, and that Motlanthe's lamentation may be a tad too late for his beloved movement. Historically, the elevation of material interests over values has been the fate of most liberation movements that have turned into political parties. The ANC's loss of electoral support over the years should be seen more like a miners' canary: a warning that the mine is about to implode, and everyone will start gunning for the exit. That has not happened yet because the ANC – or, more precisely, a faction of it – is virtually in control of state patronage.

But if the experience of other post-colonial societies is anything to go by, it would be foolhardy to think that such hegemony can last for very long. The thing about patronage is that it always creates insiders and outsiders. Not long ago I was in Nairobi, and stupidly asked the taxi driver how KANU, the party of independence, was doing. The guy burst out laughing, and I soon realised just how I had embarrassed myself. Thankfully, there was just the two of us.

The sociologist Carl Boggs once drew a distinction between two types of social movements. There are those whose primary existence is the instrumental capture of state power under the guise of transforming society. No sooner is the movement in power than it lapses into the same corporate greed and bureaucratic culture it purported to challenge in the name of the people. Calls are made for unity and discipline, but it soon becomes apparent that these are no more than an outward appearance; a cover for factional mobilisation for gaining access to resources. Either you are with us, or against us. Leadership battles become vicious precisely because they are life-and-death issues.

Frankly, what is happening to the ANC is the coming apart of a political model that predates Malema.

It is a political model of material accumulation through the state that was started by his parents in the ANC when he was barely able to walk. Before you knew it, the leadership of the party was implicated in every corruption scandal imaginable. The former national police commissioner is in jail, and many of the ANC's leaders have seen the other side of prison gates.

I was sitting with some friends in a shebeen the other day when a young man walked in singing a tune to the words 'the ANC . . . the African National Criminals . . .' Everybody cringed, because this is not an accurate description of the good men and women in the ANC. The truth though is that those good men and women have failed to assert their values over a leadership that cynically fights over the distribution of spoils while insisting on unity and discipline.

The larger question for this society – and particularly for black people in whose name this struggle was launched – is whether we can imagine ourselves surviving the ANC's shenanigans, and what institutional form this would take. The problem with moral outrage is that it doesn't easily turn into political and institutional clarity.

I don't think other political parties are the solution to our problems, for they too will turn around to exhibit the same behaviour. But I also don't think the ANC's expulsion of someone it used as its 'useful idiot' for so long will do the trick either. After all, whose hands are clean in this fight among political millionaires? The ANC expelling Malema and his cronies amounts to no more than throwing a few chairs off the decks of the *Titanic*, while the leadership insists: 'The movement is everything, the goal nothing'.

South Africa – and the black community in particular – requires a leadership and values revolution. As it starts out on the path to the bloodbath of Mangaung, the ANC leadership would do well to keep in mind the following definition of leadership by Robert Sobukwe, whose passed this week: 'True leadership demands complete subjugation of self, absolute honesty, integrity and uprightness of character, courage and fearlessness, and, above all, a consuming love for one's people.' Those qualities are sorely lacking in our national life right now, with or without Julius Malema.

Our invisible lineage is gone
City Press, 21 July 2012

All our great leaders have learnt from great teachers, but from whom will tomorrow's leaders take their cue? Celebrating Nelson Mandela's life is not a mere indulgence or fancy. It is the expression of a deep-felt yearning to return to something wondrous in the black struggle for freedom since the middle of the 19th century. Prior to that, black people – first the Khoisan on the Northern Cape frontier, and the Xhosa on the Eastern Cape frontier – were engaged in military warfare against the Dutch and the British colonists. When they were defeated, they heeded I W W Citashe's famous poem 'The Cattle Are Gone' (1882):

Your cattle are gone, my countrymen!
Go rescue them! Go rescue them!
Leave the breechloader alone
And turn to the pen.
Load it with ink
For that is your shield.
Your rights are going!
So pick up your pen.
Load it, load it with ink.
Sit on a chair.
Repair not to Hoho
But fire with your pen.

Thus emerged a group of African intellectuals who began to grapple with the question of how to respond to emergent European modernity, which was a combination of violent conquest and missionary education. Through their writings and public debates, those intellectuals – among them Tiyo Soga, John Knox Bokwe, John Tengo Jabavu, W B Rubusana, Sol Plaatje and S E K Mqhayi – provided the philosophical foundations for the vision of a society that would begin to emerge more than a century later. This included Plaatje's historic resistance against the 1913 Natives Land Act. Among other things, Plaatje challenged Jabavu to a public debate in King William's Town over the latter's support for the Land Act. And in December 1913, Plaatje wrote in his newspaper *The Friend of the People*: 'God forbid that we should ever find that our mind had become the property of someone other than ourselves; but should such a misfortune ever overtake us, we should at least strive to serve our new proprietor diligently, and whenever our people are unanimously opposed to a policy, we should consider it a part of our duty to tell him so; but that is not Mr Jabavu's way of serving a master.'

This public intellectual work was institutionalised through the formation of the South African Native Convention in 1909 and the South African National Native Congress in 1912, which was renamed the African National Congress in 1923. The idea of freedom that inspired the organisation would be hotly contested within the black community, leading to the emergence of other intellectual traditions in the All Africa Convention in the 1930s, the Unity Movement in the 1940s, the PAC in 1959, and the black consciousness Movement in 1968.

Nelson Mandela's birth in 1918 comes midway between the advent of this African intellectual response to European modernity in the 1840s – through its various permutations – and the onset of democracy in the 1990s. He becomes, through the ANC, a constituent part of the chain for the transmission of ideas through time. These ideas constitute what the American academic Paula Backscheider calls 'invisible lineages'.

The young Mandela was shocked to the core when S E K Mqhayi, whom A C Jordan described as 'the soul of his people', visited Healdtown College and lambasted white people in their presence, and even in the presence of the school principal, Dr Arthur Wellington. Years later, Mandela reflected on this 'invisible lineage' as follows: 'I could hardly believe my ears. His boldness in speaking of such delicate matters in the presence of Dr Wellington and other whites seemed utterly astonishing to us. Yet at the same time it aroused and motivated us, and began to alter my perception of men like Dr Wellington, whom I had automatically considered my benefactor.' Mandela would have a similar invisible impact on those who came after him.

When locals were initially afraid to come near Steve Biko after he was banished to Ginsberg, he invoked 'the invisible lineage' of Mandela. Fikile Mlinda recalls how Biko convinced him to join the movement: 'I realised that this was trouble, but he kept on saying that this is for our children and their children, and pointed to the fact that people like Nelson Mandela were in prison for our sake.' In this way, a chain was formed between Mandela and Biko's generation by appealing to the invisible lineages of our past.

And so, in remembering Mandela, we should stop thinking about him in terms of how many houses or clinics he has brought to the community – important though such things undoubtedly are. I would rather ask us to widen our interpretative imagination, if only to locate ourselves in that chain of our invisible lineages. Sadly, such a wider framework will expose the fact that the long chain of our invisible lineages has been broken under the current generation of leaders.

Can anyone really and honestly tell me what is the animating idea of our time – something we can pass on to our children as their heritage? What is the intellectual project on which we can base the making of a new collective subjectivity as a nation? With Mandela, it was reconciliation, and with Thabo Mbeki, the 'African Renaissance'. But what big idea will Jacob Zuma be remembered for by future generations?

To use Francis Fukuyama's rather unfortunate term, it looks like we have tragically come to the end of history. The political party that contributed so greatly to our freedom is not only bedevilled by tribalism, which Mandela and Biko fought so hard to eliminate; but has also become, in Frantz Fanon's words, 'a trade union of individual interests'. What chance do you really have of leaving any intellectual tradition to your children when you cannot even provide them with the most basic educational element, textbooks, let alone proper schools? You could not ask for a more demonstrative metaphor for the end of our intellectual tradition.

Leaders don't plunder: The ANC has become a union of individual interests
Sowetan, 14 August 2012

The redoubtable *Sowetan* editor Aggrey Klaaste once observed: 'It is increasingly the responsibility of blacks to help this country from certain ruination. It is our responsibility, because it is also our country and we are, after all, in the majority.' Klaaste wrote those prophetic words in the 1980s, when the black community was tearing itself apart because of ideological differences. It was as if, Klaaste continued, we were 'a nation accursed'. That article was inappropriately titled 'The thinking behind nation-building', maybe because it was given at the launch of *Sowetan*'s nation-building programme.

I've re-read this article countless times over the years, and remain convinced that it amounted to a pivotal redefinition of our conception of leadership. Indeed, because politics was such a dominant aspect of our public life at the time, we reduced our definition of the concept of leadership to the party-political sphere. And yet leadership is a much broader social concept.

Klaaste also wrote: 'We are asked in times of crisis: A*phi amadoda*? Where are the men? The answer has almost always pathetically been that they are in jail, in detention or in exile. What an insulting thing to say about the many black men and women who are doing excellent work that can make them fit the cap of leadership effortlessly.'

A decade after the publication of that article, I invited Klaaste to an international conference on community-building with the likes of the late Mwalimu Julius Nyerere. At that conference, Klaaste acknowledged that what he had been talking about was not so much nation-building than community-building: 'At that time, I decided to write about what I called nation-building, but I actually meant community-building. I said what needed to happen was for blacks, as in the language of black consciousness, to recapture and rebuild community structures.'

Klaaste's insights are particularly germane to how we think about leadership in South Africa today. We are stuck in a political conception of leadership. As a result, we automatically conflate politicians with leaders, when that has proven not to be the case. Leadership, James MacGregor Burns famously argued, is the ability to take one's people to a higher moral plane. The politicians who run South Africa do not fit the cap, because they have been consistently doing the opposite.

Our government has become the closest thing to what Richard Joseph called prebendalism – a term he borrowed from the sociologist Max Weber, and applied to Nigeria. A prebendal government is one in which politicians reward their families, friends and supporters with loads of money. In such a government, there is no distinction between public and private property. As a friend put it to me recently: '*Kuyadliwa nje*' (everyone is eating).

The ruling ANC – the party of freedom – has turned into what Frantz Fanon called 'a trade union of individual interests'. It will have a national gathering in Mangaung in December under the pretext of electing a new leadership. But we know the gathering is about a changing of the guard, so that a new lot can have its turn at the public trough. Stop calling it a leadership elective conference, for crying out loud. A rotation of office-holders sounds more like it. If the gathering was really about leadership, we would be hearing more about values and priorities than songs about Jacob Zuma, Kgalema Motlanthe or Tokyo Sexwale. It is a real embarrassment that the party of John Dube, Albert Luthuli, Oliver Tambo and Nelson Mandela has not been able to stretch itself intellectually beyond semantic shuffles about 'second transitions' and 'second phases'. Can anyone really call that leadership?

The challenge lies not with the current or the future crop of office-holders. It really lies with those of us who respond with rapturous applause every time those individuals smile. Because they are human, the adulation has turned them into preening peacocks. The mildest criticism has turned them into self-satisfied plutocrats at best, and rowdy autocrats at worst. The time has come for black people in particular to deflate the inflated egos of party political officials by refusing to call them leaders until they have earned the title. Office-holders is what they must remain.

For that to occur, there must first be a change in consciousness along the lines suggested by Klaaste, and Steve Biko before him. Just as Biko asked black people to stop their dependence on white liberals, the time has come for the black community to end its dependence on politicians who have proven over and over again that their interests and those of their families come first.

Developing a new order of business in South Africa must start with a new consciousness about the meaning of leadership, and who really deserves such a worthy title to be bestowed upon them. Call it a new leadership consciousness, if you like. Its message must be that we cannot continue to call leaders those who have proven themselves to be predators on our communities. That change in consciousness must start at the community level, ward by ward.

ANC has sold out on struggle
Sowetan, 22 October 2012

Back in the 1980s, those of us in the black consciousness movement used to joke that ANC-aligned student leaders could not really be trusted with the struggle. We argued that, given their non-racialism, they were too enamoured with their white colleagues in the National Union of South African Students (NUSAS). Whenever a 'mediocre' member of our movement defected to join ANC-aligned student bodies, we would predict that they would soon assume leadership positions. The worst amongst us would become the best amongst them, we gloated, perhaps to console ourselves about our dwindling membership.

I cringe now when I reflect upon our intellectual arrogance. But a part of me also says there might have been an element of truth in what we were saying. The ANC has all but sold out our struggle, in ways that are unlikely to be reversed. What used to be a black political culture bursting with ideas has been reduced to an amorphous culture with nothing to offer beyond officious platitudes about this or that economic plan. The other day I turned off the radio while listening to yet another media conference the president had called about how to respond to the crisis in the global economy, and the wildcat strikes on the mines.

None of this government-speak is likely to bridge the ever-widening gulf between the government and the citizenry. The reality is that there is no vanguard movement, no political leadership, and no institutional platforms through which citizens can really become part of any collective imagination about what kind of society we might want to become. The only leadership that exists is an alternation between two extremes: Julius Malema, who stoked Marikana; and the priests, who saved Marikana. There is nothing in-between.

Wherever I go, people seem to be asking themselves the same question: 'Where did it all go wrong?' One answer, of course, is that we have invested our hopes and dreams in individual leaders and political parties instead of asserting our roles as citizens. And yet, the source of authority in democracies does not lie with individual leaders or political party bosses, but with citizens. Mitt Romney and Barack Obama are in a neck-and-neck race for the presidency of the United States because without an active citizenry they cannot receive political authorisation to become president. And because the political authorisation rests with citizens, there is no guaranteed return to office by the winner.

In this beloved country of ours, we seem content with a 21st century version of 'indirect rule'. We vote for the party, and the party decides who will rule over us. All of that is interspersed with ominous threats about 'the enemy within'. People who were once part of arguably the most dynamic social movements of the 20th century are now just floating along, hoping that somehow the solution will present itself. Well, fellow citizens, I have news for you. The solution will not present itself, not any time soon.

The solution might well begin with a frank admission that the political movement that used to be the source of political and moral authority has turned us into a global laughing stock, and that it is merely a matter of time before the international community abandons us to fend for ourselves. Fending for ourselves will be no more than the tragedy of the commons, where everyone takes as much from the public purse as they possibly can before everything goes out. When asked why they loot, they would point to the R238 million boondoggle that is being constructed at Nkandla for the president, at our expense. Those better able to fend for themselves will be the educated and well-off, as well as the politicians, which will make their efforts to corrupt the system even more vicious. The victims will be the mineworkers, and the young people who have been failed by the education system. The other day, I listened to the minister of education, Angie Motshekga, wishing students good luck, and I concluded that this was indeed an ironic country. To wit, not only is the ruling party faced with a loss of authority but a loss of credibility too – and without the latter, it cannot possibly establish the former.

I have tried to imagine scenarios in which we could avoid this path, but someone said I care too much, and that 'the horse has already bolted' – which shows you the kind of generalised cynicism that has begun to grip the imagination in this country. He also said that maybe Zuma should win at Mangaung and run this country down further over the next decade, which might bring us to our senses. But will there be a country left to save at that point? I'm not so sure. Perhaps the road to clarity begins with the words of the 19th century African intellectual Isaac Wauchope: 'The cattle are gone, my countrymen.' We might as well think about the next decade as the lost decade, and engage honestly with the young people to whom we have bequeathed this mess.

Taste the coffee, comrades; things are bad
Sunday Times, 28 October 2012

I had a lump in my throat reading Thabo Mbeki's Oliver Tambo Memorial Lecture at the University of Fort Hare last week. What moved me most was his frank admission of the mistakes made under his leadership: 'In this regard,' he said, among other things, 'I must accept that during the years when I served in the leadership of the ANC, we failed to achieve the objective of sustaining the calibre of a membership made up of politically mature and committed cadres.'

This public admission of a 'failure of leadership' is noble and courageous. It certainly does not deserve the contemptuous response it received from the current leadership of the ANC. Other countries have more respect for their former presidents than the vitriol that has been thrown at Mbeki. If the ANC could forgive apartheid's executioners, why would it find it difficult to forgive one of its own? But then again, we black people tend to be more vicious and brutal towards each other than towards others, for reasons that psychologists should be best able to explain.

Through his words, Mbeki reminded me of Julius Nyerere towards the end of his life. On every platform, Nyerere spoke openly about the mistakes of his leadership and how, having realised those mistakes, he became the leading spokesperson for multiparty democracy in Tanzania. If Mbeki is confused about what he should do 'to respond to what is obviously a dangerous and unacceptable situation of directionless and unguided national drift', he ought to look to Nyerere's example and become a trailblazer for democracy in this country.

The lump in my throat also had to do with Mbeki's recognition of the other liberation movements: 'I must, as well, pay tribute to the broad liberation movement in our country, in the rest of Africa and the world, not only the ANC.' Well, thank you, Sir. This is the moment some of us have been waiting for. It really hurt when you, your party and the government defined our movements and the leaders who inspired us out of history. I take issue of course with your characterisation that the 1960s and 1970s were a period when 'serious national organised opposition collapsed', except for the 'resurgence of university student resistance'. That might be true of the early- to mid-1960s, but the rise of black consciousness beyond the university campuses, leading to the formation of the Black People's Convention, resulted in 'serious national organised opposition'. I therefore take further issue with your contention that 'in the absence of what was done outside our country, there would have been no organising centre representing the oppressed majority'. As Amílcar Cabral put it, 'claim no easy victories'.

On the whole, however, I am happy with your recognition that it took more than the ANC to sustain our struggle, and that it is going to take more than the ANC to restore the historical expectation that South Africa would become 'the exemplar of African independence, self-determination and African pride'. At the rate the country is going, and with the level of national looting going on, we will soon be in hell in a handbasket.

The lump in my throat, I suspect, also had something to do with what happens when our best minds go into party-politics and government. Maybe the ANC had no choice, and Mbeki had to assume the leadership mantle when he did. But if we are indeed going to be the 'exemplar of African independence, self-determination and pride', we must think seriously about the implications of having everyone serving in government instead of all the other strategic institutions in this country. On 5 June 1998 I published an article in the *Mail & Guardian* urging black people, especially the rich ones, to seriously reflect on what I called 'black intellectual empowerment'.

Maybe that is what Mbeki is now doing with his foundation, for it is in such times of crisis that countries need to engage in a process of critical intellectual discussion. Therefore, the failure was not just one of 'building politically mature and committed [ANC] cadres'. There was also a general failure to draw into the African Renaissance thousands of talented young people who would have provided our country with the compass it needs at this time of 'directionless and unguided national drift'. The last time Mbeki spoke with such clarity and acuity was in 1996 on the occasion of the adoption of our constitution, when he was deputy president. Becoming president deprived us of his clarity and acuity of thought. Now that he is out of power, may we see more of that political and intellectual leadership.

The lump in my throat, I also suspect, had something to do with something Mbeki said which reminded of me of Robert Sobukwe's famous words: 'It is meet we speak the truth before we die.' Whatever the party leadership says in response to Mbeki, or this article, the reality is that there is a 'pervasive sense that there is no certainty about our future, and therefore the future of the nation'. I see and hear this sense of foreboding all the time, wherever I go. To deny its reality would be to do exactly what we were accusing Mbeki of doing when he was president.

Taste the coffee, comrades, things are bad. Or as Mbeki put it: 'I also know this as a matter of fact, that it will not be possible to correct whatever might have gone wrong, and therefore address our challenges in this regard, unless all of us have the honesty and courage publicly to state what we believe is true.' Well said, Sir, and welcome back to the public domain.

There's a fire, so better put it out
Sowetan, 5 November 2012

The Italian Marxist philosopher Antonio Gramsci could have been describing South Africa when he wrote: 'The crisis consists precisely in the fact that old is dying and new cannot be born; in this interregnum a great variety of morbid symptoms appear.' Another relevant saying at this juncture is of more ancient vintage, and comes from the Greeks: 'Whom the Gods seek to destroy, they first make mad.' This idiom usually depicts a situation in which rulers fail to provide a creative response to Gramsci's 'morbid symptoms'.

The Romans had yet another term to depict a situation in

which the rulers were not only failing to see the crisis around them, but continued to party nonetheless. Those rulers, like the Roman emperor Nero, are said to be 'fiddling while Rome burns'. The French equivalent of this same attitude among the privileged classes is captured in the saying '*Qu'ils mangent de la brioche*' (let them eat cake).

Only rulers who are blind to the reality of their societies could possibly deny that our country is in a state of what former president Thabo Mbeki described as a 'dangerous and unacceptable situation of directionless and unguided national drift' in which 'we are allowing ourselves to progress towards a costly disaster of a protracted and endemic general crisis'. I always admired Mbeki's turn of phrase more than his policy decisions. But at least the man has had the decency to own up to his mistakes.

The last idiom which springs to mind, which is of either Danish or Spanish origin, is that 'the emperor has no clothes'. It refers to a country in which a leader who is obsessed with material things is promised an expensive piece of clothing by designers. The clothing is so exclusive that it is invisible to anyone who is stupid. Afraid to be seen as stupid, the emperor goes around the country in this invisible clothing. The people, also careful not to be seen as stupid, applaud the emperor's designer clothing until a little boy sees the emperor and says: 'But he isn't wearing anything!'

Of course, this saying depicts a situation in which the leader and the led are in a collective game of pretence that everything is well under the sun. They are in a state of denial – one of those words that only entered our public lexicon in the Mbeki era. All leaders, I suppose bring about, wittingly and unwittingly, their own lexicon. 'Shower' was not part of our public lexicon before Jacob Zuma moved to the centre of our political stage. But I digress.

The point I am making is that the diversity of the origins of these idioms suggests there is something universal about leaders being blind to the circumstances around them, until it is too late. Responding to my claim in a recent column that the ANC has 'sold out', the party's secretary-general, Gwede Mantashe accuses me of – wait for it – 'pointing fingers' ('Let's find solutions for SA's problems and not point fingers', *Sowetan*, 24/10/2012). In other words, I am the little boy who is disrupting the narrative of pretence that the emperor is wearing clothes when he is actually naked. The nakedness of our situation is there for all to see – from Marikana to the R250 million Nkandla construction and the rampant corruption in Limpopo and elsewhere, while our children go without schoolbooks.

Mantashe also complains that I have not been part of discussions between the ANC and intellectuals: 'Even if we assume he was never reached, he never inquired about these sessions.' But, truly, dear brother, it doesn't really matter that I am not part of those particular discussions. We all make our contributions in different spaces, and in my case that space happens to be the university. What really frustrates me is that the young people I teach don't even think about a political career because of the closed, corruption-ridden networks in the ANC. And yet, successful democracies are those that provide pathways for that youthful genius to bubble up into the political system.

The solution, it seems to me, is a political culture that allows young people from different sectors of our society to collectively shape their future through the political process. One proven way of doing this is to allow them to vote for leaders of their choice, instead of those leaders being chosen by party branch leaders whose sole interest in politics is the advancement of personal interests. The tricky part of course is that it is precisely those with vested interests in the current system who would have to change it. But there are instances of leaders acting against their own interests for the betterment of their societies, including Costa

Rica, Tanzania, China and Cuba – your comrades, I presume, Comrade Mantashe.

And so, I should perhaps conclude with yet another idiom, most famously coined by William Shakespeare in *Henry IV*: 'Don't shoot the messenger.' The unrest that is currently extant in the nation is not a figment of my imagination. As we say in our indigenous languages: '*Kunganuka kubasiwe!*' (there is fire in the land; put it out).

Give SA service without gain
Sowetan, 19 November 2012

I'm on a flight from Johannesburg to Cape Town. Seated next to me is a young black professional woman. There is the initial awkwardness that comes with the prospect of being stuck with a stranger for the next two hours, accompanied of course by the nerves about whether you are all going to make it this time. The pilot announces that we are 33 000 feet above sea level – it's never 31 000 or 34 000. He also announces, and it's always in English or Afrikaans, that flight service is about to start. No great anticipation there – it's chicken or beef, Bells or J&B. Heart-breaking stuff.

We are now above the clouds, fairly sure that we might indeed make it. The only other nervous anticipation is about the landing, but we can push that to the back of our minds for now. The lady and I begin the usual exchange of pleasantries. It always begins with whether one is returning home or on a business trip. To fill the awkward silence, I think to steer the conversation in the direction of Mangaung, if you know what I mean. 'So who would it be', I ask, 'JZ or Kgalema?'

She wastes no time in saying how uninspiring the whole spectacle is, drawing the inevitable comparison with the recently concluded contest between the American presidential candidates Mitt Romney and Barack Obama. Indeed, I know a few friends who deliberately arranged their business trips so they could be in the United States just to experience the excitement of a real election – one in which the people actually elect their own leaders. I ask the young lady what she thinks about the idea of direct elections of individual candidates. She reckons that would seal the fate of the ruling ANC, because she could not identify even one figure who could get her heart to beat faster. And then she says she might be coming back to Cape Town to study: 'And I'll be wearing a blue DA t-shirt, jeans and takkies.'

The following day I relay the story of this young lady at a gathering to launch my book *Biko: A Biography* (2012) in Gugulethu. Someone in the audience responds: 'What's wrong with that, Xolela? The t-shirt is blue, and jeans are blue.' At a subsequent launch of my book in Langa Township, an older member of the audience says something similar to the young woman: '*Sesikulemeko yalo mbutho wethu – sesixhomekeke kuwo, kodwa ke abantwana bethu bazakuzikhethele bona*' (the reality is that there is nothing we can do – even if we wanted to leave the ANC, our lives depend on it, but the children will be freer to choose as they please).

The implication of all this is that the ANC will over time lose its followers to the DA. That would be the case if politics were mathematics – where what you take from one side is added in equal proportion to the other. The reality of course is that while the ANC may lose the support of young black professionals and the disenchanted children of the woman in Langa, this will not automatically translate into a DA majority.

In Cape Town there is an interesting ambivalence about the DA among the black middle class, many of whom live in DA-controlled wards. They like the fact that their garbage is picked up on time. What holds them back is that the DA's leadership structure is not African. They have a real sense that poorer African communities do not get the attention they deserve from the DA government. In this regard, the upcoming contest for the chairmanship of the DA between Masizole Mnqasela and Wilmot James looks set to be a symbolic referendum about the party's identity.

Africans alienated from an increasingly corrupt ANC and a white-led DA tend to opt out of politics. Unfortunately, this serves to leave the political space to the wolves. Maybe it's time to find a new space for the disillusioned and disenchanted by organising them into a non-party, non-parliamentary body whose sole purpose would be to weigh in with their voice during and between elections, in the same way in which the 'independent voter' determines election outcomes in the United States. To be effective, such a pressure group would have to go beyond the suburbs to every village and township. It would have to consist of people with no interest in going to parliament, or holding any government position. The philosophy for such a body would have to be 'service without gain'.

It has been a long time since we have had principled, service-oriented leadership in this country. It is time to bring it back if we are going to create a political future for the young professional woman on that flight with me, and overcome the despondency of the woman in Langa. As Steve Biko taught us in so many ways, no community can survive such despondency and dependency.

ANC degeneration to accelerate after Mangaung
Sowetan, 18 December 2012

I almost started this column by saying I would leave the ANC if it re-elects Jacob Zuma as its president in Mangaung later this week. Then I remembered that I never had the privilege of belonging to this august 'movement of the people'. I laugh whenever people use this phrase – whose movement it would be, really, if it was not of the people?

Moving right along. Never having enjoyed this privilege, I am unlikely to be faced with the big trade-off many ANC members will face post-Mangaung. On the one hand is the real prospect of staying with an increasingly corrupt party under Zuma for the next seven years. On the other is the prospect of joining a growing, multiracial opposition alliance, albeit one that may still have racists within it. While historical attachments may counsel sticking with the party of corruption, realistic calculations may suggest coexistence with the racists in a broader coalition.

But one does not have to be a member of a political party to feel the tension between history and the future. I find myself bound by my own history in the liberation movement while Frantz Fanon's prophetic words ring continuously in my head: 'I am not the prisoner of history . . . I should not seek there the meaning of my destiny. In the world through which I travel, I am endlessly creating myself.'

In the best of circumstances, this tension between the bonds with history and the call of the future should be the source of a creative tension in nation-building. In one of my edited volumes, *Becoming Worthy Ancestors* (2011), the sociologist Benedict Anderson argues that the 'goodness of nations' lies in the ability of the present generation to draw a linkage between the dead and the unborn. Even as we know that some of the dead were terrible people, and some of the unborn will grow up to be terrible people, the present generation extracts the idea of goodness to sustain the idea of the nation into the future. However, nations unravel when the present generation themselves have no sense of doing what George Bizos suggested at Arthur Chaskalson's funeral the other day. He asked what should be a blindingly simple question: Whether we are able to make the distinction between 'what is right and what is wrong'.

Many others, including members of the clergy and civil society, have been pointedly asking the same question of Zuma's ANC. Without the moral sensibility to distinguish between right and wrong, the present leaders – if we can really call them that – have no way of retrieving the best from the past to chart a way into the future. Zuma's ANC is unable to bridge the bonds of history and the call of the future because the phrase 'it's our turn to eat' is the extent of their collective imagination about the nation in the present.

But this malaise extends beyond the ANC. There is a general failure of black leadership in this country. The PAC and AZAPO provide hardly a murmur, COPE and the Inkatha Freedom Party are reduced to theatrics, and who knows what happened to Bantu Holomisa's United Democratic Movement.

Black people may find it hard to swallow this bitter truth: we have been defeated in a battle we thought we had won. Our condition recalls a conversation in Arundhati Roy's book *The God of Small Things* (1997): 'Chacko told the twins . . . that they were all pointed in the wrong direction, trapped outside their own history and unable to retrace their steps because their footprints had been swept away.'

It's the atrophy of the ANC that really matters at this point, because it has occupied the centre of the political space these past two decades. With Zuma at the helm for the next seven years, that atrophy will soon become a complete meltdown as the party haemorrhages from a loss of support among both the upper and the lower rungs of black society. There is no point even talking about its support among other racial groups at this point in its history. Younger members of the black middle class are less likely to be attracted by its promises of a 'better life for all', and members of the lower rungs have long realised how hollow those platitudes ring.

As the ANC and black political leaders fail to provide moral leadership for this country, the former rulers will reappear as the voice of reason – as knights in shining armour. And who in their right mind would argue with them at that point? If not, a new public discourse may yet emerge within a new opposition alliance, which may include putting back on the agenda the long postponed question of what actually constitutes a racially inclusive and more equal society. A new political middle may still be in the offing, based on a creative tension between the bond with history and the call of the future. For all its history, that conversation may not be led by the ANC. Kgalema Motlanthe may well be the party's last best chance before the final meltdown.

Biko would cringe at our return to the 1960s
City Press, 4 December 2012

There are some interesting parallels between South African politics now and in the late 1960s just before Steve Biko came up with the idea of black consciousness. This may seem like a startling observation, given that we now live in a democratic order. However, political transitions do not necessarily translate into changes in cultural behaviour; hence the need for a change in consciousness. What, then, are these parallels?

First, as in the 1960s, the black community is for all intents and purposes leaderless. True, we do elect parties that choose their own preferred individuals to represent us in parliament in turn. Those individuals take their instructions from party bosses, and more often than not those instructions have to do with how to protect the leadership. One only need to look at how members of parliament acted on HIV/AIDS, the arms deal, and now the secrecy bill. They vote in pretty much the same way that the National Party MPs used to do – like a herd. Second, as in the 1960s, they preside over ghettoized homelands called provinces in which they pilfer the state with abandon. Sure, they speak a different language, sing revolutionary songs, wear different badges and carry differently coloured flags, but their behaviour is no different from that of the former homeland leaders.

The situation is even worse in the municipalities where there is a 'generally corrupt relationship' between branch leaders and ward councillors. Their slogan is, 'it's our turn to eat'. Second, while the black politicians, like the homeland leaders of yore, gluttonously burrow their heads in the excrement of black people's misery, the public domain has been captured by white left and liberal pressure and lobby groups. Some time ago I described this as the knowledge–ideas complex that defines the moral and intellectual temper of the times, whether in the media or the universities or in civil society. Look around, and almost every major constitutional protection of people's rights have been brought about by white-led civic groups.

There is nothing wrong with that, save to say, like Biko did, once other people articulate your rights on your behalf, you cannot blame them when they claim the right to lead, as the DA is beginning to do now. As a result, there is an overall schizophrenia about race, and any expression of race consciousness is immediately dismissed as backward and not belonging in a non-racial society. This is because those who define race now do so purely in terms of skin colour, which is the opposite of Biko's conception of race as a way of life. I still hold on to this concept of race as a social identity, a recognition of whose political and intellectual richness is the best way to create a democratic, pluralist society. But because there is no black political and intellectual leadership to speak of, the debate about race has been left to white left and liberal intellectuals who question the relevance of race as a social category.

The third similarity has to do with the rise of ethnic and tribal identities as part of the internecine competition for resources. Suddenly Indians, coloureds and Africans have found that their interests are mutually exclusive. Biko would cringe at these developments. The concomitant rise of tribalism can be seen in the unanimous support for Jacob Zuma in KwaZulu-Natal. I can understand Zuma gaining the support of the majority of provincial delegates, but how is it possible that a man who has shown such flawed leadership can gain the support of all of them? I know of no other province in which there is such unanimity over leadership.

Fourth, the overall effect is that what was once a black struggle infused with themes of Pan Africanism, cultural pride and self-reliance has all but disappeared in an amorphous procedural democracy in which politics has been reduced to showing up at the polls every five years, and hoping that things will turn out just fine.

Some years ago I was invited to address the central committee of my old comrades in AZAPO. My central point, which I repeat now, was that AZAPO should de-register as a political party. There was – and is – no point expending all that energy and money for one seat in parliament. I suggested that AZAPO should return to the voice of conscience it once was in the black community before it degenerated into multiple socialist factions. If it did that, it might fill the civic vacuum in the black community – and indeed co-operate with white-led civil society organisations. The days of going it alone are over. While these organisations have enough resources to mount legal challenges against the government, no one will solve the crisis of black education except black people themselves, going out there and teaching our children ourselves when the teachers walk out on them.

Interestingly, Biko's idea of black consciousness was that of a cultural movement. He was defeated on this score by his more radical comrades who wanted a political organisation, which became the Black People's Convention and later the Azanian People's Organisation. Maybe the time has come to go back to Biko's original idea of a cultural movement aimed primarily at creating a new way of life in our communities. If Kwame Nkrumah said, 'Seek ye first the political kingdom and the rest will follow', I say, 'Grab ye first the cultural initiative and the politics will follow'.

As Biko said, it might take twenty years for such a cultural organisation to translate into a political movement, but that may well be the best our generation can do for those who come after us. Like Biko, we must lay the groundwork through consciousness-raising, and hope future generations will reap the benefits. We do not all have to be parliamentarians to begin the process of repairing our badly damaged political culture.

Beginning or end of the ANC?
City Press, 17 December 2012

Five years ago, I made a plea to ANC delegates at their fateful national conference at Polokwane to choose Jacob Zuma over Thabo Mbeki. At that time, our people were dying unnecessary deaths under the Mbeki's autocratic leadership. In the latest edition of the prestigious medical journal *Lancet*, Bongani Mayosi, Joy E Lawn, Debbie Bradshaw, Ashley van Niekerk, Salim S Abdool Karim, and Hoosen Coovadia write about 'the unscientific health policies and disastrous mistakes of the Thabo Mbeki era (1999–2008) made in respect to the HIV epidemic'. And so, Kgalema Motlanthe was right the other day to praise Zuma for his leadership on HIV/AIDS, which has led to life expectancy rising from 49 under Mbeki to 60. But what Zuma has given with one hand, he has taken with the other.

If HIV/AIDS was Mbeki's Achilles' heel, Zuma's administration has become synonymous with corruption. Our public reputation is in tatters because of all the reports of personal and financial impropriety surrounding the head of state. The daily reports of flows of money from questionable sources to the president and his relatives sap the energy of the people, create cynicism among young people, and lead to a generalised loss of confidence in the rest of the world. At the rate the ANC government is going, it's just a matter of time before the global ratings agencies downgrade South Africa yet again – surely a certainty during the next seven years of a Zuma party presidency. In a functioning democracy, all these foibles would have been enough to disqualify any president from a further stay in office. So what prevents members of the ruling party from seeing this impending disaster, and acting to forestall it?

The answer may lie in the paradox of freedom and democracy identified by the British philosopher Isaiah Berlin in his famous essay 'Two Concepts of Liberty'. Berlin wrote that 'freedom . . . is not, at any rate logically connected to democracy', and that 'there is no necessary connection between individual liberty and democratic rule'. Translated into our context, this can be taken to mean that fighting for freedom did not automatically turn us into democrats. At the heart of democracy is a requirement to respect certain types of institutions, such as the judiciary. By contrast, the attacks on the judiciary, the media and universities by the former freedom fighters betray a political leadership that understands the concept of freedom as keeping the institutions of constitutional democracy at bay.

To be sure, the assault on democratic institutions started under Mbeki. But those of us who supported Zuma in his battle against Mbeki thought he would reverse this decline. Instead, Zuma institutionalised the decline even further with his attacks on the judiciary, the media, 'clever blacks', and his construction of a R250 million compound in one of the most poverty-stricken areas in the land. I predict his palace(s) will prove to be the single most important monument to institutional failure in this country. In time, it may even prove to be a reminder of when institutionalised wrongdoing set in: when the worst instincts of former freedom fighters prevailed over the best instincts of democratic accountability and sensibility.

Edmund Burke once described institutions as 'a partnership with future generations', but this particular construction stands as a signal of a break with future generations. It may help our government officials to be reminded of the example of the great Mwalimu Julius Nyerere – a leader beloved by his people, who continued to live in the same modest home he had owned before becoming president of Tanzania. Nyerere combined a lack of ostentatiousness in both his personal demeanour and public conduct.

Motlanthe comes across as having that sense of probity, although like any other leader he could still turn out to be just as bad as his predecessors. But that is no reason not to test his mettle in practice. Too many dictators have blackmailed their people by telling them that they had better stick with the devil they know. That is how the African continent has found itself saddled with corrupt potentates who built themselves palaces as large as Zuma's at taxpayers' expense. I would be among the first to call for Motlanthe's ouster should he behave like his predecessors.

There has been much speculation about whether Motlanthe will stand against Zuma at the forthcoming ANC national conference at Mangaung. I certainly hope he does, if only to highlight the distance we still have to travel before we can align the values of our freedom struggle and the challenge of building a democratic society based on solid, unsullied institutions. If the ANC chooses Zuma over Motlanthe – in other words, the institutionalisation of wrong over right – then the duty will fall on the opposition parties to save us from certain ruination in 2014. We would not be the first country to jettison a liberation movement because it would have failed to align its historical values with the challenge of building a democratic society based on solid, unsullied institutions.

Unwittingly, Zuma may have helped bring about the end of South African exceptionalism. Like many other African countries, the ruling party would have taken us over the brink, but in the process brought about a new political alignment. The irony is that this week the ANC is going back to the place of its birth for what could be its burial. Don't we all, for our final resting place?

SA on the threshold once more

23 December 2012

'The ANC is dead, long live the ANC!' For me that about sums up the meaning of the party's national conference at Mangaung. After listening to the organisational reports about how the ANC had grown, I found myself saying: 'Who can argue with the numbers?' But as a sociologist I could also not help asking myself questions about the meaning of the numbers, the people behind the numbers, and the identity of the post-Mangaung ANC. The answer seems to be that of an organisation which has indeed grown, but has done do in a way that goes against its best traditions.

Before it was unbanned, the ANC, through its internal proxies in the civic, student and mass democratic movements, used to pride itself on its nonracial character, even though I would suggest you read multiracial for that, dear reader. After all, the Freedom Charter proudly proclaims that South Africa consists of four nations: Whites, Africans, Coloureds and Indians. The late Neville Alexander showed how problematic that conceptualisation was in his book *One Azania, One Nation: The National Question in South Africa* (1979), published under the false name of No Sizwe as it was banned in South Africa, and we in the black consciousness movement rejected the ANC's use of those ethnic categories. We preferred to refer to coloureds and Indians as black people. Those were the days. I digress, of course.

The point I am getting to is that despite its multiracial character the ANC has become a party populated and led only by Africans, its non-racial pretences and rhetoric notwithstanding. If it was truly non-racial, would the party not have elected some whites to its top six? I did some bean-counting of members of the NEC, and found only three whites among them: Rob Davies, Derek Hanekom and Sue van der Merwe. Whatever happened to the white comrades the ANC and its proxies used to defend so fiercely in the 1980s? Or have they been repelled by the rise of racial nativism in the party since the reign of former president Thabo Mbeki?

My bean-counting further revealed that the total number of Indians and coloureds put together is no more than five – two Indians, and three coloureds out of the entire 86 members of the NEC and the top six put together. I can see a swift correction from Jackson Mthembu that I have it all wrong, and that the total is actually six or seven. I would plead guilty as charged – I struggle to make distinctions among black people, in the Biko sense of the term.

But is this non-representative nature of the ANC not a plain disinvitation of members of these groups from its much-vaunted 'big tent'? And can the party then expect their support in 2014? C'mon. I can't argue against the breast-beating about the growth in membership that went on at the conference, but the numbers also tell a story of a party that is not as non-racial/multiracial as it used to be. They also reveal yet another paradox: the non-availability of some of its most talented leaders for the NEC, including Trevor Manuel, who was probably freaked out by Archbishop Desmond Tutu's admonition that he did not belong in this government.

Thus the ANC that has emerged out of Mangaung has become less representative of the country as a whole. Not only has it become demographically homogenous (but then, the ANC does not have a long history of accepting whites and other groups into its NEC – that decision was only taken at the Kabwe Conference in 1985) but more temperamentally homogenous as well. Maybe this is what Motlanthe was alluding to when he complained about the problem of 'slates' in respect of elections at the ANC's national conferences. This is the practice in terms of which a group of people are presented to the conference on one election ticket – resulting in people gaining positions because they curry favour with factions, and not on merit. This practice leads to the self-selection of the same type of people as leaders of the organisation. One need only look at the ferocity with which the movement's 'cadres' belted out their tunes while insulting and denigrating their opponents. It is one thing to have preferences for individual candidates, but the incivility towards Motlanthe, who has served the organisation with distinction for so long, has become something of a culture in the ANC. Is it perhaps not time to ban the singing from your conferences, comrades, and just get on with the business at hand?

Some might say the uniformity I am talking about is disproved by the election of Cyril Ramaphosa (whom Gwede Mantashe has christened as our new prime minister) as deputy president of the party. I am not convinced that Ramaphosa is the cross-over candidate who will appeal to the broad cross-section of South African society – the business elite, the middle class, the 'clever blacks', and the other three 'nations' consisting of the coloureds, Indians and Whites. Don't blame me for that last formulation; just read the Freedom Charter.

The 'cross-over appeal' argument would probably work if we had an electoral system in which Ramaphosa would appeal directly to the voters. But under our current system his path to the top must go through the branches first. Now, does anyone seriously believe that he would stand up against the people who delivered him to his position, sometimes frothing at the mouth? Ramaphosa will have to please his new masters if he has any chance of reaching the pole position in 2017. But he would have to become more like them first.

Why is Mantashe so afraid of Ramphele?
Sowetan, 25 February 2013

Will someone please urgently tell ANC secretary-general Gwede Mantashe that he is not God? In the process, please convey a message from the African-American scholar Cornel West that like all of us mere mortals, his body will also be 'the culinary delight of the terrestrial world one day'.

Okay – I just could not resist using that line, from my edited book *The Meaning of Mandela* (2007). Mantashe's rhetorical statement that he hopes Mamphela Ramphele's new party is not an American initiative is, quite frankly, disgusting. And Ramphele was quite right to ask him not to underestimate the intelligence of the South African public. What is Mantashe so afraid of that he will not wait for the people of this country to make their views known about Ramphele's party through the ballot box? As ANC secretary-general, he may be entitled to gerrymander elections in his own party, but he has no special rights to decide who can form or join a political party in this country.

Mantashe's outburst bespeaks a greater problem: the ANC's proprietary approach to this country and its history. The fact of the matter is that we all fought for this freedom, including Ramphele. We are entitled to exercise our political choices. That freedom extends even to those who never lifted a hand, or were born after the fight was over. No amount of scaremongering is likely to affect how these young people exercise their choices. And what will the ANC's S-G do if they do not heed his scare tactics? Will he call them American agents as well? Will he then follow through and do what is done to American agents?

I write as a survivor of the violence of the 1980s when ANC-aligned organisations brooked no ideological or philosophical disagreement. I lost many friends in the ensuing mayhem. All it took was for someone to claim that black consciousness-aligned organisations and individuals were sponsored by the CIA. I have written before about my memories of ANC/UDF/civic organisations chanting in front of Steve Biko's home: 'Steve Biko, i-CIA'. It is to the memory of those who died on both sides of the ideological warfare that I make this appeal: 'Get a hold of yourself, *Mqwathi*. As a senior political figure, your job and responsibility is to plant the seeds of tolerance, not to create conditions for the elimination of opponents.

And what to make of the argument that Ramphele will appeal

only to the middle class? It is as if 'middle class' has become a status to be shunned in this country. It is as if to be poor and working class is a badge of honour. Well, try asking a poor or working-class person, my dear fellow analysts, how much they enjoy being trapped in their status. They might just surprise you by how much they want to be part of the middle class.

If we are not willing to defend the 'middle class' status, then why do we bother sending our children to school? Why should we want them to be teachers, nurses, doctors, engineers, and accountants if we don't want them to be middle class? Why do our children form endless lines to register at our universities? Or could the anti-middle class sentiment among the politicians be the reason why they are neglecting our public schools? If I were Ramphele, I would not run away from the middle class, I would embrace it. I would want to be the education and jobs president. As Malcolm X would say, 'Make it plain'.

Those who write about the middle class as if it is a sin forget that the people who occupy this stratum are embedded in social relationships. Through these relationships they affect the lives of their communities, and indeed influence others to vote. Or could that be the real fear: that the rise of the middle class will be accompanied by a more independent political culture?

Every revolution I know about – from the French Revolution to the Russian Revolution to our own liberation struggles on the continent – was led by the middle classes, by lawyers and teachers such as Nelson Mandela, Robert Sobukwe and Zeph Mothopeng, medical students such as Steve Biko and Amílcar Cabral, and medical doctors such as Che Guevara. Cabral was adamant that the petit bourgeoisie must lead the struggle in Guinea-Bissau. Besides, the most stable democracies are those with an ever expanding middle class.

So, if I were Ramphele, I would not run away from the middle classes. If there is one thing we all have in common – young and old, black and white, male and female – it is the desire for a good education and secure jobs for our children. There is no way to achieve those things outside of a middle-class vision. It is an aspiration that only the dishonest dare to denounce. The denunciations are a political posture belied by their actions, their lifestyles, and the choices they make for their own.

How money has poisoned us
Sowetan, 26 August 2013

Truth-telling in writing requires that we admit our mistakes, openly and without equivocation. Does anyone remember the time I suggested that Mosiuoa Lekota could be president? Eish! I have a confession to make – I was smoking something. And then there was the big one: my endorsement of Jacob Zuma when it became clear that the 'third way' candidacy of Tokyo Sexwale was not viable. Could I really not have just kept my trap shut?

I have now decided not to make it my business whom the ANC elects as its leader, and to seriously reconsider whether I should make it my business which party the country elects as its leader. The election campaigns are making me nauseous already – 'a better life for all' while they are stealing from the people, or giving government money to their boyfriends. This country is really something else – an ANC member of parliament has just urged us to congratulate the disgraced minister of communications, Dina Pule, for admitting to her wrongdoing. What choice did she have, given that she was caught with her hands in the cookie jar? Wrongdoing by public office-bearers has become so normalised, it seems, that their admission is an extraordinary event calling for national celebrations.

The other *faux pas* has to do with an argument I used to make about how different we were from other African countries. While studying at the Massachusetts Institute of Technology and Harvard and Cornell universities in the 1990s, I was often invited to give seminars and dinner talks about South Africa's prospects. Oh man, did I hold forth about why we would never be corrupt, or come under the dominance of one individual. I was so wrong that I now run for cover whenever I see my former colleagues from those institutions. I avoid them like the plague, because I cannot possibly explain how and why we have become what we have become in such a short space of time.

So what have we become? In short, a people whose minds have been poisoned by a mindless chase for money – the most common denominator in everything that is going wrong in this country, from the presidency right down to the con-man wearing a shiny suit, trying to bribe his way to a tender. The other day I was re-reading Marshall Berman's lovely book *All That is Solid Melts Into Air* (1982). The title is drawn from the *Communist Manifesto*, in which Karl Marx describes a dialectic in which the bourgeoisie have to destroy what they create in order to rebuild it for capitalism to sustain itself. Joseph Schumpeter described the same process as 'creative destruction'.

The thing about Marx missed by many of our comrades is that he never envisioned communism as a society of poor people. He understood the bourgeoisie as the most productive class in the history of humanity – except that it reduced everything to sale. Instead, Marx wanted those productive energies to be used for the development of the broader society, hence his longing for a society in which 'the free development of each will be the condition for the free development of all'. In this kind of society, 'enough will be a feast', to borrow from Neville Alexander. But our bourgeoisie do not even pretend to be productive. Instead, they live and flaunt lifestyles gained from stealing from their own people.

All of this leads me to 'never say never' about anything about South Africa, including the fact that we could become another Syria or another Egypt, where a violent counter-revolution is unfolding. A few years ago, the Egyptian people thought they were being liberated from Hosni Mubarak's dictatorship, just as we thought we were being liberated from the apartheid regime. Now, the Last Pharoah, as they call Mubarak, is being released on bail. I bet you the next step will be to drop the charges.

We are also busy stoking our own counter-revolution in this country. The former rulers are linking with the disenchanted 'natives' to replace a corrupt ANC government. Through different discursive strategies and institutional configurations, white South Africans now occupy the intellectual and moral high ground in South Africa. You hear it in the self-satisfied commentary on radio and TV, in the newspapers, and in the revisionist books and reviews about the past. 'Look at them, look at them, we told you so', some of them say gleefully to a watching world. Who can honestly say they are lying? And who can blame them when black people have hardly created any new intellectual spaces or institutions?

Don't let anyone fool you – white people are not doing these things because they seek to bring back apartheid. What their re-fashioned political parties are doing is what similar parties would do elsewhere – they are seeking to marry their interests with those who have been maltreated by the post-liberation government so they can regain power. And don't you dare think this will never happen in your lifetime; only pray that when it happens we will not find ourselves on the road to Syria. Or is it Gomorrah?

When the head rots, the body will follow
Sowetan, 9 September 2013

The Alliance is dead; long live the Alliance! From the days of its return from exile, the ANC leadership never seems to have accepted that no political party can thrive on the multiplication of factions. I remember writing a column in the early 2000s advising the ruling party to look to a book by Myron Weiner on how the Indian Congress Party was able to hold its various factions together. Those were the days before the party spoke of black intellectuals as 'clever blacks', or 'foot-lickers of the white man'. It has been a slippery slope since then, with Mbeki dispensing of his detractors, and Zuma outdoing him by far. If Mbeki was accused of building a Xhosa-nostra, Zuma could be accused of building a Zulu kingdom within the government.

Every appointment the government makes, especially in the justice cluster, seems to be coming from KwaZulu-Natal. I would not mind if these people had any pedigree, but a lot of them look like they have been just pulled off from the street. I don't think there has been any government whose appointments have been overturned quite like the present, either because the courts have seen fit to protect us, or the media has uncovered a scandal. If you see a group of South Africans moving their heads from side to side at the same time, just know the president has just announced a new appointment. And by the way, who really is the boss at the SABC: the chief operating officer, Hlaudi Motsoaneng, or the chief executive officer, Lulama Mokgoba? Just asking.

Now here's what beats me. If the ANC is the head of the tripartite alliance, and the ANC is falling apart, why does it surprise anyone that the alliance is also falling apart? If the head rots, surely the body will follow? I can claim to speak with some authority when it comes to COSATU. Some 27 years ago, Tsepo

Taolo and I submitted a joint industrial sociology research project to Duncan Innes at Wits University. The last time I heard, someone was carrying it around in London, having pilfered it from the Wits University library. Take that as a hint, dear reader, just in case you have a comrade or relative carrying a bound document that he or she could not have possibly authored.

The project was about the formation of COSATU and the decision to align it with the United Democratic Front, a decision that was countered by the formation of the Council of Unions of South Africa (CUSA), which was more aligned with the black consciousness movement and the National Forum. COSATU and its brand of non-racial political unionism won the day. This has always been a strange kind of non-racialism, though, when everything else suggests it is a federation of African workers. The credibility of COSATU's claim is as believable as the ANC's claim to the same principle. Out of an NEC of 90 members, there are only two whites, two Indians and three coloureds. You go figure!

The romance between the ANC and COSATU was fine for as long as the latter knew its place. Now the National Union of Metalworkers of South Africa (NUMSA) is taking COSATU to court for suspending its general secretary, Zwelinzima Vavi. NUMSA's president, Irvin Jim has thrown down the gauntlet at Gwede Mantashe and Blade Nzimande, respectively ANC secretary-general and SACP general secretary (it's important to get the word order right on these matters, even if the lexical difference is not that clear). While the comrades are snuffing each other out, literally and figuratively, the workers are 'catching hell', as Malcolm X would have put it. And the mine bosses are gleefully watching the battle, saying to themselves, '*Sizakutya efileyo*' (like vultures, the bosses will feast on the carcass of the vanquished without doing any of the killing themselves).

This self-satisfaction is itself testimony to the irrationality of

273

rational self-interest. It is incredible how South African business people can think they can run this economy on the cheap, and still have stability. Could they really not enter into long-term agreements that will make their workers happy for a long time to come, even if they give up their bonuses and perks in the present? Where are the latter-day equivalents of Henry Ford, the American magnate who paid his workers $5 a day, and thereby ensured not only a happy workforce but a potential market for his cars? Sadly, South Africa's business leaders, it seems, are only interested in coining it now as if there is no tomorrow – which is probably true, given the quality of our political leadership.

Both business and political leaders will get their come-uppance when the economy blows up in their face and the masses desert the ruling party. Without Julius Malema and Vavi on his side, Jacob Zuma may find it hard to retain the voters' attention. Faced with the choice of voting for Zuma and the ANC on the one hand, and the opposition parties on the other, many will decide to stay at home. At that point, Zuma may find himself asking: 'Where are your friends when you really need them?' Well, you left them along the way, Mr President, in old ANC tradition. Political unionism is dead; long live political unionism!

Republic of Banana slipping on landing
Sowetan, 7 October, 2013

Breaking news! A senior military officer informs the nation that the head of the Republic of Banana sanctioned the illegal landing of a civilian aircraft full of foreign nationals from the Republic of India at one of the country's air force bases. It is not as yet clear what reason the President of the Republic of Banana could possibly have had to allow such a serious breach of the nation's security. Our sources in the Republic of Banana tell us that this is not the first time a military aircraft has breached the republic's airspace. The president's spokesperson, Mac the Knife, denies that there was any wrongdoing on the part of the president.

'It's all lies to smear the President,' he declares earnestly. 'For some reason, people, especially the media, have this ability to concoct stories about our President. As a result, we have urged parliament to disband itself, like the Americans have done. Independent media are now banned, and the SABC is the only recognised source of news. The courts are now also suspended. These measures are all temporary until matters have normalised. In the meantime, we urge investors in the Republic of Banana to remain calm; everything is under control.'

This may be a fictitious approximation of what is happening in our country following allegations by Lieutenant-General Christine Anderson that President Jacob Zuma sanctioned the landing of a private aircraft carrying guests to the Gupta wedding at the Waterkloof Air Force Base. I hope against hope that this is not the case. No citizen enjoys the prospect of their country's president going to jail.

If I was a member of the ANC, I would be worried about what else in the president's closet will come out between now and the next election. I honestly know of no liberation movement that has ever given up its moral and intellectual high ground as quickly as this one. It is as if its members are in a permanent state of hypnosis, as its leaders tear it down piece by piece, or is it scandal by scandal. Chief Albert Luthuli and Oliver Tambo must be turning in their graves. Nelson Mandela should have stayed in office for one more term. His successors were just not worthy of the name, and are bequeathing to our children a polarised and corrupt society.

I am one of those columnists who insisted throughout Zuma's

trials and tribulations that he was innocent until proven guilty, despite many of my colleagues in the media baying for his blood. We must still hold dearly to that principle if we are to be worthy custodians of our constitution. However, if I was Zuma I would be really worried this time around. It would be hard to convince the South African public that a senior military officer has her guns out for the president.

Anderson says she was phoned by the Chief of State Protocol, Bruce Kholoane – who seems to be the fall guy in all of this – telling her that he had 'just returned from the president and that the president wanted to know if everything was still on track for the flight'. Now that is a bombshell of an allegation. Presidential spokesperson Mac Maharaj has been quick off the mark to dismiss her allegations as hearsay. This, then, becomes a matter of credibility. Who would you rather believe, dear reader: Lieutenant-General Anderson or Comrade Mac? Wink, wink.

One thing about military officers, especially at that level of seniority, is that they operate in terms of a certain code of honour, whether they serve the good guys or the bad guys. That is why many of them spent their lives supporting apartheid, only to turn around to be loyal servants of Nelson Mandela. What should really worry the current president is that Anderson's lawyers have promised to subpoena him: 'It is likely that President Zuma will be on the witness list – we will ask that, in terms of the Defence Act, he (Zuma) is subpoenaed. We think his evidence might be crucial. And if we need to go to the high court to get him into court to explain, we're prepared to do that.'

I don't know how Zuma is going to wiggle himself out of this one, or how much stamina he has left to run more of these marathons with the law. The thing about the law and constitutions is that they rarely run out of stamina. I really pity the president, who has to go through yet another allegation of illegality. I pity more the political party that will go into elections with its 'Number One' candidate, Jacob Zuma, clouded in a shroud of allegations of illegality for favours to the Gupta family. But I pity most the nation that has lost the capacity for reinvention. And for this, citizens and opposition parties must take responsibility for fiddling with their fingers while Rome burns. Even political parties that know they don't have a chance in hell of forming a new government will contest the elections as one-man or one-woman self-employment agencies. Such vanity is hard to explain, let alone stomach. Damn!

Be afraid, be very afraid, for the future
Sowetan, 4 November 2013

Some people call me a prophet of doom, and they're probably right. The truth is that I am afraid for this country; very afraid. Every waking day brings depressing news. No sooner had Jacob Zuma told us to stop thinking like Africans – to the accompaniment of his ANC chorus – than his supporters heckled DA leader Helen Zille at a government function. The president sat in stony silence like he used to when Julius Malema attacked everyone who walked. Upset and angry, Zille went up to him, apparently telling him that Mandela would not have stood for it, and then walked off the stage. True, but that's just not Zuma's way of solving conflict. He would rather look away. Not long ago it was Smuts Ngonyama who was howled down by an unruly ANC crowd. Who knows who it will be next time.

I frankly doubt whether we have the consciousness that is needed to sustain a democratic society. A people who have been humiliated and degraded are often tyrants in the making. But then again, we don't seem to have much of a choice when it comes to alternatives both within the ruling party and outside it. If they want their party to hold on to power and retain their positions, party members are going to fall behind a leader who tells them to stop thinking like Africans, as he did during an address at Wits University in an apparent attempt to get people to pay e-tolls. It seems as if Africans don't want to pay for anything – or so the president would have us believe.

Under Thabo Mbeki, the crime was not to think like Africans. Don't be un-African, was the injunction. Under Zuma, the crime is to think like Africans. Don't be too African *maan wena*, is the new injunction. Which is which, comrades, to be or not to be? I hear you say, the president was just joking, and I should get over it. Please forgive me, I'm just a humour-less academic; I don't get the joke.

As if falling behind JZ will not be enough of a quandary, party members also have to fall in line behind a deputy president who is being accused of masterminding democratic South Africa's first massacre, the shooting at Marikana – of workers, *nogal*. Whether those accusations are true or false, the question that will not go away is: on what constitutional authority did Cyril Ramaphosa, a member of the Lonmin board, give orders to the minister of mineral resources, Susan Shabangu? The party is in a bind on this one as well. Even though the folks down in Kwa-Zulu-Natal might want to replace Cyril Ramaphosa with Nkosazana Dlamini-Zuma, a Zuma–Zuma ticket might just not sell (pardon the pun).

Today's ANC reminds me of the Soweto boxing sensation of the early 1970s, Anthony 'Blue Jaguar' Morodi – no offence to 'Blue Jaguar'. When asked which opponent he feared the most, Blue Jaguar would say, '*akakazalwa ozakubetha u 'Blue Jaguar'* – no such boxer has yet been born. That was until Mdantsane's Happyboy Mgxaji came along and gave him a wallop.

Zille may of course present herself as the Happyboy of our times. But I can also hear Gwede Mantashe say, in a paraphrase of Lloyd Bentsen's memorable rebuttal of Dan Quayle: 'Helen, I knew Happyboy. I grew up with Happyboy. Happyboy was a friend of mine. Helen, you're no Happyboy.' Fair enough, but then Mantashe should not be too reticent, because he also knows how a lion can be brought down by a pack of hyenas.

The hyenas at least have a strategy. Not so our opposition parties. And that's the real nub for South Africa. The mere fact that opposition leaders cannot even form an effective alliance gives an indication of the kind of rulers they would become. They would be what in isi-Xhosa is called '*oo-zwilakhe*'- it's their word, or the highway. We have seen, on our continent and elsewhere, how former democrats have turned into tyrants. What then, if neither the rulers nor the opposition offer any hope?

My secret plan, which comes out of desperation more than anything, starts with running for president of AZAPO – please don't take this literally, comrades, it's just a manner of speaking. I would then do what Oscar Arias did when he was elected president of Costa Rica. A respected military man, he abolished Costa Rica's military. No country has attacked Costa Rica ever since. Similarly, my first order of business would be to de-register AZAPO as a political party. What's the point of spending all this money and energy to put one person in parliament so he or she can speak for a few seconds during question time? AZAPO would then do what AfriForum does for its constituents, or progressive white-led organisations such as Section 27 and Equal Education are doing for our own children, while we sit on the sidelines and watch. Biko must be turning in his grave.

The party would have a goal of re-entering party politics only in 25 years. Old geezers such as the Class of 1943 would all be dead, and so would the 1980s activists with their intolerant culture. The focus would be on nipping the creeping intolerance in our young in the bud. The struggle for power and positions would be replaced by a new struggle for consciousness. A generation – say, 25 years – might just be what the doctor ordered for our gravely ill political culture.

Culture of illegality has taken over government
Sowetan, 18 November 2013

What a joke we have become. As I wrote in a previous column, not even bananas would want to live in our republic. Almost every institution we touch turns into a mess. The government's so-called 'security cluster' takes the cake. Former police commissioner Jackie Selebi started it when he made it okay for law enforcers to become law-breakers. And if Vusi Pikoli's book *My Second Initiation* (2013) is anything to go by, former president Thabo Mbeki made it okay to intervene to protect wayward and even criminal comrades.

Mbeki and Selebi's successors have taken the art – or is it the clumsiness – of cover-up to higher and more brazen levels. To brazenly threaten to stop the report of a Chapter 9 institution before it is cleared by the executive is not only unlawful, but speaks to the culture of illegality that has taken over our government. The whole thing begs the purpose of establishing Chapter 9 institutions in the first instance. I experienced the disrespect for these institutions at first hand when I worked for the Human Sciences Research Council. I walked out in a huff. I hope the public protector, Thuli Madonsela does not do the same. Too much is at stake in her case.

I laughed hard when I heard the ministers' reason for backing off from challenging Madonsela's report in court, namely that the courts were not the best place to air the dirty linen of Zuma's palatial compound at Nkandla Duh, what a stroke of genius. And this is my point exactly – a sediment of systemic ineptitude at the highest levels of our government. How else can you explain the fact that the national police commissioner, Riah Phiyega – herself under criminal investigation – has appointed several people to critical police positions without verifying their suitability for the jobs. Some did not have the proper qualifications, and the latest does not have security clearance.

Poor Cyril. I watched him on television telling the Afrikaners how they were all going to *saamtrek* together. Amazing, the things that politics will make otherwise respectable people do. It turns out that elsewhere he was giving a contrary message about how the 'boers' might be coming back to haunt us. I know he apologised later, and that seems to have sufficed. Shouldn't it have sufficed for Julius Malema as well? After all, shouldn't the same crimes or misdemeanours be subject to the same punishment? Julius must be fuming, but then again he can't complain too much right now. He's got his own party, the Economic Freedom Fighters. He wouldn't want his comrades to start singing the old O'Jays tune: 'Your body's here with us, but your mind is on the other side of town'. Just do it under the breath, Commander-in-Chief, so as to avoid confusion among the ranks. But then again, my old friend Dali would be waiting in the wings, if he could get security clearance from the other commanders. Where was I? Oh yes – the security cluster.

Now that Madonsela has stood her ground, some shocking revelations are coming out – except that nothing about Zuma is shocking anymore. We now hear that the president's architect oversaw the project, and pocketed a cool R18 bar, as we say in Gugs. And parliament's own standing committee on intelligence has found that there was so much low-lying fruit that queues reminiscent of the 1994 elections could be seen outside the president's homestead. When a journalist asked whether they had any security clearance, they responded with blank stares. 'Security what? *Ungazosijwayela wena*', they said as they chased the journalist away.

I have been desperately trying to find my copy of Ngugi wa Thiong'o's *Devil on the Cross* (1987). I now suspect one of those guys must have stolen it. But I can tell you that Nkandla makes even *Devil on the Cross* look like a walk in the park. AT the same time, South Africans really have nothing to complain about. Some of us – including yours truly – cheered the man to power. Even as his shortcomings became apparent, men and women who should have known better to speak out remained silent and joined the feast instead. Kgalema Motlanthe tentatively tried to beat the man to the presidency of the party, but it was too late. I don't know what it will take for me to forgive Motlanthe for that tentativeness. And so here we are, poised to return the great charmer to power. What a country, and what a people. Because of apartheid, we're suckers for punishment, addicted to it.

The question no historian I know has ever been able to answer is, why do the bad guys win and the good guys lose? And does this historical regularity also mean that Madonsela will suffer Vusi Pikoli's fate? After all, she's standing between the looters and the safe. In any other country where there was a modicum of respect of the rule of law by politicians, Pikoli and Madonsela would be fêted with Medals of Honour for seeking to keep the wolves at bay. I'm not a religious person. However, I thank God for both of them, and I pray for Madonsela as she tries to get to the bottom of what could turn out to be a bottomless pit.

The undoing of Mandela's legacy has begun
Sowetan, 17 December 2013

I share with President Jacob Gedleyihlekisa Zuma the distinction of being booed by members of the ANC. The difference of course is that I am just a talking head, while he is a head of state for whom the booing is like a canary in a cage, warning miners of the presence of lethal gas. To be sure, no one could have seen it coming, and it will not help for ANC and government spokespersons to spin their way out of this one.

In fact, it is this tendency to treat us like children that makes everybody angry with Zuma. People feel that he has no respect for their intelligence or moral sensibilities. Maybe staying in exile for too long makes it difficult to understand that we just don't like to be taken for granted. That is the cheek Zuma encountered at Nelson Mandela's funeral. It must have been the longest moment of his life as the booing spread like a wave across that stadium. It seemed more like the wrath of the gods.

The ANC's spin doctors complain about how booing embarrassed the president, but they say nothing about how the shambolic organisation of Madiba's last farewell embarrassed the country. Take a few examples.

First, what were Cyril Ramaphosa and Baleka Mbethe doing presiding over a state event when they are not government representatives? Where was Kgalema Motlanthe, the deputy president of the country; Max Sisulu, the speaker of parliament; or Paul Mashatile, the minister of arts and culture?

Second, why were Nelson Mandela's closest friends Ahmed Kathrada, George Bizos and Desmond Tutu, and his beloved assistant, Zelda la Grange, kept out of the programme? Where were representatives of Madiba's flagship institutions, the Nelson Mandela Children's Fund and the Nelson Mandela Centre for

Memory? By the end of that programme, I was convinced that the erasure of Madiba's memory had already begun.

Third, why was there no acknowledgement of the presence of dignitaries who were part of Mandela's inner circle of elders – Jimmy Carter, Bill and Hillary Clinton, George W Bush and, above all, Kofi Annan? Those people must have sat there and thought, what a bunch of jokers we really are. And did the South African president really have to walk in with two of his several wives for this event, in what surely came across as a show-off? I don't know what roster the president follows, but I missed the presence of his older wife, MaKhumalo, on this solemn occasion.

Fourth, and this one takes the cake, how did a fake and schizophrenic sign language interpreter get to stand next to Barack Obama? I shudder when I hear he was seeing animals and things. In that mental state, he could have lashed out at Obama at any moment. And now nobody knows who hired him, which is hardly surprising in a government where even high-ranking police officers are appointed without security clearance, and a German con-man can meet the president without any background check. The hiring of the interpreter is emblematic of everything wrong with this government. You will inevitably lose sight of the ball when you spend your time thinking about who to keep out of things, whether its funerals or the appointment of government officials.

It took Obama and Desmond Tutu to prevent the whole thing from turning into a total disaster. It took the head of another country to soothe us while our own president was hidden behind a sheaf of papers, reading a speech no one was listening to. Did anyone care to remind the president that this was a funeral, for crying out loud? As a friend put it, 'Barack Obama was the Mark Antony who came to speak about our Caesar'. It took Desmond Tutu to put a stamp of authority on the occasion. In one second he told the crowd he wanted to hear a pin drop – and indeed, you could hear a pin drop. There is no greater demonstration of moral authority than that.

At this painful moment of our national life, we would like to tell ourselves that Nelson Mandela died a satisfied man. I just find it hard to imagine that a man of such moral principle would have been happy with Nkandla. I cannot imagine Madiba being happy with the way the Guptas do as they please with our country. I cannot imagine Mandela going along with the resurgence of tribalism in the ANC. I cannot imagine Mandela, a proud African, being happy with Zuma's statement that we must stop thinking like Africans.

But maybe this is more about our honesty than it is about Zuma. Maybe we are just crying crocodile tears while Mandela's values are being trampled on a daily basis. Or maybe the booing is an embryonic, if inarticulate, expression of our disgust at what is happening to Madiba's legacy. The ANC will either continue blindly into the future with Zuma, or face a mass revolt at next year's polls. What a choice.

When freedom betrayed his twin
Sowetan, 13 January 2014

This is the story of a deadly rivalry between a set of twins, one called Freedom and the other called Democracy. The Afrikaners call such rivalries a '*broedertwis*'. While Freedom and Democracy have the same parents, they are not identical twins. They were both born to their mother Modernity during the transition from feudalism to the Enlightenment after the 16th century. Freedom developed faster and uncontrollably while democracy was the late developer, coming of age only in the 18th century. And so, in the house of Modernity, Freedom stood for vibrancy and Democracy for steadiness. When people saw them together in public in the 19th century, they called them Liberal Democracy – liberal being freedom's middle name.

The German sociologist Max Weber spent a lot of time observing the relationship between these twins. Freedom's most defining quality was her beauty and 'charisma'. Weber noted that freedom inspired millions of people around the world to march under her charismatic banner, but had absolutely no skills for managing the household of Modernity. This is not surprising, given that Freedom was raised on breaking rules and defying authority. Democracy, on the other hand, was more deliberative and always sought to cool Freedom's passions by putting in place certain laws and institutions by which they would abide.

Weber described Democracy as the more rational of the twins. When Nelson Mandela was the leader of the country, he thought he should ask Freedom and Democracy for their views regarding a subpoena by rugby strong-man Louis Luyt, who resisted transformation of the largely white national team. 'How dare this *mzungu* (white man) say you did not apply your mind? He is saying you don't have brains, Mr President,' said Freedom. He paced around the room, pounded the fist on the table, and declared: 'You're not going there, Mr President.'

Mandela then turned to Democracy for his view. Democracy began by citing a number of countries that had followed the rule of law and compared them with those that had fallen under the rule of the 'Big Man'. In the long run, he said, the former were always more successful and the latter always ended in disaster, especially on the African continent. 'There he goes with his American propaganda', interrupted Freedom, 'this is Africa. Africa for the Africans.'

Mandela waited for Freedom to finish, and asked Democracy

to continue where he had left off. Democracy starting by citing the American academic Hugh Heclo's book *Thinking Institutionally* (2008): 'To think institutionally is to understand there is something estimable and decisive beyond me, and my immediate personal inclinations. In approaching a major choice, the question is not, how can I get what I want. It is the duty-laden question that asks, what expectations and conduct are appropriate to my position and the choices I might make. What is it larger than myself into which I am drawn.'

After both had finished, Mandela reflected on how those accustomed to bringing down institutions and defying laws were suddenly confronted with the challenge of building institutions and the rule of law. This is what Mandela said to the twins: 'Suddenly, in April 1994, the same fire-eaters who had mastered the art of resistance, and who had worked relentlessly for the total destruction of white supremacy, without any previous training and experience in governance, were entrusted with the awesome task of governing the most advanced and wealthy country on the African continent.'

As he stood up to leave for the courthouse, he described the transition that freedom fighters had to make from ungovernability as 'the real Rubicon to cross . . . now the former "terrorist" had the task of uniting South Africa . . .' and build confidence in its national institutions. He said it was his 'duty-laden task' to obey those institutions for the sake of posterity.

Freedom was miffed, to put it mildly, and marched out in a huff. He questioned Democracy's loyalty to the house of Modernity. He went straight to their oldest brother, Tradition, to tell him about Freedom's disloyalty. Something had to be done about Democracy, he insisted. And then he got to the point and asked if Tradition would do the honourable thing and do the deed – in return for a contract or a job in the government.

Now, Tradition is an interesting fellow. History had taught him to be both resistant and pliable. That is how his people had adapted to the vicissitudes of time. But he also felt unappreciated in the House of Modernity. An honest fellow, Tradition could not, however, resist, wily Freedom's offer. Not only could he have a contract or a government job; Freedom told him the two of them could take over the entire government. Democracy and his institutions were the only thing that stood in their way. Life could be really good if they put their minds to it. How about a house in their village for about R200 million to get the ball rolling? asked Freedom with a smile.

Splitting hairs while Zuma takes SA into the abyss
Sunday Times, 23 March 2014

Following public protector Thuli Madonsela's damnation, Jacob Zuma should resign. That would free his party of a presidential candidate who is more of a liability than an asset. Otherwise the ANC is going to spend the next six weeks explaining away Nkandla – as his government ministers have vainly started to do. The party should just cut its losses, lick its wounds, and put up a candidate with a modicum of credibility. That could translate into temporary confusion, and a loss of some supporters. Depending on what remedial action they take, that could be the basis for future rejuvenation. The Indian Congress Party, whose popularity has waxed and waned over the past 60 years, is a useful study in this regard. But it is to Nkandla that I must return.

If the ANC could fire Thabo Mbeki for manipulating state institutions for political reasons, the case for firing Zuma is much stronger. The legal reasons are plentiful, but I should like to highlight a handful of political ones. First, Madonsela found that Zuma failed to protect the resources of the country from misuse even as he knew the costs of the project were escalating. How does a project that starts at R27 million rise to R65 million and then to R215 million without anybody knowing, let alone the president of the country? As one official reportedly put it, 'we went from humble beginnings to establishing a township'. What a cruel joke on township residents, whose resources were illegally diverted to construct what Madonsela correctly described as 'opulence on a grand scale' for just one individual. In sociology, we describe this kind of rule as 'praebandal authority', where no distinction remains between the resources of the state and those of the leader. What is even more damning is Madonsela's reference to a Constitutional Court ruling that a public functionary is duty-bound to act on any suspicion of wrongdoing. No, not our Jacob Zuma; nothing would stir him to action, not even repeated newspaper reports.

Second, this is not the first time that Zuma has been accused of failing to apply his mind. The Supreme Court of Appeals found that he had failed to apply his mind in his appointment of Menzi Simelane as National Director of Public Prosecutions. As someone entrusted with the laws of this country, should it not have crossed Zuma's mind that there was something wrong with appointing his private architect as the principal agent on a state project? As Madonsela has pointed out, even if there was a need to co-ordinate work on the inner and the outer perimeters of the Nkandla homestead, security experts could have consulted him from time to time. Eventually, the president's personal architect, hired on a percentage basis, kept on making additions to the project that increased his earnings from R400 000 to R16 million. Bravo! What a country!

And is it really not stretching the bounds of credulity to argue that the president did not know that a whole community adjacent to his home had been removed? How do you wake up one morning to find that your long-term neighbours are no longer there, and not raise questions about it – especially when you're the head of state? Simply put, if the president cannot apply his mind to matters pertaining to his own residence, how can he possibly apply his mind to matters of state?

Third, a culture of lawlessness has taken hold under Zuma's presidency of the ANC and the country. People caught with their hand in the till have been sent back to parliament despite their rebuke by the party's own parliamentary representatives. Can there be a greater insult to our intelligence than the assertion by the minister of public works, Thulas Nxesi, that the swimming pool was a 'fire pool'. What do you take us for, chief?

Fourth, Madonsela asked a question I have been asking myself ever since Zuma became president. Why all these exaggerated concerns about his security? Why would Zuma need a medical facility, a police station and a bunker at his home when neither Thabo Mbeki nor Nelson Mandela had any need for one? What will happen to all these resources after Zuma dies? Will they pass on to his children and his wives? In that case, who will be responsible for their 'lifelong maintenance'? Have we so lost our senses as a country that we cannot see this wrong for what it blatantly is?

Fifth, Madonsela's finest moment came when she 'directed' the president to appear before parliament within the next 14 days. By law, the president must account to parliament, and he is definitely not above the judiciary. Memories of Mandela came gushing over me when she said: 'we do not make the laws, we are keepers of the laws.' Mandela always obeyed the instructions of these other institutions, even when they ruled against him. In their wisdom, our founding fathers crafted a constitution and created institutions that anticipated the kind of malfeasance identified by Madonsela. It is these institutions that stand between us and kleptocracy.

Madonsela cut Zuma some slack by saying his utterance to parliament – that his family built Nkandla – was 'untrue'. She stopped short of saying he lied to parliament. But what is the difference between saying something is 'untrue' and lying? Then again, is this not the entire edifice upon which Zuma's presidency is based – a continual splitting of hairs? How long can this be sustained before irreversible damage is done to the moral fabric of this society? I suspect that we have not seen the end of this debacle, as investigators try to get to the bottom of the question: 'What did the president know, and when did he know it?'

Madonsela's most profound message, though, was that those who seek to undermine her authority do not deserve to be in public office in the first place. The trouble of course is that you and I put keep putting them there by the way we vote. It is time to send the ANC a message by voting against it at the next elections – unless they present us with a candidate we deserve. With the tales of corruption under Zuma's rule, anything else becomes appealing. Whatever choices we make, putting Zuma back in that office would be condoning his actions. It's as simple as all that.

Let Nkandla stand as a symbol of corruption
Sowetan, 24 March, 2014

To better grasp the obscenity of spending R200 million of our money on President Jacob Zuma's homestead at Nkandla, consider the following statistics from a recently completed master's thesis about the Nkandla area. Nkandla is the poorest area in all of KwaZulu-Natal. Only 0.5 per cent of the income in the area comes from formal wage jobs. The other 99.5 per cent comes from a combination of government grants, migrant remittances, informal services, and simply eking out a living off the barren soil. The place gives a literal meaning to the phrase 'dirt-poor'.

Compare that description of this community to Madonsela's description of Zuma's homestead as 'opulence on a grand scale', and tell me if you can honestly believe the president when he speaks about Batho Pele. Nkandla cruelly evokes the comment attributed to King Louis XVI's wife, Marie Antoinette, after being told the poor were suffering from bread shortages in 18th century Paris. 'Let them eat cake', she said.

When you look at the actual breakdown of household incomes in Nkandla, you find that 98 per cent of households earn less than R76 000 a year. That's virtually the whole population. I bet that is what the consultants on Nkandla spent on an evening of single malt and Cuban cigars, after they had relocated the people, apartheid-style, from within sight of the president's house.

According to Madonsela, the president's personal architect, who also doubled up as the state's principal agent on the project, started out making R400 000. Because he was running the show and was paid on a percentage basis, it was in his interest to make unending expensive additions. By the time of the investigation, his earnings were in the order of R16 million. I am not against enjoying a decent standard of living, but stealing from the poor to finance the lifestyles of the well-connected is just evil. Zuma's defenders are going to fall back on race – and before you know it, ethnicity – to justify this obscenity. But if this is what it means to be black, then please, by all means, count me out.

When asked why resources such as the medical and police facilities should not be shared by the broader public, Zuma's defenders refer to P W Botha's construction of the George Airport as their precedent. It turns out Botha was actually more sensitive to his surroundings. The airport he built is a distance from his home, and benefits a broader area.

In terms of schooling, 87 per cent of the population of Nkandla have not gone beyond secondary education. Only 10 per cent have matric, and 2 per cent have a higher education. Since higher education includes technikons and FET colleges, the figure for university education is likely to be even much lower, especially if you consider that only 0.5 per cent have formal wage jobs. Can you imagine how many university bursaries R200 million could fund, let alone classrooms? Cabinet ministers may protest to the high heavens if they like, but no one is likely to pay them any attention – at least not there.

Given that Zuma's defenders use P W Botha as their moral yardstick, let me also go back to the apartheid era to draw a parallel with Nkandla. Like the Voortrekker Monument, Zuma's house should not be taken down. It should stand there in the middle of the prairie as a permanent monument to public corruption. As Madonsela put it, the Nkandla project was a 'licence to loot'.

I now hear there is another 'arms deal' in the making. The government is going to manufacture locomotives worth R50 billion, in a recently concluded deal with the Chinese. Mark my words, it's only a matter of time before the thieves corner this one as well. One wonders how many private businesspeople have been 'introduced' to government decision-makers already. Our public coffers are there for the taking by our modern-day 'robber barons'. The public philosophy of our times is, 'take a million here and a billion there while the sun shines'. What offends me no end – and I have said this like a broken record – is that Thuli Madonsela is the only one left standing against the barbarians at the gate. Without our support, she has no chance in hell against the ANC juggernaut.

The other day I wrote about how proud I was of the actress Lupita Nyong'o. Thuli Madonsela has made me even prouder. In any other country, she would be headed for the constitutional court, the cabinet or the presidency. Not here. She will soon be grabbed by an international organisation or another country that has a use for talented people. Our universities should have endowed professorships for people like her, should they be willing to take the salary cut – and it is not a small one, I'm afraid.

We are indebted to Madonsela for unearthing the muck that went into the construction of the worst symbol of conspicuous consumption and corruption in our country: the president's home. Where have you ever heard of this – except in Zimbabwe or some other kleptocratic state. It's a sign of the times, I suppose.

It's a bling thing
City Press, 30 March 2014

The African-American songstress Roberta Flack began her classic song 'Go Up Moses' with lyrics that have not left me since I was a little boy: 'Black people, let Pharoah go! You've been down too long. Let Pharoah go! You don't need his tricks, you don't need his trinkets. Just let him go!' The skulduggery of Nkandla has got me asking whether President Jacob Zuma has not effectively become the black community's own Pharoah.

You may wonder why I should be addressing myself to black people on a national matter that transcends race: the pilfering of state resources by those who are constitutionally obliged to protect them at the highest levels of our government. My answer comes from the late Aggrey Klaaste's seminal article *The Thinking Behind Nation Building*: 'I have written somewhere that it is increasingly becoming the responsibility of blacks to help this country from certain ruination. It is our responsibility because it is also our country, and we are, after all, in the majority.'

I also address myself to black people for a reason outlined by Steve Biko in *I Write What I Like* (1978): 'While it may be relevant now to talk about black in relation to white, we must not make this our preoccupation, for it can be a negative exercise. As we proceed further towards the achievement of our goals, let us talk more about ourselves and our struggle, and less about whites.'

Finally, it is only when black people throw their toys that the ANC will pay attention, especially as we get closer to the 2014 elections. More than anything else, the 2014 elections will be a referendum on black values. We generically refer to these values as *Ubuntu*, at the heart of which is the principle of human solidarity. This principle has been expressed by our political movements throughout the ages as they have sought to establish a more equal society. How consistent with this historical principle is the construction of a R200 million homestead for one individual in one of the poorest areas in the country? Only 0.5 per cent of the population here earn formal wages; the other 99.5 per cent live on grants and agricultural subsistence.

But Zuma building a R200 million compound in the midst of all that poverty is a manifestation of a new value system in our communities. To possess multiples of what others possess is the new status symbol. Inequality has become the new badge of honour. Bling makes up for generations of poverty and damaged self-worth. Cornel West describes bling as the 'paraphernalia of suffering' – an attempt to distance yourself from the suffering of the past by wearing masks of accumulated wealth obtained by stealing from the poorer and weaker among us. That is what Nkandla is: the diversion of state resources for the titillation of the president. I say 'titillation', because no human being needs a R200 million house. Instead of being a leader who uses the 'bully pulpit' of the presidency to combat the materialism of the bling culture, Zuma has become its embodiment. This crossroads between the historical principles of human solidarity and the contemporary culture of bling highlights even more the need for a 'consciousness of blackness'. While 'black consciousness' was mostly a political movement in a context of oppression, 'consciousness of blackness' is an inquiry into our historically generated values as a guide for the way forward.

Instead of helping us locate Nkandla in relation to these historical values, the ANC leadership obfuscates. Its ministers in government muddy the waters with technicalities such as 'fire pools'. The party sends crooks back to parliament in the full knowledge that you and I will vote for them. If we do that, I submit, we become accomplices to our own downfall. We give up any right to complain about corruption in the future.

One African country after the other has fallen to its knees because of this nationalist blackmail. The blackmail rests on a Faustian bargain: keep us in power so we can accumulate the billions, and we will guarantee you the trinkets – the social grants and temporary jobs. Wait until they have divided the R50 billion deal to build locomotives among themselves, and tell me I did not say so.

When asked why we should have Zuma as president until 2019, ANC leaders tell us that we do not vote for the individual but the organisation in this country. Yeah, right. The truth of our experience is that ANC leaders shape the organisation in their own image. We have a *de jure* party system and a *de facto* presidential system in which 'Number One' – a term that goes back to the Mbeki years – reigns like a king. But even if you cannot bring yourself to vote for the white-dominated political parties, you cannot really tell me there is not a single black man or woman who can become president among the various parties. There is also nothing to stop parliamentarians from choosing a different president among themselves. That is all the constitution requires – not that the president should be the person whose face is on the ballot paper. This is a long shot in a parliament that acts like a herd of cattle. But as citizens we need to 'free ourselves from the mental slavery' of voting for corrupt individuals because they present themselves to us in certain colours, like Father Christmas. That is a mockery of our intelligence, our history and our democracy.

As the 2014 elections approach, I suggest we take to heart the presidential historian Richard Neustadt's warning: 'Choose your president carefully, because at the end of the day no one can save him from himself.' Frankly, we don't need Neustadt to know that, if Zuma's example is anything to go by. We need to let our own Pharoah go, with all his tricks and his trinkets. We've been down too long with him. We need a break. We need to write a new history.

Acknowledgements

As noted in the introduction, this volume contains a selection of columns written for various South African newspapers over the past 15 years. I would like to acknowledge the various newspapers in which they first appeared, namely *Business Day, City Press, Mail & Guardian, Sowetan, The Sunday Independent, Sunday Times,* and *The Weekender.*

I am very grateful to John Battersby, former editor of *The Sunday Independent,* for taking a leap of faith and giving me not only the leader page column but also appointing me as an associate editor. I fondly remember my colleagues there, including Jeremy Gordin, Maureen Isaacson and Robert Greig. After my spell at *Sunday Independent,* I joined the exciting team led by Peter Bruce at *Business Day* and *The Weekender.* In well over a decade I never missed a column, nor do I remember them telling me what to write about. Janet Parker and Kevin O'Grady were the most professional editors one could ever hope to work with.

I must mention my friend Mondli Makhanya, former editor of the *Sunday Times.* He almost guaranteed that I was published if and when I wished, if we could find a way to get around his features editor, Fred Khumalo – yet another great professional. It helped matters a great deal that we shared a liking for a particular drink of Scottish origin. Phylicia Oppelt and Brendan Boyle continued to give me space. Of all the editors I have worked with, I have known *City Press* editor Ferial Haffajee the longest, going back to our undergraduate years at the University of the Witwatersrand where I led the black consciousness student movement – sorry, my friend, if I have outed you. Without Ferial and Dumisane Lubisi, many of my ideas would not have seen the light of day.

No journalist had a better turn of phrase or a deeper social commitment that the late Aggrey Klaaste, editor of *Sowetan* from 1988 to 2002. I once invited him to a conference hosted by the Rockefeller Foundation in Bellagio, Italy. I still have this memory of both of us sitting on the floor of his hotel in Milan as we waited for our flights – his to South Africa, and mine back to New York, where I was working for the foundation. Nothing gives me a greater sense of honour than the thought I could be writing in his space in *Sowetan*. I loved him dearly. And so, thanks to the current editor of *Sowetan*, Mpumelelo Mkhabela, for this honour, and to his colleagues Phumla Matjila, Nompumelelo Runji and Loretta Ndlovu – Loretta in particular for helping me to find the various columns.

Finally, my thanks go to my favourite publisher, Erika Oost-huysen of Tafelberg, and the copy-editor, Riaan de Villiers, whom I last saw in 1999 when we worked under Steven Friedman at the Centre for Policy Studies in Johannesburg. He has been as painstakingly attentive to detail in editing this manuscript as he was back in those early years of my writing apprenticeship.

Over the years, many people have asked me when I would publish a collection of my columns. I wasn't sure I would until I started hearing revisionist renditions of history. Hopefully, the columns will set the record straight about when I got it right and when I got it wrong. Columns don't lie, so to speak.

XOLELA MANGCU
July 2014

Select bibliography

Alexander, Neville (No Sizwe). *One Azania, One Nation: The National Question in South Africa*. London: Zed Press. 1979.

Alinsky, Saul D. *Reveille for Radicals*. New York: Random House, 1969.

Anderson, Benedict. *Imagined Communities: Reflections on the Origin and Spread of Nationalism*. New York: Verso, 1983.

Arendt, Hannah. *The Origins of Totalitarianism*. New York: Harcourt Brace Jovanovich Press, 1951.

Arendt, Hannah. *Between Past and Present*. New York: Viking Press, 1961.

Arendt, Hannah. *Eichmann in Jerusalem: A Report on the Banality of Evil*. New York: Viking Press, 1963.

Armah, Ayi Kwei. *The Beautyful Ones Are Not Yet Born*. London: Heinemann, 1968.

Badiou, Alain. *Metapolitics*. New York: Verso, 2005.

Barber, Benjamin R. *A Passion for Democracy: American Essays*. Princeton: Princeton University Press, 1998.

Bayart, Jean-François, Stephen Ellis and Béatrice Hibou. *Criminalization of the State in Africa*. Oxford: James Currey, 1999.

Berlin, Isaiah (edited by Henry Hardy). *The Crooked Timber of Humanity: Chapters in the History of Ideas*. London: John Murray, 1990.

Berlin, Isaiah. *The Sense of Reality: Studies in Ideas and Their History*. New York: Farrar, Strauss, Giroux, 1997.

Berman, Marshall. *All That is Solid Melts Into Air: The Experience of Modernity*. New York: Simon & Schuster, 1982.

Biko, Steve. *I Write What I Like*. Johannesburg: Picador Africa, 2004 [1978].

Boggs, Carl. *Social Movements and Political Power: Emerging Forms of Radicalism in the West*. Philadelphia: Temple University Press, 1986.

Bryce, James. *The American Commonwealth: Volume I*. New York: The MacMillan Company, 1897.

Burns, James MacGregor. *Leadership*. New York: Harper Row Publishers, 1978.

Carter, Stephen, L. *Integrity*. New York: Basic Books. 1996.

Clavel, P and W Wiewel. *Harold Washington and the Neighbourhoods: Progressive City Government in Chicago, 1983–1987*. New Brunswick: Rutgers University Press, 1991.

Dahl, Robert A. *Democracy and Its Critics*. New Haven: Yale University Press. 1989.

Elkin, Stephen. *City and Regime in the American Republic*. Chicago: The University of Chicago Press, 1987.

Fanon, Frantz. *The Wretched of the Earth*. New York: Grove Press, 1963.

Fanon, Frantz. *Black Skin, White Masks*. London: Pluto Press, 1967.

Freire, Paolo. *Pedagogy of the Oppressed*. NewYork: Continuum, 1986.

Freire, Paolo. *Pedagogy of Hope: Reliving Pedagogy of the Oppressed*. New York: Continuum, 1994.

Fukuyama, Francis. *The Origins of Political Order: From Prehuman Times to the French Revolution*. London: Profile Books, 2011.

Gergen, David. *Eyewitness to Power: The Essence of Leadership: Nixon to Clinton*. NewYork: Simon & Schuster, 2000.

Gerhart, Gail M. *Black Power in South Africa: The Evolution of an Ideology*. Berkeley: University of California Press, 1978.

Gladwell, Malcolm. *Outliers: The Story of Success*. NewYork: Little, Brown, 2008.

Goldfarb, Jeffrey C. *Civility and Subversion: The Intellectual in Democratic Society*. Cambridge: Cambridge University Press, 1998.

Havel, Václav. *The Power of the Powerless: Citizens against the State in Central-Eastern Europe*. NewYork: Routledge, 2010.

Heclo, Hugh. *On Thinking Institutionally*. Boulder, CO: Paradigm Publishers, 2008.

Heifetz, Ronald A. *Leadership Without Easy Answers*. Cambridge, MA: The Belknap Press of Harvard University Press, 1994.

Hirschman, Albert O. *Exit, Voice and Loyalty: Responses to Decline in Firms, Organizations and States*. Cambridge: Harvard University Press, 1970.

Huntington, Samuel. *Who Are We?: The Challenges to America's National Identity*. NewYork: Simon & Schuster, 2004.

James, William. *The Varieties of Religious Experience: A Study in Human Nature*. NewYork: The Modern Library, 1902.

Jordan, Pallo Z. *Oliver Tambo Remembered*. Johannesburg: Pan Macmillan, 2007.

Katznelson, Ira. *Liberalism's Crooked Circle: Letters to Adam Michnik*. Princeton: Princeton University Press. 1996.

Klaaste, Aggrey. 'The Thinking Behind Nation Building'. Paper delivered at the launch of Sowetan's Nation Building Programme, Shareworld, Johannesburg, October 1988.

Krugman, Paul. *Pop Internationalism*. Cambridge: MIT Press. 1996.

Krugman, Paul. *The Return of Depression Economics and the Crisis of 2008*. New York: WW Norton, 2009.

Laclau, Ernesto. *On Populist Reason*. London: Verso, 2005.

Macpherson, Crawford Brough. *The Political Theory of Possessive Individualism: Hobbes to Locke*. Oxford: Clarendon Press, 1962.

Macpherson, Crawford Brough. *The Life and Times of Liberal Democracy*. Oxford: Oxford University Press, 1977.

Mangcu, Xolela (ed). *The Meaning of Mandela: A Literary and Intellectual Celebration*. Cape Town: HSRC Press, 2007.

Mangcu, Xolela. *To The Brink: The State of Democracy in South Africa*. Durban: University of KwaZulu-Natal Press, 2008.

Mangcu, Xolela. *The Democratic Moment: South Africa's Prospects Under Jacob Zuma.* Auckland Park: Jacana Media, 2009.

Mangcu, Xolela. *Becoming Worthy Ancestors: Archive, Public Deliberations and Identity in South Africa.* Johannesburg: Witwatersrand University Press, 2011.

Mangcu, Xolela. *Biko: A Bibliography.* Cape Town: Tafelberg, 2012.

Mbembe, Achille. *On the Postcolony.* Los Angeles: UCLA Press, 2001.

Michels, Robert. *Political Parties: A Sociological Study of the Oligarchical Tendencies of Modern Democracy.* New York: The Free Press. 1962 [1915].

Mills, C. Wright. *The Power Elite.* New York: Oxford University Press, 1956.

Nehru, Jawaharlal. *The Discovery of India.* London: Meridian Books, 1947.

Neustadt, Richard. *Presidential Power and the Modern Presidents: The Politics of Leadership from Roosevelt to Reagan.* New York: The Free Press, 1991 [1960].

Nyerere, Julius K. *Freedom and Development: A Selection from Writings and Speeches 1968–73.* New York: Oxford University Press. 1973.

Obama, Barack. *Dreams From My Father: A Story of Race and Inheritance.* New York: Random House Large Print, 2006.

O'Meara, Dan. *Forty Lost Years: The Apartheid State and the Politics of the National Party, 1948–1994.* Johannesburg: Ravan Press, 1996.

Pateman, Carole. *Participation and Democratic Theory.* Cambridge: Cambridge University Press, 1970.

Pikoli, Vusi. *My Second Initiation: The Memoir of Vusi Pikoli.* Johannesburg: Picador Africa, 2013.

Polanyi, Karl. *The Great Transformation: The Political and Economic Origins of our Time.* Boston: Beacon Press, 1944.

Putnam, Robert D. *Making Democracy Work: Civic Traditions in Modern Italy.* Princeton: Princeton University Press. 1994.

Rousseau, Jean-Jacques. *The Social Contract.* New York: Hafner Press, 1947 [1762].

Roy, Arundhati. *The God of Small Things.* New Delhi: Penguin Books, 1997.

Said, Edward W. *Representations of the Intellectual.* New York: Pantheon Books, 1994

Sandel, Michael. *Democracy's Discontent: America in Search of a Public Philosophy.* Cambridge: The Belknap Press of Harvard University Press, 1998.

Schön, Donald A. *Beyond the Stable State.* New York: W.W. Norton and Company, 1973.

Schön, Donald A. *The Reflective Practitioner: How Professionals Think in Action.* New York: Basic Books, 1983.

Shonfield, Andrew. *Modern Capitalism: The Changing Balance of Public and Private Power.* Oxford: Oxford University Press, 1976.

Soyinka, Wole. *You Must Set Forth At Dawn: A Memoir.* New York: Random House, 2007.

Soyinka, Wole. *Of Africa.* New Haven: Yale University Press, 2013.

Thiong'o, Ngũgĩ wa. *Devil on the Cross.* London: Heinemann Educational Books, 1987 [1982].

Thiong'o, Ngũgĩ wa. *Wizard of the Crow.* London: Harvill Secker, 2006.

Walzer, Michael. 'The civil society argument'. In Chantal Mouffe (ed), *Dimensions of Radical Democracy: Pluralism, Citizenship, Community*. London: Verso, 1992.

Weiner, Myron. *Party Building in A New Nation: The Indian National Congress*. Chicago: University of Chicago Press, 1967.

West, Cornel. *Race Matters*. Boston: Beacon Press, 1993.

West, Cornel. *Restoring Hope*. Boston: Beacon Press, 1997.

Wills, Garry. *Certain Trumpets: The Nature of Leadership*. New York: Simon & Schuster, 1994.

Wrong, Michela. *It's Our Turn to Eat: The Story of a Kenyan Whistle Blower*. London: Harper Collins, 2009.

Zaleznik, Abe. 'Managers and leaders: are they different?' *Harvard Business Review*, 1977, reprinted in *The Best of the HBR*, January 2004.

About the author

PROFESSOR XOLELA MANGCU is Associate Professor of Sociology at the University of Cape Town and Oppenheimer Fellow at the Hutchins Centre for African and African American Research at Harvard University. He has held fellowships at the Brookings Institution, the Rockefeller Foundation, the Massachusetts Institute of Technology and Harvard. He was also a Distinguished Fellow and Executive Director at the Human Sciences Research Council. He holds a PhD from Cornell University.

Mangcu, a regular columnist for *Business Day*, the *Weekender*, the *Sowetan* and the *Sunday Independent*, has authored and co-authored seven previous books, including *The Meaning of Mandela* (2007), *To the Brink* (2008), *The Democratic Moment* (2009) and *Becoming Worthy Ancestors* (2011). His *Biko: A Biography* (2012), a South African bestseller also published in the UK and US by IB Tauris, was shortlisted for the Recht Malan Nonfiction Prize as well as the *Sunday Times* Alan Paton Award. Mangcu was the founding Executive Director of the Steve Biko Foundation and grew up in King William's Town.

Index

317

www.ingramcontent.com/pod-product-compliance
Lightning Source LLC
Chambersburg PA
CBHW052121270326
41930CB00012B/2709